WITHDRAWN

THE HISTORY OF
THE ENGLISH NOVEL

THE HISTORY OF
THE ENGLISH NOVEL

By Ernest A. Baker, D. Lit., M.A.

THE HISTORY
OF THE
ENGLISH NOVEL

By Ernest A. Baker, D. Lit., M.A.

Volume III

The Later Romances and the
Establishment of Realism

New York
BARNES & NOBLE, INC.

First published 1929

Reprinted 1967 by special arrangement with
H. F. & G. Witherby, Ltd.
326 High Holborn, London, W. C. 1

Printed in the United States of America

27409

PREFACE

SOME of my very good-natured critics have complained that in the two preceding volumes of this supposed history of the English novel the novel itself has hardly yet appeared. It will not appear in its complete form till the next volume, which deals with the age of Richardson and Fielding. My tentative definition of the novel was " The interpretation of human life by means of fictitious narrative in prose." So far, the works of fiction or the studies of life and character considered have been defective either as stories or as interpretations of life. It was perhaps worth while to trace the process of natural selection by which a form evolved combining the two elements, a form that may be regarded as the type, even though fiction has developed since in many directions and become almost as protean as the kinds of literature out of which it grew.

In the preceding volume, and still more in the present, I feel myself under a peculiar obligation to Mr Esdaile, whose famous *List of English Tales and Prose Romances printed before 1740* has been for long the chief map and guide to those who would explore the jungle of prose fiction during this period. The spade-work of Dr Secord and M. Dottin on Defoe and his predecessors has also been invaluable in helping to form an estimate of that great pioneer's relative originality and indebtedness to others. Lastly I have to acknowledge the kindness of Dr F. S. Boas in looking through

5

the proofs, and of Mr Egbert E. Smart in again undertaking the analytical index. It is only fair to mention that Dr Boas does not see eye to eye with me on several points ; for instance, he thinks I have done less than justice to *Grace Abounding*. Mrs Boas, who is a devoted student of Bunyan, reminds me also that the second part of *The Pilgrim's Progress* displays acute insight into women : see, for example, the gathering of the neighbours before Christiana's departure ; their very names—Mrs Know-nothing, Mrs Bats-eyes, Mrs Light-mind, etc. It contains, perhaps, the most poetical lines Bunyan ever wrote : " Who would true valour see . . ."—now often used as the sole hymn at a wedding. Think also of the beautiful passage at the end where the pilgrims who have journeyed together await their final summons, each alone to pass the river. Each speaks in character to the last. " The words of Valiant-for-truth have, to my knowledge, impressed hearers of many types ; and, of course, the passage about the sounding of the trumpets is among the most-quoted in our literature." I quote her remarks without any serious dissent.

E. A. B.

July, 1929

CONTENTS

7

THE LATER ROMANCES AND THE ESTABLISHMENT OF REALISM

CHAPTER I

THE REVIVAL OF ROMANCE

IN the seventeenth century novel-writing became a regular business, affording remuneration to a number of experienced hands. *Advent of the professional novelist* This was due to the steady multiplication of those who read, and also to a growing responsiveness between authors and readers. Booksellers and authors studied the public taste, instead of trying to lead it. The university wits and their humbler rivals in the previous age were not, of course, unmindful of the commercial side of their work; Greene, for instance, depended on the proceeds of his stories and miscellaneous pamphlets, probably more than on his productions for the stage, to keep body and soul together. But, at any rate, Greene made his own choice of the kind of writing with which his customers were to be regaled, whilst such arbitrary persons as Nashe and Dekker were more inclined to dictate what their admirers should like than wait to be told what was wanted. It was a season of effort in tried and untried directions. All sorts of fashions were started or brought in from abroad, not one of which was finally accepted as the very thing that all were in quest of, the most interesting way of picturing life or retailing a story. But in the course of the following century certain stock forms gradually came to be recognized, and large groups of readers began to look for a steady supply of their favourite article. Before the end of the seventeenth century, one of these forms began to be described as novels, in distinction from romances and such special varieties as the rogue-story. The modern novel, the more elastic and comprehensive form which was to absorb all the others, was still in the distance. Before that came into being, the training of readers was as necessary as the training of writers.

*Gradual
emergence
of the
novel
as the
favourite
kind of
fiction*

In the meantime, there was not one reading public eagerly waiting for the next new novel, but a number of different publics, each wedded to a particular type of fiction.[1] Those high-bred enthusiasts who welcomed the French heroic romance were not more different from the vulgar who still cherished the old-fashioned romance of chivalry than from the wits who amused themselves with the Theophrastian character. The heroic romance was superseded by heroic drama, when the theatre reopened at the Restoration. But its high-flown sentiment and counterfeit sublimities went into the romance of real life, which speedily succeeded it. From this evolved, on the one hand, the domestic novel of sentiment, and on the other, the scandalous chronicle caparisoned as fiction. There were still other kinds, as distinct as Ingelo and Bunyan's religious allegories and the realistic tales of low life and rascality coarsely translated from Spanish or French. Readers of the one kind of book would look askance at readers of the other. Writers plodded on in the path they marked out for themselves at the outset, without much deviation, and without any sudden brilliant advance. They were not, however, merely marking time. These mere day-labourers had their share in the final establishment of the novel, since they habituated readers to look to fiction for their amusement and to expect to find in it some reflection of real life. We owe something to the predecessors of Shakespeare, and we are equally indebted to the obscure predecessors of Fielding. It was not merely that the predecessors showed the artist when he arrived how to start writing plays or novels, but also that they provided him with a public and a livelihood.[2]

[1] A public that probably held most sorts of fiction in abhorrence, the serious Puritans addressed as "Christian Readers," gave a warm reception to a collection of admonitory *novelle* by John Reynolds, *The Triumphs of God's Revenge, against the crying, and execrable Sinne of Murther : or His Miraculous discoueries and seuere punishments thereof : In thirty seuerall Tragicall Histories (digested in Sixe Bookes) acted in diuers Countries beyond the Seas and neuer till now published* (3 vols., 1621-1623). This was reprinted, amplified, and abridged in numerous editions down to 1688.

[2] The disuse of the old custom of dedication to a wealthy patron is a rough-and-ready index of the changed relations between author and public. With a ready market for his wares, the novelist became more dependent on the tastes of the average reader.

At the time when the character-writers were compiling their Examples
annotated catalogues of human virtues and vices, as related in of older
the preceding volume, the booksellers were well stocked with fiction
reprints of both the fiction that appealed to educated tastes still
and that which was adapted for popular consumption. The current
old-fashioned romance, now fallen into a very trite and dilapi- in the
dated condition, was still in demand, not solely, perhaps, seven-
among the uneducated. New editions and crude imitations teenth
kept the printers at work. But it was not for the common herd century
that Sidney's *Arcadia* reappeared in expensive folios every
few years, or that Underdowne's version of Heliodorus was
frequently reprinted, until ousted from favour by the new
translation done by a Person of Quality. There was a brisk
demand for Lyly's *Euphues* down to the sixteen-thirties, and
Lodge's *Rosalynde* had a fair sale. On the other hand, the class
of readers who exhausted edition after edition of Deloney's
histories of the clothiers and cordwainers, which they were
probably very far from recognizing as in any way fictitious,
were voracious consumers of romantic tales, such as *Valentine
and Orson* or *Paris and Vienne*, which had come down from
the Middle Ages in a form not less but more primitive than
when they first set out. Caxton's *Recuyell*, considerably
altered and given a new title, *The Auncient Historie of the
destruction of Troy*, went on being reprinted until it was in
an eighteenth edition in 1738. Mandeville also kept up his
vogue, and so too with such chap-book stories as *Dr Faustus*
and even *Fortunatus*. Greene's *Pandosto*, usually under the style
of *Dorastus and Fawnia*, and his *Ciceronis Amor*, were extra-
ordinarily popular well into the century after his death ; but
the *Groats-Worth, Never too Late*, and other of his confessional
tracts, were also long in request.

The new productions that had most success as chap-books Survivals
were Richard Johnson's *Seven Champions of Christendom* and from old
History of Tom a Lincoln, and Emanuel Forde's *Parismus*, popular
Ornatus and Artesia, and *Montelion, Knight of the Oracle*, romance:
debased travesties of an already degenerate form of authentic
romance. And Johnson and Forde had to stand the com-
petition of numerous though less prolific authors. A glance

at the contemporary registers shows such entries as these—
The Heroicall Adventures of the Knight of the Sea (1600) ; *The
First and Second part of the History of the famous Evordanus
Prince of Denmark ; with the strange adventures of Iago Prince
of Saxonie* (1605) ; *The Moste famous and delightfull History of
Urano otherwise called the Grene knighte and the moste bewtifull
Princess Beroshia Daughter to the Kinge of Brittaine* (1605) ;
*The most Famous and renowned Historie of that woorthie and
illustrious knight Mervine, Sonne to that rare and excellent
Mirror of Princely prowesse, Oger the Dane* (1612). The last-
named, which was published the same year as Shelton's translation of the first part of *Don Quixote*, was the second edition [1]
of a tale that began its course as a *chanson de geste*. It was
Englished from a late French prose redaction by that omniv-
orous scholar Gervase Markham, who also took it upon himself
to invent an *English Arcadia, Alluding his beginning from Sir
Philip Sydnes ending* (2 parts, 1607-1613).

These sequels or supplements to Sidney, by Sir William
Alexander, Gervase Markham, Richard Beling, and divers
others who had the assurance to detect and rectify what they
regarded as defects,[2] together with Lady Mary Wroath's *Urania*,
written in hero-worship of her renowned kinsman, are further
signs that romance was not yet a drug in the market. Readers
of all classes craved for it still ; and, if it had to contend in
popular esteem with the plebeian literature mentioned, those
who plumed themselves on having superior taste and refinement were soon entirely subjugated for a while by a renovated
form of the time-worn genre that had come into vogue across
the Channel, the heroic romance. When a French princess
became queen of England, in 1625, it was not long before not
merely French fashions and etiquette, but also the new style

---

[1] First ed. licensed 1596.

[2] " A young Gentlewoman," Anne Weamys, wrote *A Continuation of Sir
Philip Sydney's Arcadia ; Wherein is handled The Loves of Amphialus and Helena,
Queen of Corinth, Prince Plangus and Erona* (1651) ; and a novel, *Almanzor and
Almanzaida*, was passed off as " written by Sir Philip Sidney and found since
his death amongst his papers " by a certain Mlle de la Roche Guilhem (1678),
who was the author or translator of some half-dozen similar effusions. The
chap-book versions of the *Argalus and Parthenia* episode were evidently much
in demand in the last quarter of the century.

of French romance and the standards of breeding, speech, and conduct derived therefrom, were taken up as eagerly at the English Court as the poetry and the doctrines of chivalry and gallantry of the Provençal courts of love had been adopted by English knights and dames under the Angevins.

The pastoralism of Honoré d'Urfé, author of the *Astrée*, was of like extraction to that of Sidney's *Arcadia* ; but it was untainted with the exciting strain of heroic adventure which Sidney brought in from the *Amadis* and its kin. The direct ancestor, Montemayor's *Diana*, had been put into French by Nicole Collin (1578), and there had already been an imitation in *La Pyrenée et pastorale amoureuse* of Belleforest (1571). These works appear to have fallen flat ; there was as yet no public in France for the novel of sentiment. But three decades later, after the close of the religious wars, things had altered. The later years of the reign of Henry IV. saw a society idle, frivolous, eager for amusement, grouped around the Court. Here was fertile soil for the novel, and the seeds already sown began to germinate. The famous *Astrée*, the three parts of which completed by d'Urfé himself came out from 1607 to 1619, was only one, though beyond rivalry the chief, among a number of romances having the same ancestry and very similar features.[1] It was a pastoral after the manner of Sanazzaro and Montemayor, in a French setting. The time is supposed to be the fifth century, and the scene the country of Forez, where the writer had spent his boyhood. In this peaceful region Queen Amasis rules over a kingdom of shepherds and shepherdesses, who are in reality persons of rank who have betaken themselves to the pastoral existence for the sake of its quietude and purity.

French romance, d'Urfé's "Astrée"

D'Urfé's is the usual motive : to depict a golden age of innocence and simplicity, in contrast with the vicious and jaded life of the modern world. The contrast is complete but for many curious mannerisms and ingrained affectations which it was not easy for a contemporary to eliminate. Obviously, the shepherds and shepherdesses are really denizens of polite society, and, as we are warned in the preface, none of your

[1] Reynier, Gustave, *Le Roman sentimental avant Astrée* (1908).

needy villagers obliged to drive their flocks out to pasture for their living. They are, in truth, poets and idealists in masquerade, with a fluent command of amorous dialectic and neat versification, anxious to pay their way as settlers in Arcadia and to observe all the conventions. The main occupation of that happy land is the making of love, according to the rules, and the rules have been thoroughly learned. In conversations long drawn out, in diffuse letters and sententious *billets-doux*, which were prized by d'Urfé's readers as gems of the epistolary art, he lingers reverently over the most tenuous vibrations of sentiment, illustrating the moral casuistry of life and love by both example and precept: all this in an elegant, highly elaborate, seductive style, which quickly found numerous imitators.

The story is enormously long, with some seventy or eighty stories attached to the main thread. This in itself is comparatively simple, but it is entangled and protracted to suit the writer's whim. The two lovers in chief, Céladon and Astrée, belong to families who are at enmity. Céladon has to disguise himself as a woman before he can declare his love, and then to avoid suspicion feigns that he is enamoured of all shepherdesses alike. Astrée cannot contain her jealousy, and treats him with disdain. From this situation all the rest of the action languidly flows. The story meanders on, interspersed with islets of verse in the traditional style, the one thing in which we can still take unfeigned pleasure being the descriptive stretches in which d'Urfé shows us the beloved scenery of Forez and the meads and groves watered by the Lignon.

Yet there is true feeling in the *Astrée*, if the form selected for its expression seems to us stilted and overwrought. D'Urfé was an idealist who depicted his vision of a world where all the women were beauteous and good, and all the men their adoring slaves, with his back deliberately turned to the ugly facts of life. Women in France were indeed beginning to acquire a new status, a new freedom, culture, and dignity; and d'Urfé, believing that such was their right, and that there was a high place and function for women in a reformed society, painted them as he would have them be, and as a result helped materially in their emancipation. Love in the *Astrée* is a lofty cult, with an intricate and well-recognized ritual. That cult was soon to be accepted in all its rigours by the coteries of superfine ladies and gentlemen who met in the Hôtel de Rambouillet and other salons. Captivated by make-believe in fiction, they went on to make-believe in earnest. Life itself became an esoteric art, and the romances that reciprocally inspired and were inspired by it far outwent the *Astrée* in extravagance.

It was the same in this country as in France, though the movement had no native momentum here and was not very productive, except in translations. D'Urfé's romance was published in English almost as fast as the successive instalments appeared in French. It was licensed as early as 1611, and an anonymous version of the first part came out in 1620 with the title *The History of Astrea*. There was another translation, this time of the whole work, by " A Person of Quality," [1] in three folio volumes, entitled *Astrea* (1657-1658). Many amateurs of leisure, either single-handed or with professional assistance supplied by the booksellers, dealt with the still longer productions of d'Urfé's followers, cutting them down to such a length as English readers would endure ; and the work seems to have been very poorly done, to judge by the strictures of Dorothy Osborne, and also of Mrs Lennox, who in the course of time was to deliver another of the death-strokes that always failed to finish off romance.[2]

Translations of "Astrée"

But before going on to the later performances of the school established by d'Urfé, let us glance at a famous romance that belongs in strictness neither to French nor to English literature, though it has certain important links with both.[3] The *Argenis* of John Barclay was written and first published in Latin, at

Barclay's "Argenis"

---

[1] John Davies of Kidwelly, who soon became an old hand at the business. For a general account of the English translations of French romances, see Charlanne, L., *L'Influence française en Angleterre au 17ᵉ Siècle*, 1906, pp. 387-404.

[2] The Lady Arabella goes as mad as Don Quixote through making too good use of her father's library, " in which, unfortunately for her, were great store of romances, and what was still more unfortunate, not in the original French, but very bad translations " (*The Female Quixote*, Bk. I., c. 1). See also *Letters from Dorothy Osborne to Sir William Temple*, ed. E. A. Parry, pp. 160-161.

[3] Professor Saintsbury declines to regard it as a French novel, and apparently was unable to get on with it very far (*Hist. of French Novel*, i. 152).

Paris (1621),[1] with a dedication to Louis XIII., and was the work of a young man, half-Scottish, half-French, born in France, and a subject of the French king, though he spent some part of his life in England and Italy, and when it suited him claimed that he had been officially connected with the Court of James I. Barclay was a scholar and what would now be termed a publicist. He had already brought out a commentary on Statius, a collection of his own Latin poems, a survey of the European peoples entitled *Icon Animorum* (1614),[2] and among other works a satirical novel of a picaresque character, *Euphormionis Lucinini Satyricon* (1605-1607), in which, along with a great deal rather in the vein of Petronius than of the Spanish novelists, there are attacks on the Jesuits, philosophical disquisitions on matters of current interest, disguised portraits of living notabilities, and some allegorical treatment of contemporary politics. Barclay was on dangerous ground, and did not escape censure; nor did his *Euphormionis Satyrici Apologia* (1610) safely exonerate him. In the *Argenis*, which is a critical account of the affairs of France during the epoch of the religious wars, put into the oblique form of an heroic romance, he employed the allegorical machinery with more discretion, and, for reasons which he sets forth in a discourse by his mouthpiece, Nicopompus, in the middle of the book, instead of a preface at the beginning, he leaves the real incidence of many episodes, and even the identity of various actors in them, doubtful for those of his own time and still more difficult for later readers to make out with certainty.

After explaining to Antenorius and Hieroleander that he purposes to show the king how he hath done amiss, " and what anchor the history of former times doth yet offer him in his now near shipwreck," and hearkening to their remonstrances that he will only excite further animosity by unmasking the vices of factious men, Nicopompus unfolds the length and breadth of his scheme :

I will compile some stately fable, in manner of a history ; in it will I fold up strange events, and mingle together arms,

---

[1] The Clavis (key to the countries and personages) was first provided in the edition of 1623.   [2] Translated as *The Mirrour of Mindes* (1631).

marriages, bloodshed, mirth, with many and various successes. The readers will be delighted with the vanities there shown incident to mortal men ; and I shall have them more willing to read me when they shall not find me severe or giving precepts. I will feed their minds with divers contemplations, and, as it were, with a map of places. Then will I with the show of danger stir up pity, fear, and horror ; and by and by cheer up all doubts, and graciously allay the tempests. Whom I please I will deliver, and whom I please give up to the Fates. I know the disposition of our countrymen : because I seem to tell them tales I shall have them all ; they will love my book above any stage-play or spectacle on the theatre. So first, bringing them in love with the potion, I will after put in wholesome herbs ; I will figure vices and virtues, and each of them shall have his reward. While they read, while they are affected with anger or favour, as it were against strangers, they shall meet with themselves, and find in the glass held before them the show and merit of their own fame. It will perchance make them ashamed longer to play those parts upon the stage of this life for which they must confess themselves justly taxed in a fable. And that they may not say they are traduced, no man's character shall be simply set down : I shall find many things to conceal them which would not well agree with them if they were made known. For I, that bind not myself religiously to the writing of a true history, may take this liberty. So shall the vices, not the men, be struck ; neither can any man take exceptions, but such as shall with a most shameful confession discover his own naughtiness. Besides, I will have here and there imaginary names, to signify several vices and virtues, so that he may be as much deceived, that would draw all in my writing, as he that would nothing, to the truth of any late or present passage of state.[1]

Disarmed by this reasoning, Antenorius withdraws his objections, and, " merely rubbing his hands," says :

Bestow, I pray you, this pains upon the commonwealth : you are bound to it, if you respect either yourself or this age. Such a book would wear out many ages, and make his author glorious to all posterity, besides the infinite profit in laying open and confounding the frauds and practices of the wicked, and arming honesty against them.[2]

---

[1] Kingsmill Long's translation, Lib. II., c. 14.   [2] *Ibid.*

If such declarations were lost sight of, and the book accepted for what on the surface it appears to be, the *Argenis* would be read as another complicated romance of love and heroic adventure, of like architecture to that erected by Sidney on the Heliodorian plan, but more heavily didactic, with its sermons and reflections on the moral and political truths exemplified in the events, and especially on the excellence of monarchy in comparison with all other forms of government. The action begins in Sicily, in the time-honoured way, with the arrival of a stranger, Archombrotus. His services are straightway invoked to assist Poliarchus, who is found valiantly defending himself against a band of robbers. Having discomfited these marauders, the pair converse at the house of Timoclea, the lady who had sent Archombrotus to the rescue, and he is then enlightened concerning the revolts and cabals that are disturbing the peace of the kingdom. No doubt, the robbers are from the camp of Lycogenes, a disaffected noble, who had plotted against the king, Meleander, refusing to recognize the succession of his daughter, the Princess Argenis, had aspired to her hand, and being refused had tried to carry her off by force. Lycogenes for the time being has been defeated, but Meleander is still too weak to extinguish opposition, and is about to enter into a league of peace with the factious nobles. To this accommodation Poliarchus, who is secretly beloved of Argenis, strenuously opposes himself.

Hard pressed by his enemies, Poliarchus takes refuge in a cavern, and is given out for dead. He makes his way, however, first to Italy, and then to Mauretania, the queen of which, Hyanisbe, is supposed to be the mother of Archombrotus, who is likewise a suitor for the hand of the fair Argenis, and is regarded favourably by her father. There is also a fourth claimant, Radirobanes, king of Sardinia, who does not stick at fraud, but corrupts the princess's waiting-maid, and even attempts abduction. Poliarchus frustrates all the conspiracies against the person of his lady, kills Radirobanes in single combat, and is relieved of rivalry on the part of Archombrotus through the discovery that this prince is Meleander's son. All complications are eventually adjusted, and the royal lovers united.

This is the merest sketch of an enormously involved and

enigmatical story, which becomes absolutely cryptic if much exactness is sought in the allegorical meanings. But Barclay expressly warned his readers that he was writing " a fable like a history." He provided a key, but left many of the doors *Key* ajar because there was nothing to conceal. At this time of *to the* day, it would be of little interest to identify the host of *allegory* individuals glanced at in the princes and nobles and knights and ladies who are the minor characters. Enough to recognize the central personages and the main lines of the events figuratively narrated. Sicily is obviously intended to represent France, during the troublous times that ended with the concordat under Henry IV. This prince, apparently, had duality of representation, Archombrotus standing for his earlier character and career when he was prince of Béarn, and Poliarchus for the statesman and monarch of mature years. Meleander is Henry III., and his daughter Argenis personifies the succession to the throne of the Valois. All the French nobility implicated in the wars of the League, and a crowd of foreign potentates, politicians, and dignitaries of the Church, figure in appropriate rôles. The names of some are anagrammatized : Ibburanes is Cardinal Barberini ; Dunalbius, Cardinal Ubaldini ; Dereficus Comes, Frederic, Count Palatine ; and so on. Usinulca is Calvin, and his followers, the Hyperephanians, are of course the Huguenots. Mergania is Germany ; Mauretania, the country over against Sicily, is manifestly England, with its queen, Hyanisbe, of limited prerogative, as clearly signifying Elizabeth. The rapacious and high-handed Radirobanes, king of Sardinia, must of course be Philip of Spain, and his disastrous expedition against Mauretania typifies the ill-starred Armada. The narrative should be read, however, as a metaphorical version of human history in general, with particular applications, but also *Trans-* with philosophical lessons of universal import. *lations*

The book had immediate and enormous vogue. Latin editions *and* abounded, and it was translated into the leading European lan- *influence* guages, affording plots for a number of dramas.[1] A translation *of "Ar-* *genis "*

---

[1] See Bibliography in the edition of the *Argenis* by K. F. Schmid (Berlin, 1904), and A. Collignon's *Notes historiques, littéraires et bibliographiques sur l'Argenis* (*Mem. de l'Académie de Stanislas*, Paris, 1902).

by Ben Jonson was entered at Stationers' Hall (1623); but the first English version printed was Kingsmill Long's *Barclay his Argenis, or, The Loves of Polyarchus and Argenis* (1625), which was republished (1636) "with a Key Prefixed to unlock the whole Story." There followed another translation, " upon his Majesty's command," the prose by Sir Robert le Grys and the verses by Thomas May, Esq. (1628); an *Epitome of the History of Faire Argenis and Polyarchus*, translated from a French abridgment by " a yong Gentlewoman," Judith Man (1640); and *The Phœnix ; or, the History of Polyarchus and Argenis*, translated by " a Lady," Clara Reeve, the novelist (1772).

Barclay's was one of the influences that went to the shaping of the heroic romance, in the hands of Gomberville, La Calprenède, and Mlle de Scudéry. In England, his method was followed, without much skill or intelligence, by the author of *Nova Solyma*, for instance, and by Richard Braithwaite, in his *Panthalia : or the Royal Romance. A Discourse Stored with infinite variety in relation to State-Government* (1659), in which Panthalia represents England recovered from the incendiaries by Charicles, who is of course Charles II. Another imitator was the " Honourable Person " responsible for *Cloria and Narcissus. A Delightfull and New Romance. Imbellished with divers Politi-call Notions, and singular Remarks of Moderne Transactions* (1653). Boyle was indebted to Barclay for some of the pomposities of his heroic romance *Parthenissa*. Mackenzie, in the stories interspersed in his *Aretina*, was under more obligations, although his allegorical reference to the political relations of England and Scotland is far from lucid.

Ingelo's " Benti-volio and Urania "   Any one dipping into the didactic romance, *Bentivolio and Urania* (1660), described by the late Sir Walter Raleigh [1] as marking for the historian of literature " the lowest depth to which English romance-writing sank," may see the Rev. Nathaniel Ingelo, D.D., laboriously plodding after Barclay and

---

[1] *The English Novel*, 117. The first issue of *Bentivolio and Urania* was in four books (1660); a fifth and sixth were added in the second issue the same year. In the third edition (1673) along with " some amendments " there was inserted a (very desirable) marginal glossary to the obscure terms. The fourth had " large amendments " (1682),

striving to adapt the heroico-allegorical style to the exigencies of religious teaching. Ingelo abjures romantic love and all its sensual works, and puts before us in its stead an etherealized passion of the soul, personified in Urania, or Heavenly Love, the sister of Bentivolio, and in Agape his mistress. This may have been one of the books that gave John Bunyan the idea of a pilgrimage. Bentivolio forsakes the deceitful Lady Inganna and the wicked land of Argentora, and after many perils and trials of endurance reaches the blessed country of Theoprepia, where he receives the hand of Agape. Perhaps the swampy lake that all but swallowed up Borborites suggested the Slough of Despond, and Ingelo's military and naval engagements the *Holy War*. But there could hardly be a greater contrast than that between Ingelo's learned and ponderous diction or his cumbrous allegorizing of abstractions and Bunyan's racy English and vivid story-telling.

The same year as the original Latin edition of *Argenis*, there appeared the first of three works by Marin le Roy, Sieur de Gomberville, who was to change the character of sentimental romance decisively by infusing it, as Sidney had done in the *Arcadia*, with the stirring spirit of warlike adventure. In this initial work, however, *La Carithée : Contenant sous des temps, des provinces et des noms supposes plusieurs rares et veritables histoires de nostre temps* (1621), Gomberville was content to follow d'Urfé. His shepherd and shepherdess, Cérinthe and Carithée, are another Céladon and Astrée ; and he was not untrue to his master in allowing the one to stand for Charles IX. and the other for a famous beauty of his Court. It was in his second romance, *Polexandre* (1629-1637), that he inaugurated the new fashion and gave the first example of the novel of gallantry. Though imbued with the sentimental philosophy of d'Urfé, the narrative of wild adventure is almost the same as the *Amadis* and its suite all over again. Gomberville ranges as far and as recklessly over the Old World and the New, from the Canary Isles, of which Polexandre is king, to Morocco and the fabulous regions of the Niger, and thence to the Inaccessible Isle, somewhere in the ocean of Nowhere, of which Alcidiane, the object of his superhuman pursuit, is queen. He does not abstain from

French heroic romance — Gomberville

giants and dragons. Yet he makes a great pretence of local
colour, and brings in Spaniards, Turks, and Mexicans, fighting
in authentic battles like Lepanto, as well as in those of his own
invention. In *Le Jeune Alcidiane*, he began a recital of the deeds
of Polexandre's son, but left this to be finished by a late admirer,
Madame Gomez.[1] The immense prolixity is largely due to the
practice, already well established, of using the novel as a means
of imparting miscellaneous knowledge. Gomberville's characters deliver harangues on history, ancient and modern, geography, moral philosophy, and most other branches of learning.
Last, but not least important, he inserts romantic portraits of
his contemporaries under names that are but a thin disguise—a
practice that necessarily had one satisfactory result, it made for
some attention to verisimilitude. The book had an enthusiastic
reception, in England as well as in France, and was done into
colourless English by no less a person than William Browne of
Tavistock, in *The History of Polexander* (1647). No English
translation is known of *La Carithée* or Gomberville's later
romance *La Cythérée*.

Jean Desmarets de Saint-Sorlin, who was no disciple of Astrée,
although he made one of d'Urfé's ancestors play an heroic part
in his metrical romance, *Clovis, ou la France chrestienne* (1657),
produced something more definitely like historical romance in
his *Ariane* (1632). He laid the action in the reign of Nero, and
localized the scenes in Rome, Syracuse, and Thessaly. Thus was
originated that passion for romanticized historiography which
in the vast chronicle-novels of La Calprenède and Mlle de
Scudéry gave currency to a spurious history and geography of
the ancient world, with Alexandria, Babylon, and Parthia for
chief theatres of action, and heroes such as Darius or Alexander,
Scythian kings or emperors of Persia, engaged in war and
hazards of mighty states for the love of a Statira or a Roxana.
The tone of these many-volumed narratives is as grave and
austere as if the writers were relating facts of world-wide import.
La Calprenède actually gave his novel *Faramond* the sub-title,
"The History of France," although his true motive in selecting
a remote and obscure period was to have a free hand for

*Des-
marets*

[1] *Suite de Polexandre* (1733).

invention. To nothing indeed does Bacon's definition of fiction as "feigned history" apply so literally as to these elephantine effusions of a ponderous fancy. *Ariane* was one of the first of the new romances to be Englished, appearing as *Ariana* (1636) with later editions (1641 and 1663).[1]

With the multiplication of characters, all having their several histories to tell, and of under-plots and episodes with labyrinthine connexions, the prolixity of the romances grew more and more overwhelming. They exceeded the vulgate romances of Arthur and Perceval ; like a Chinese novel, it seemed as if they might go on for ever. La Calprenède's *Cassandre* (1642-1650) was in ten volumes, his *Cléopâtre* (1647-1658) and *Faramond* (1661-1670) in twelve volumes each. The scene of the first is Babylon, of the second Alexandria and Parthia; the third is laid on the banks of the Rhine in the time of a legendary king of the Franks. Madeleine de Scudéry, whose romances were discreetly published under the name of her brother Georges, covered larger realms and wider stretches of chronology in her *Ibrahim, ou l'Illustre Bassa* (1641), in four volumes, *Artamène, ou le Grand Cyrus* (1649-1653), in ten volumes, *Clélie* (1654-1661), also in ten, and *Almahide* (1661-1663) in eight volumes.[2] *La Calprenède and Mlle de Scudéry*

La Calprenède took more liberties in handling historical matters than his fair rival would have sanctioned. As already mentioned, he had what was to all intents and purposes a blank canvas in his *Faramond*. In the others, he carefully avoided the lady's custom of making the chief figure in an historical episode the central figure of his story. His Cassandra is not the Trojan princess, but Statira, daughter of Darius and wife of Alexander, *La Calprenède's treatment of history*

---

[1] How many different tastes were being catered for is illustrated remarkably by the different sorts of fiction that were being translated at this period —*e.g.* Carlos García's picaresque novel, *The Sonne of the Rogue, or, The Politick Theefe. With the Antiquitie of Theeves.* Englished by W. M., and the cognate French *Histoire des Larrons, or the History of Theeves,* translated by Charles Godwin (both in 1638); the mythological romance in which Gombauld celebrated his amorous worship of Marie de Médicis under the names of Endymion and Cynthia—Keats is said to have read it—a book Englished as *Endimion, An Excellent Fancy first composed in French by Mounsieur Gombauld. And now Elegantly Interpreted by Richard Hurst Gentleman* (1639) ; Cervantes' *Exemplarie Novells,* by James Mabbe; and Quevedo's *Visions,* under the piquant title of *Hell Reformed or a Glasse for Favorites* (both in 1641).

[2] A lengthy epitome of the most famous of all these romances, the *Grand Cyrus,* is given by Professor Saintsbury (*Hist. of French Novel,* i. 178-217).

under a name which she is known by when wooed and won by her ancient lover, the Scythian monarch Oroondates. Cleopatra is the daughter of her famous namesake and of Antony, and her far-ramifying story brings Julius Cæsar, Augustus, Tiberius, Juba, and other historical persons on the stage, chiefly in the guise of lovers. On the other hand, Mlle de Scudéry's Cyrus and Clelia are the identical persons known to history; her Ibrahim is grand vizier to Solyman the Magnificent, and Almahide a Moorish queen at the time of the conquest of Granada, of which she gives a romantic account. Both writers were desirous, in the first place, of presenting matters that were picturesque and impressive, and were compelled from time to time to falsify history for the sake of effect. But their embellishments were carefully contrived so as to make the story sound even more credible than if they had kept strictly to facts, which are proverbially often stranger than fiction. They take elaborate precautions not to excite distrust, and occasionally debate the question how to make fiction at once interesting and convincing. The proper way is to exhibit motive as the intelligible reason for acts that might else strain credulity. In short, they saw that the secret of verisimilitude is a reasonable psychology.[1]

The novel of sentiment by La Calprenède and Mlle de Scudéry

The prime motive of action in the romances of either is love, love at once of a grandiose and of a delicate order. Though in La Calprenède ambition and heroic prowess may seem to be the mainsprings, it is clear that these motives are subordinated to the loftier aim. But it is Mlle de Scudéry who set out in form the psychological view that is the basic principle of the sentimental novel. She tabulated this psychology in *Clélie*, in the celebrated Carte de Tendre, and conveyed it succinctly in *Le Grand Cyrus*, in the characterization of herself as Sapho:

She even expresses so delicately those sentiments which are the most difficult to express, and she knows so well how to anatomize the amorous heart, if one may put it so, that she can describe exactly all the jealousies, all the anxieties, all the

[1] Their scattered pronouncements on this problem are cited by Dr A. J. Tieje, in *The Theory of Characterization in Prose Fiction prior to 1740 (University of Minnesota Studies in Language and Literature,* 5, 1916).

impatience, joys, chagrins, all the complaints, despairs, hopes, rebellions, all the tumultuous sentiments which none has ever understood save those who feel or have experienced them.

Such is the main theme of La Calprenède and Mlle de Scudéry ; this the emotional aim of their complicated but carefully articulated plots ; of their grave disquisitions in letters, speeches, and dialogue ; their studied situations, displays of valour, trials of constancy, chastity, and magnanimity, and long-withheld rewards for devotion. Mlle de Scudéry was a rapt admirer of d'Urfé. *Astrée* was an inspired book to the coterie in which she reigned. But the original novel of sentiment was a very different thing from the pseudo-historical novel of heroism and gallantry in which the genre culminated. In narrative and dramatic interest La Calprenède is the better of the twain. His rival was too ardent a daughter of the Précieuses. Her conversations on the casuistry of love are more sensitive and fine drawn, the standards of etiquette and becoming attitudes more fastidious, she soars to rarer altitudes of sensibility. Yet in spite of this exalted ideality her novels have a realism of their own. They reproduce the mental atmosphere of the salons, as the bourgeois novels which were written in mockery of heroic romance reproduced the life and manners of the lower orders—who had been deliberately ignored by all the romancers. This counterfeit sentiment (counterfeit, however earnestly and tenaciously held) and this artificial punctilio were the accepted rule of life in the society of exquisites which was her world. There she found the originals for her idealized portraits. The lineaments of her most renowned contemporaries and the salient lines of their careers may be traced, and were easily traced by her readers, in the figures of ancient conquerors, princes, and incomparable queens. This was the regular usage of the romancers, not discarded in the briefer compositions of Mme de la Fayette, and one that gives a supplementary interest even to *La Princesse de Clèves*, the story in which far-fetched adventure and fine-spun sentimentalism are abandoned for the more tragic motive of a soul tortured by the ironies of circumstance.

Platon-ism in the novel of senti-ment

The history of heroic romance is closely parallel to that of mediæval romance in the hands of Chrétien de Troyes and his disciples. In the one case as in the other, the cult of love and gallantry was carried to extravagant lengths ; in both, the mania for sentimental analysis went to the same extremes of over-subtlety and deviation from nature. Ovid's *Art of Love* was the text-book from which the trouvère and the troubadour learned the erotic science which was their chosen philosophy of life. The later romancers drew their inspiration, filtered through various intermediaries, from a different master, Plato. From the time of d'Urfé and his school to that of Mlle de Scudéry, and in this country down to the circles of kindred spirits who reverently translated and imitated the French romances, Platonism is an element whose traces are easily detected. The *Cortegiano* of Baldassare Castiglione, in which Platonic doctrines are laid down in the form of rules for practical life, was as well conned and as influential in France as in England, where at the date now reached a homelier manual, Henry Peacham's *Compleat Gentleman* (1634), was the conduct-book likeliest to be found on a drawing-room table. And that too is the work of a Platonist. Platonism degenerated into formalism and pedantry ; yet it remained a great refining principle, and, coupled with the growing influence of women in social life, helped to cleanse fiction of the sensuality and grossness which had pervaded those romances that Gomberville and La Calprenède followed when they could not brook the narrow bounds of d'Urfé's pastoralism. It engendered a loftier and purer ideal of sexual relations, even though the sophistical psychology and artificial codes of be-haviour evolved through self-conscious endeavours to live and love according to Plato led to the affectations and absurdities that gave so much sport to the satirists.

Heroic romance in England

The year after the downfall of the Cavaliers at Worcester, three translations from the two chief French romancers were published in London.[1] *Cassandra. The Fam'd Romance . . .*

---

[1] It is noteworthy that this same year (1652) the egregious Francis Kirkman brought out a " sixt Part never before Published " of *Amadis de Gaule*. More at home in compiling chronicles of roguery from Spanish and French sources, he was always at the service of readers. The fifth book was translated by T. J. (1664).

now rendered into English by an Honourable Person (1652) con-   *—trans-*
sisted of only the first three books.   The whole work was sub-   *lations*
sequently translated by Sir Charles Cotterel, going through at   *from the*
least three editions ; and there was a later abridged version " by   *French*
several hands " described as *The Famous History of Cassandra*
(1703).   The first part of *Cléopâtre* was Englished as *Hymen's
Præludia :   or, Love's Master-Piece* (1652), with a " succinct
Abridgement of what is extant of the succeeding Story.   By the
same Hand." The remainder came out part by part, done by
Loveday and others, John Davies of Kidwelly among them,
down to the final instalment, the eleventh, twelfth, and last
parts (1659).   The first to appear of the Scudéry series was
Ibrahim, Or the Illustrious Bassa . . . Englished by Henry
Cogan, Gent. (1652) ; of this there was another edition (1674).
Of La Calprenède's last work there were two translations.   The
industrious John Davies did the earlier, *Pharamond : Or, The
History of France. A New Romance. In Four Parts* (1662).   The
later was fathered by John Phillips, Gent., nephew of Milton,
and included the later books written by Pierre d'Ortigue de
Vaumorière (1677).   The rest of the Scudéry romances, all set
down to the credit of Madeleine's brother, " that famous
Wit of France, Monsieur de Scudéry, Governour of Nostre-
Dame," as he is described in the title to *Le Grand Cyrus,*
were Englished still more promptly : *Artamenes or the Grand
Cyrus* (1653-1655), by a certain F. G., Gent., was in five folio
volumes, and there was an octavo edition in ten (1691).   John
Davies took *Clélie* in hand, parts 1-2 appearing as *Clelia : An
excellent new Romance* (1655-1656), in two folio volumes, and
the whole in five volumes (1656-1661).   There was another
edition of this, by different firms of publishers, who brought
the later volumes out before the earlier (1677-1678).   The last
of Mlle de Scudéry's romances had to wait seventeen years for
a translator, and then John Phillips officiated again.   *Almahide ;
or, the Captive Queen* (1677) appeared in one volume folio.[1]
It has already been mentioned that the complete translation

---

[1] Milton's rather disreputable nephew was a busy and very miscellaneous
translator.   He did versions of *Don Quixote* (1681) and of Scarron's *Typhon ; or
the Wars of the Gods and the Giants* (1704)

English romantic- ists—the matchless Orinda and her circle

of d'Urfé's *Astrée* was another production of the romantic sixteen-fifties.[1]

The form in which these translations were published shows that they were intended for people who could afford expensive books, and also that even among the class chiefly addicted to idealistic romance a great many, perhaps a majority, found it more agreeable to do their reading in English.[2] But there were others not a few deeply versed in the French originals, as may be ascertained from allusions in the letters of the Duchess of Newcastle and of Dorothy Osborne. These fervid students of the sacred texts read not only for amusement but also for edification, and trained themselves to think and feel and speak and behave according to the best French standards of breeding. Groups of lofty souls formed themselves into clubs or fraternities that were a distant copy of Mme de Rambouillet's salon. Such was the Society of Friendship gathered round her by the poetical Mrs Katherine Philips, at Cardigan Priory, all the members renamed in proper romantic style : Katherine herself as Orinda, " the Matchless Orinda " as she deservedly came to be known to wider and wider circles ; her scant sympathetic husband as Antenor, her bosom friend Anne Owen as Lucasia, Sir Edward Dering as Silvander, Sir Charles Cotterel, who translated La Calprenède's *Cassandre*, as Poliarchus, and so on. Was it at her instigation that John Davies of Kidwelly helped in the translation of *Cléopâtre* and *Clélie?* It is strange that she prompted him to do a like service for the facetious Scarron.[3] Another who paid homage to Orinda was Roger Boyle, Lord Broghill, afterwards Earl of Orrery, author of the first English attempt to rival Gomberville and La Calprenède on their own ground. Boyle, with his eminence in soldiering, statesmanship, and literature, was almost another Philip Sidney.[4]

---

[1] See p. 17.
[2] Charlanne, 391-392.
[3] See preface to *The Unexpected Choice*, from Scarron (1670). He also translated Sorel's burlesque attack on *Astrée*, *The Extravagant Shepherd* (1653).
[4] For an account of this circle see "The Matchless Orinda " (Gosse, Sir E. *Seventeenth-Century Studies*, 4th ed., 1915, pp. 228-258). Orinda translated Corneille's *Pompée* (1663) and four acts of *Horace*, the translation of which was finished by Sir John Denham (1669).

Another aspirant to romantic honours was Margaret, the *The* "thrice-noble" Duchess of Newcastle, who also had her com- *Duchess* pany of eager devotees of the new culture at Welbeck or in her *of New-* house in London. Her fondest wish would have been to queen *castle* it as a Statira or Cleopatra, and in her own eyes the husband whose life she wrote was the peer of any Oroondates or Cyrus of them all. Fortunately, in spite of the nine volumes of her works, she had a shrewd idea of her own limitations, and in her few essays in fiction did not try to emulate the French luminaries whom she admired. Her *Blazing World* is a mad effort in a different style.[1] *Natures Pictures Drawn by Fancies Pen to the Life* (1656), containing " several feigned stories . . . comical, tragical, and tragi-comical, poetical, romantical, philosophical, and historical, both in prose and verse," is a rather dull miscellany enlivened by some touches of domestic portraiture ; and the *CCXX Sociable Letters* (1664) are an early example of the familiar painting of life and incident which was to be cultivated by writer after writer until it matured into the art of Richardson and Fanny Burney. But her life of her husband and her own autobiography are of more intrinsic interest ; the veracious memoir was now pointing out to the novel how it should proceed.

Roger Boyle's *Parthenissa* appeared at Waterford with a title- *Boyle's* page announcing six tomes (1654-1655), but only four were *"Parthe-* published then, a fifth tome (1656) and a sixth (1669), each *nissa"* described as the last part, appearing in London, and the whole book in six folio volumes (1676).[2] *Parthenissa* assuredly outdoes all other English romances in length, extravagance, and bombastic gravity. Even the friendly Dorothy Osborne, infatuated as she was by the French romances, whose cumbrous methods and mannerisms Boyle indefatigably copied, felt bored at the excessive monotony and the dearth of originality, though she freely acknowledged his " handsome language." The scenes shift

[1] Vol. ii. 338.
[2] The story goes that Henrietta, Duchess of Orleans, daughter of Charles I., entreated the author to go on with the book, and say what happened after the perplexing incident at the end of the fifth volume. He wrote the sixth volume, but failed to clear up the mystery. See Jusserand, J. J., *Eng. Novel in the time of Shakespeare*, 1899, pp. 386-387.

from country to country of the ancient world. Boyle's hero is a prince of the blood royal of Media, and in the long vicissitudes of his courtship of the peerless Parthenissa, a lady at the Court of the king of Parthia, he encounters the rivalry of or otherwise comes into collision with such historic individuals as Mithridates, Spartacus, Massinissa, Hannibal, Pompey, who are somewhat unlikely to have been in the supposed time or place. Boyle aims ambitiously at the structural complexity affected by the French romancers, with their ramifying episodes, personal histories re-counted at first hand, unfathomable oracles to be unriddled by events, and all the rest of it ; but he breaks down lamentably.[1]

Mac-kenzie's "Are-tina"

Sir George Mackenzie's youthful indiscretion, *Aretina ; Or, The Serious Romance* (1660), which ends abruptly with the first part, though likewise an essay in the exotic style, has some measure of originality and in places not a little beauty. Both Lyly and Sidney are brought to mind by the high-flown diction. Mackenzie proposed, as his sub-title hints, to write fiction in the manner of a philosopher. Hence he abounds in aphorisms and paradoxes, which are tortured into euphuistic conceits. These are too often grotesque and annoying, yet they do sometimes adorn. In a witty preface, he pledged himself to avoid the improbabilities of the old romances and the " soaring style " of the new ; but to make good such an undertaking was beyond him. The essays interlaced are the most entertaining things in the book. As to the allegory, Mackenzie, following *Argenis* at a distance, but coming right in the wake of Harrington's *Oceana*, tried manfully to expound a view of English and Scottish relations under the guise of Athens and Sparta, but failed to shed a clear light on the situation.

Some other imita-tions of French romance

If Mackenzie's *Aretina* is the most tolerable of these imita-tions, a mercenary production of John Crowne, afterwards a playwright in some esteem, is the dullest. *Pandion and Amphi-genia : Or, The History of the Coy Lady of Thessala* (1665), which he planned if he did not finish whilst in his teens, is a flagrant and invertebrate copy of the *Arcadia*. Crowne is to Sidney as Forde to the authors of *Amadís de Gaula* and *Palmerin*

---

[1] For a brief summary of the plot, see Morgan, Charlotte E., *The Rise of the Novel of Manners*, N.Y., 1911, pp. 138-142.

de Inglaterra. Yet for this bad eminence he has competitors in John Bulteel with his *Birinthia* (1664) and the perpetrators of such late specimens of the outworn mode as *Eromena : Or, The Noble Stranger* (1683), a romantic story condensed out of Chamberlayne's heroic poem *Pharonnida,* and the anonymous *Celenia : Or, The History of Hyempsal, King of Numidia* (1736). *Birinthia* is a tawdry piece of would-be heroic romancing, with a vague and ineffective setting in some remote age and country. *Eromena* is even more stilted though not so vapid, preserving the loftiness of tone and the bigoted royalism of its original, and also the incoherence. *Celenia* is a belated attempt to resuscitate an effete style. Actually, the one English novelist who assimilated the heroic idea and made it work was Mrs Behn, who applied it with a change of costume to the history of her swarthy paragon Oroonoko and to the lovelorn heroes and heroines of her tales of intrigue. And the inspiration in her case was derived from English heroic drama rather than directly from French romanticism.

The exiled Royalists who came back at the Restoration, after wasting some of their best years in idleness and indigence in France and the Netherlands, with only one ardent wish remaining, to devote the rest of their lives to the pursuit of pleasure, were faithful adherents of the heroic creed, howbeit they interpreted its articles in a way of their own. They were well-versed in the romances, from *Amadis* and *Palmerin* to *Cassandra* and the *Grand Cyrus,* and the names of the invincible paladins and matchless beauties were continually on their lips.[1] A soldier of the old stamp who had fought and bled on many fields would be nicknamed the Cid ; a man of honour and gallantry was an Amadis; one with a reputation for not over-scrupulous amours a Galaor. There was no lack of Almahides and Cleopatras, Medeas and Roxanas, among the gallant ladies and maids of honour at Whitehall. But the demure Platonic doctrines taught and put in practice at the Hôtel de Rambouillet, " where love and honour are to be weighed by drachms and scruples," [2]

Pseudo-romanticism at the Restoration Court

---

[1] See Charlanne, 396-398, on the prevalence of romantic names, especially as *noms de guerre.*

[2] Dryden on "the French Standard " (" Essay on Heroic Plays " in *Essays of Dryden,* ed. W. T. Ker, i., 157).

had no meaning to these converts, or were employed to throw a glamour on mere licentiousness. Detached observers like Evelyn might deplore the frivolity and scandalous vices of the great. The Puritans might denounce the court as a brothel and the king as a whoremaster. But even vice must see itself idealized. The noble rakes and ladies of easy virtue saw their own glittering figures, not as a worthless set of idlers ·and debauchees, but in the hues of romance. Their gallantries were a distorted kind of chivalry. Erotic adventure and the gratification of appetite were glorified with the high-sounding phrases which Mlle de Scudéry and her friends applied to the devotion of an Aronce or the chaste affection of a Mandane.

Rise of Heroic Drama

Parthenissa and *Aretina* had no successors. In the ceaseless round of gaiety now in fashion there was little time or taste for such a pastime as reading long-winded novels or romances. Boyle never brought his story to a satisfactory conclusion ; Mackenzie did not go on to a second part. Toys like these were a good enough resource in the dull years when there was no theatre. But now the ban was removed, and masks and spectacular plays were a much better outlet for the new romanticism. Morally decadent as it was, the society that had its whole being in London and its centre at the court lived. at the highest pressure. And to such a feverish intensity of social existence the only literary activity that could be adequately responsive was the drama.

Life itself at the court of King Charles was a perpetual masquerade. So it is depicted, with complacent cynicism but with frank veracity, in the *Gramont Memoirs*. The sham heroics and rodomontade of what Dryden called " serious plays " were a true image of the time. Like the Elizabethans, the Stuart dramatists imitated nature ; but, as he put it, " 'tis Nature wrought up to an higher pitch. The plot, the characters, the wit, the passions, the descriptions, are all exalted above the level of common converse, as high as the imagination of the poet can carry them, with proportion to verisimility." [1] " A play . . . to be like Nature, is to be set above it ; as statues which are placed on high are made greater than the life, that they may descend

[1] " Essay of Dramatic Poesy " (*ibid.*, i., 100-101).

to the sight in their just proportion." [1] The new version of the heroic creed, with its deification of love and valour as the ruling aims of life, was more than adequately expressed in the inflated figures and the bombastic rhetoric of Dryden, Otway, and Lee's tragedies.

The author of the first English heroic romance was also the author of the first English heroic play. Boyle, now Earl of Orrery, in 1662 or 1663 brought out a play, *Altamira*, at an Irish theatre, which he afterwards altered and improved, and produced again in London under the new designation of *The General*.[2] It was followed by *The Indian Queen* (1664), a joint work of Sir Robert Howard and the poet Dryden, in which Dryden's brother-in-law had the larger share. Then came another play of Orrery's, *Henry V*. Dryden provided *The Indian Queen* with a much finer sequel, *The Indian Emperor*, which with *Tyrannic Love* and *The Conquest of Granada* makes up a trio, in magnificence and in absurdity, towering above all the other heroic plays. For twenty years this was the school of drama that held the stage. The posturing cavaliers and ladies looked admiringly on at a more monstrous world of make-believe, where titanic souls, Montezumas, Maximins, Almanzors outranted even the Tamburlaines of the first Elizabethans and the Vittorias and Vendices of the last. Fortunate it was for the novel that it escaped the worst of the hurricane. There are absurdities enough in Mrs Behn's romantic stories; she had written heroic plays herself. But the grandiosity and bombast had spent most of their force when she turned to novel-writing. There was a long interval, also, between her stories and the latest of the French romances. The Laureate and such rivals as Settle and Banks often utilized those of Mlle de Scudéry for their plots and personages; [3] Mrs Behn, Nat Lee, and others

---

[1] "Essay of Dramatic Poesy," 102.

[2] See *Times Literary Supplement*, 2nd Sept. 1926, p. 580, where Mr B. M. Wagner produces evidence that *Altamira* had appeared in Ireland probably in 1662, and had been altered in form as well as title by 3rd Nov. 1663. *The Indian Queen* was presented at the Theatre Royal on 27th Jan. 1664. *The General* afterwards resumed its first title, *Altamira*.

[3] But as Saintsbury remarks (*Hist. of French Novel*, i., 230), it was from La Calprenède, the heroic romancer *par excellence*, that Dryden borrowed the "hectoring heroic style" of his plays.

took a number of theirs from La Calprenède. Then, at length, the factitious splendour waned, and heroic drama was almost entirely eclipsed by the comedies of Wycherley, Congreve, and Vanbrugh; Congreve's one tragedy, *The Mourning Bride*, being a return, however, to the former style.

Roman-
ticism in
Restora-
tion
Comedy
Comedy must of necessity keep closer to the average of actual human existence than tragedy need or ought. Congreve and his associates painted manners and characters with a faithfulness and accuracy not hitherto approached. Yet the question whether they were realists at all has been keenly debated, ever since Lamb described the world presented on their stage as a mere Utopia of gallantry, a region of pure comedy " where no cold moral reigns," and Macaulay retorted that gallantry was only a fine name for seduction and adultery, and that the town rakes with their simpering partners were drawn exactly as they lived.[1] The truth is, the playwrights did depict the fops and idlers in this later period very much as they saw them, and made it perfectly clear how these people saw themselves. They did not satirize, nor did they consciously idealize ; their object was to make comedy out of the life of gallantry to which the fast set dedicated their whole existence. There was an improvement in manners under James II. and William III., but morals in the society brought upon the stage were as corrupt as ever.[2] If due allowance be made for the literary heightening required even of comedy—a different matter from the exaggeration claimed for heroic drama—the wit and polish and charm of Congreve's dialogue are perhaps not a fantastic version of the talk actually heard in this frivolous world. But that world itself was funda- mentally romantic ; it was still the world of the Restoration, saturated through and through with a debased idealism, not the heroic cult of love and ambition, but the cult of gallantry and of a brilliant if heartless wit. Sentimentalism had degenerated into sensuality, varnished over but hardly concealed by an urbane cynicism.

The dramatists and, with less genius but in the same spirit,

---

[1] Macaulay's *Essays*—" Leigh Hunt."
[2] *Cp.* the picture of social demoralization in France, by Le Breton (*Le Roman au dix-septième siècle*, 235). Le Breton imputes it to " l'enseignement des casuistes et la vie de cour."

such novelists as Mrs Behn, Mrs Manley, and their imitators, portrayed this gay and heartless society as it appeared to those who were in it and of it. This is not the piercing realism of the detached and clear-eyed observer who sees things as they really are and calls them by their right names with ruthless exactitude. But it was the only realism within their reach, unless they could have changed their natures and looked at the world about them from a point of view outside. They were unaware of the problem of relativity that was to be solved. The greatest of them, Congreve, had little of the universal imagination that enables the delineator of humanity to stand aloof and contemplate the object in a more absolute perspective. But, moral questions apart and the romanticism admitted, the masterly way in which characters in action are presented by Congreve and his followers, the skill with which individuals are made to reveal unwittingly the springs of their most ambiguous conduct, and the naturalness and humour of the dialogue, furnished a model for prose fiction that was to be followed in the course of time. But at present the standard set in comedy was far beyond the abilities of the professional novelists. Only a genius of Congreve's power could vie with Congreve, and till the advent of Fielding no such rival was to appear.

CHAPTER II

THE ANTI-ROMANCES
AND OTHER COUNTERBLASTS

*The
Anti-
Romances*

BOTH in France and in England there were readers who could not away with the hallucinations of romance and idealism. *Don Quixote* did not extinguish spurious latter-day chivalry either in Spain or outside Spain ; but Cervantes was Peter the Hermit to a whole series of crusades, the result of which was to extend the realm of common-sense, restrain extravagance, and render art a more faithful servant of life. Charles Sorel in *Le Berger extravagant* (1627) made game of the *Astrée* and its readers. His Lysis, son of a humdrum Parisian, his head deranged by the reading of pastorals, turns shepherd, and meets with grotesque adventures in La Brie, where he fancies himself wandering in the enchanted Forez. He thinks he is transformed into a woman, and then into a tree. He is fooled to the top of his bent by the cynical Anselme. It is all an exaggerated philistine parody of follies that Sorel took too seriously. He did better service in *Francion* (1622-1641), the first novel in bourgeois costume. In this picaresque story, which is partly an autobiography, Sorel gives a plain and honest account of a boy's school life, of the university, the courts of law, and of both bohemian and reputable middle-class society in Paris. It is the comedy of intelligent observation, rather than satire. Sorel was himself satirized by his friend Furetière in *Le Roman bourgeois* (1666), a novel in two books that have very slight connexion with each other. To correct romanticism, Furetière set out to show what real life was like, its pettiness, its sordid shifts, and the unsavouriness of love in a social environment not given to illusions. He was sceptical of the superhuman constancy attributed to the romantic heroes and heroines ; he poked fun at the *Grand Cyrus* and *Clélie*, and in a manner very libellous and ungallant at their

38

amiable author. But the value of his work, even in the ephemeral cause of anti-romanticism, lies in his novel use of minute particulars to give an animated picture of the life before his eyes.

Still more to the purpose was Scarron's *Roman comique* (1651), a burlesque of all that is romantic and affected, and at the same time a vivid panorama of city and provincial life, which with its gaiety and high spirits soon became a classic to those readers who cultivated the literature of low life, and took this for the peculiar domain of realism. Cyrano de Bergerac's *Histoire comique de la Lune et du Soleil* (1655) is another of the same group of satires, for there are many different ways of making the fantastic ridiculous.[1] Molière's *Précieuses ridicules* (1659), castigating the devotees of heroic romance, left the romances and romancers to be dealt with by Count Anthony Hamilton and Boileau. Hamilton's delightful *contes*, *Fleur d'Épine*, *Le Belier*, and *Les Quatre Facardins* (1704-1720), though affecting the oriental form under the influence of the *Arabian Nights* which had just been translated, are counter-blows to romanticism as truly as those already enumerated, and not the least telling.[2] Boileau's attack was not so damaging because more academic. His *Héros de Roman* (1713) is a Lucianic dialogue, in which the authors and the protagonists of heroic plays and novels carry on a full-dress debate, in the presence of Minos and Pluto and a large assembly of mythical and historical celebrities from ancient literature. It is a laboured performance, and came too late in the day to do any real execution.[3]

There were no English anti-romances till a later date,[4] which

Scarron, Hamilton, and others

---

[1] See Le Breton: *Le Roman au 17e siècle*, 94-99, for a list of the anti-romances.

[2] As Le Breton points out, in the *Gramont Memoirs*, that biography of an aristocratic picaro, he did still more to discredit the romances (*ibid.*, 218).

[3] Among later anti-romances may be mentioned Marivaux' *Pharsamond* (1712), a burlesque of *Faramond*, and G. de Bougéant's *Voyage merveilleux du prince Fan-Féridin dans la Romancie : contenant plusieurs observations historiques, géographiques, physiques, critiques, et morales* (1735). Marivaux was definitely anti-romantic, and scoffed at the snobbishness of readers who were annoyed if the heroes and heroines of the romances were not of lofty extraction. He contended that high souls and elevated sentiments are often found in those not of illustrious birth.

[4] That prose competitor of *Hudibras*, the work according to Sir Sidney Lee of Thomas Flatman, *Don Juan Lamberto, or a Comical History of the Late Times, by Montelion, Knight of the Oracle* (1643-1661), is an attack on the Roundheads, not the romances, though it adopts the plan of burlesquing the latter.

is rather surprising when we see the character-writers so often
hitting out at the protean forms of pedantry and affectation.
Butler pilloried the romance-writer, but was apparently more
annoyed by his distortion of historical fact and disregard of
probability than by the preposterousness of his whole conception of life.[1] But at all events there were readers enough with
an appreciation of the ridiculous to welcome translations of the
French satires.   Whilst the gigantic *Cassandres, Pharamonds,
Artamènes* and *Clélies* went on being published and republished,
there was a sale for numerous versions of the witty works of
Scarron, of *Don Quixote* and the *Exemplary Novels*, of the whole
crowd of picaresque stories, and for a few translations from
Sorel, Furetière, and even of so feeble a gallimaufry as *La Fausse
Clélie* of Subligny.[2]   It does not follow that the reading public
was different and distinct in the two cases.   No doubt some
could find mental entertainment in works of most incongruous
kinds, and we have already seen the ultra-romantic Orinda
urging John Davies of Kidwelly to English half-a-dozen of
Scarron's tales.[3]

John Phillips entitled his translation of Sorel's parody of the
*Astrée, The Extravagant Shepherd. The Anti-Romance : or, the
History of the Shepherd Lysis* (1653). It was in a third edition by
1660. Of *Francion* there were two versions, half-a-century apart.
The first was *The Comical History of Francion. Wherein the
variety of Vices that abuse the Ages are Satyrically limn'd in their
Native Colours. Interwoven with many pleasant Events* (1655).
This was by " a Person of Honour " ;   the second (1703), by
" Several Hands," was stated to be " Adapted to the Humour
of the Present Age."   Apparently it did prove congenial, for a
later corrected edition was published in two volumes, " Adorn'd
with Cuts."   Two different translations of Cyrano de Bergerac's extravaganza appeared : Σεληναρχια, *or, the Government
of the World in the Moon : a Comical History* (1659), and *The
Comical History of the States and Empires of the Worlds of the
Moon and Sun* (1687).   Furetière had longer to wait, and his

1 Butler's *Characters*—" A Romance writer."
2 *The Mock-Clelia. Being a Comical History of French Gallantries and Novels,
in imitation of Don Quixote* (1678).
3 See above, p. 30.

Roman Bourgeois was then turned into English under the title of
Scarron's City Romance (1671). Scarron's own works were
enormously popular. Davies published a collection of his shorter
Novels (1665) and afterwards added *The Unexpected Choice*
(1670). Scarron's *Comical Romance : Or, a Facetious History of
a Company of Strowling Stage-Players* (1676) soon followed. The
racy translation of his whole works by Tom Brown, Savage, and
others came out in 1700, and was not long going into further
editions.

Mere anti-romance is a version of reality meant as a sour
antithesis to fantasy and idealism, and the antithesis is harsher
than truth can justify. To the dreams of innocence and beauty
are opposed the squalor, ugliness, and ribaldry that can easily
be found in life at its worst. English readers were amused, but
no one took the lesson to heart. They did not become more
critical ; they did not require fiction to be saner and less
romantic than they were themselves in their attitude to existence. The fact that, in spite of these translations from Gallic
scoffers and still more numerous translations of still more scathing counterchecks to extravagance from the Spanish, no English
anti-romances appeared till heroic drama was all but played out,
is very significant. New interests were awakening in certain
sections of society which must inevitably, given a little time,
deeply affect the minds even of those who read only for amusement. Intellectual people were now taking an active part in
scientific inquiry. The Royal Society was incorporated the first
year of the Restoration, and men of letters, divines, thinkers,
and those engaged in practical research were attending its
meetings and contributing to its discussions. They felt themselves to be the leaders in a new age of enlightenment, and
rapidly made their influence apparent even in literature. One
of the earliest services of the society to humane letters was to
urge upon its members the need for eradicating the manifold
defects of English prose, which had inherited from the Elizabethans all the tropes and luxuries and redundancies inherent in
a mode of writing not clearly differentiated from the diction of
poetry, and still hampered by tricks of expression derived from
the Latinists. The gradual substitution of a style based on the

*Dawn
of the
age of
science*

*Encour-
agement
of a plain
style of
prose*

native idiom and suitable for plain dealing with actualities was of inestimable value to fiction, or was to be in the long run.

But the men of science did less than the amateurs of charactery, with their realistic inquisition into social types, to correct the faults of imaginative literature. The heroic drama flourished,[1] and those who read fiction still preferred an exciting or seducing romance to a truthful picture of themselves. If there was a growing tendency perceptible to value fact, it was to value it merely because it was fact. The more extraordinary the more was it relished. Readers who were romantic in their love of the abnormal were still more romantic in their gratification when they believed the abnormal true.

Ineradicable propensities for romance

Pepys and Evelyn were now writing their diaries ; Fuller, Izaak Walton, and Aubrey were putting together their collections of lives. The diary evinced a keen intentness on the changing spectacle of human life, the memoir a similar regard for individual character. The art of biography at a later date was to reach a much higher point of development, simultaneously with a full development of the art of fiction ; but at present writers of fiction had their eyes elsewhere. They and their readers were not yet interested in the daily humdrum phenomena of life. The new spirit of scientific inquiry did not lead fiction to study the natural history of the species. Even Bunyan, when he availed himself of the profane device of allegorical romance for the holy work of saving sinners, realistic as he was by instinct in his picturing of character and manners, stuck to the well-worn features of chivalric adventure in the framework of his scheme. We shall come to a striking illustration shortly, in the case of Mrs Behn, of the pull of the appetite for romance, and the pull the other way of the wish that romance may be true. As late as Defoe, the purveyor of literature for Demos finds himself compelled to provide an inexhaustible supply of surprising events, events verging on the incredible, and devises a special kind of realism primarily as a means of making the incredible sound matter of fact. Thus it is not to be confidently

---

[1] The mockery in the *Rehearsal* hardly went to the root of the matter, and did little to check the vogue of heroic plays.

assumed that the welcome given to realistic rogue-stories from Spain signifies any increasing preference for truth or any intelligent delight in the detection of shams and hypocrisies. The appeal may rather have been to that base love of seeing the worst side of everything, that relish for vice and depravity, which is so often mistaken for a love of honesty and veracity. Picaresque fiction, further, gave a piquant foreign seasoning to that popular old English course, the rascality and horseplay of the jest-books. The crudity and coarseness of the witless compilations that were intended to compete with the Spanish article are enough to persuade us that the acrid comedy of genuine picaresque fiction was little appreciated.

The literature of roguery

Bunyan alludes in *Mr Badman*, apparently with the resentment of one who had fallen a victim himself to their allurements, to the pernicious story-books current in his youth. He makes Mr Wiseman relate with horror how the young reprobate " would get all the bad and abominable books that he could, as beastly romances, and books full of ribaldry, even such as immediately tended to set all fleshly lusts on fire. True, he durst not be known to have any of these, to his master; therefore would he never let them be seen by him, but would keep them in close places, and peruse them at such times as yielded him fit opportunities thereto." [1] There is not much doubt which books these were, so obnoxious to Puritan feeling. Among them were unquestionably the later degraded versions of old romance, and such base imitations as those of Johnson and Forde. Bunyan evidently knew them well. It would be romances of the chap-book order, not those of more literary pretentions which were more expensive to buy, that would come in the way of the tinker's son. *The Pilgrim's Progress* and *The Holy War* are full of reminiscences of such tales, whilst the life-story of Mr Badman bespeaks some acquaintance with the literature of roguery.[2]

[1] *The Life and Death of Mr Badman*, ed. J. A. Froude, 32-33.
[2] Professor Chandler calls it " a Puritan romance of roguery," and compares Bunyan's preface with Alemán's in *Guzman d'Alfarache*, with its avouchment of a strictly edifying purpose. The thieving and other mischievous pranks of the young evil-doer, like the frauds of his later life, may be compared to the exploits of both Spanish and English heroes of roguery ; but the writer's intention is manifestly different. Mr Badman is not a picaro, in the Spanish

*Trans-
lations of
Spanish
picaresque
novels*

Lazarillo de Tormes and the continuation by Jean de Luna went on being published in different versions right through the seventeenth century ; and so too Alemán's *Guzman,* sometimes abridged, and sometimes in the form of select episodes. With the latter was conjoined in some editions Mabbe's translation of the *Celestina.* Such editions were in folio or in several volumes, and consequently expensive. Earlier than the English translations of Quevedo's *Visions* (1640) and the *Buscón* (1657), or of Castillo Solórzano's *Garduña de Sevilla,* as *La Picara* (1665), there appeared in 1638 two translations from Spanish and French respectively which pointed the way for the transition from the older compendiums of vagabondage and roguery to the later Newgate literature. *The Sonne of the Rogue, or, the Politick Theefe. With the Antiquitie of Theeves. A Worke no lesse Curious than delectable,* was Englished, through a French version of a Dutch translation, from Dr Carlos García's *Desordenada Codicia de los Bienos Agenos* (1619), an extremely full account of the professional picaros, their orders of precedence, their mode of life, and their methods of cozenage. It was reprinted as *Lavernae, or the Spanish Gipsy* (1650), and again as *A Scourge for a Den of Thieves* (1659).[1] Almost simultaneously came the *Histoire des Larrons, or the History of Theeves,* translated by Paul Godwin from a huge French collection, the *Histoire générale des Larrons* (1623-1625). Both these provided a mass of material for the use of such compilers and unabashed plagiarists as the authors of *The English Rogue.*

*Lives of
rogues
and
criminals*

The English supplement to this ample provision of picaresque literature from abroad consisted of unauthentic biographies of outlaws and reprobates whose exploits in defiance of law and order had passed into legend as soon as they were dead, and in some cases before. The black sheep of society were as popular now as when Robin Hood first graced the roll of English heroes. The so-called *Life and Death of Gamaliel Ratsey, a Famous Theefe of England* (1605), was a chronicle of light-hearted trickery and bold feats on the highway that is not very different

sense—he has no comic significance—nor an anti-hero, in the French sense, though Bunyan conceived him as antitype to his Christian hero (see *The Literature of Roguery,* i., 225-226).

[1] Chandler, i., 206.

in tone from such a contemporary jest-book as the pamphlet
fathered on George Peele;[1] it obviously owes more to the jest-
books and to the cony-catching stories than to history. Deloney's
Long Meg of Westminster, who was a living heroine of the
London streets in the time of Henry VIII., was celebrated in a
similar life, frequently reprinted down to 1636.[2] Along with her
might be reckoned such earlier hoydens and scapegraces as the
celebrated Elynor Rummyng, Mayd Emlyn, and the Widow
Edyth, heroines of Tudor ballads and broadsides. Meg was
succeeded in popular favour by Mrs Mary Frith, otherwise Moll
Cutpurse, celebrated in *The Madde Pranckes of Merry Mall of
the Banckside* (1610) and *The Woman's Champion* (1662) ; [3] and
she by a still more brazen hussy calling herself Dona Britanica
Hollandia, whose amply fortified house of ill-fame stood on a
spot south of Thames, where the lines of the ditch and curtain-
wall may still be traced in the curious figure of the modern
buildings. Shackerley Marmion made her the central figure of
a rumbustious play, and the same year he, or the accredited
author, Nicholas Goodman, recorded her achievements in the
" Kingdom of Eutopia " in the pamphlet *Hollands Leaguer : or
an Historical Discourse of the Life and Actions of Dona Britanica
Hollandia the Arch-Mistris of the wicked women of England* (1632).
A long file of highwaymen and highwaywomen, professional
foists, and other criminals kept up the succession in the only half
apocryphal annals of roguery right down to Defoe and Fielding.[4] The most notorious and the most bewritten were the
cozeners Dorothy Phillips and Elizabeth Caldwell, Marcy Clay
the highwaywoman, the versatile Mary Maunders, *alias* Mary
Carleton,[5] Captain James Hind, hero of *The English Guzman*
(1652) and of almost as many pretended histories and acknowledged fictions as Jack Sheppard or Jonathan Wild, " the Witty
Rogue," Richard Hainam, William Morrell, subject of *The
Notorious Imposter* (1692), Claude du Vall, Henry Walker the

---

[1] See vol. ii., p. 144 *n*. [2] See vol. ii., p. 180. [3] Chandler, 144-147.
[4] Chandler gives a list of them (*Literature of Roguery*, i., 144-155).
[5] Professor Bernbaum regards the various accounts of this impostor, many
of them highly romanticized and most of them full of imaginary details, as a
very important link between the vamped-up biography and the novel (*The
Mary Carleton Narratives*, 1663-1673, 1921).

Ironmonger, and that redoubtable swashbuckler, Colonel James Turner, who was hanged for a burglary.[1]   Most of the biographies of these miscreants are written in a jovial and facetious style that shows Spanish influence unmistakably.   Morrell's head seems to have been turned by the reading of picaresque stories. A middle-aged surgeon at Banbury, he abandoned a life of solid respectability, and merrily emulated the exploits of a Don Pablos de Segovia.   Several of his tricks appear to have been appropriated by Smollett in *Ferdinand, Count Fathom*, and by Mrs Haywood in *Jerry and Jemmy Jessamy*.[2]   Walter Pope's *Memoirs of Monsieur du Vall, containing the History of his Life and Death ; with his Last Speech and Epitaph* (1670), is in the same spirit.

"*The English Rogue*"   Out of all this promising material a good story-teller might have fashioned a capital English novel of roguery.   But the job fell into the hands of two wretched hacks, who had no higher ambition than to put together a loose farrago of rascality, vice, and crime, with no better seasoning of humour than the crudest horseplay, to be devoured by the kind of people who in later days battened on the police news and the penny dreadful. Richard Head and his continuator, Francis Kirkman, pilfered unscrupulously from every source, without having either the intelligence or the ability to preserve the witty flavour of picaresque tradition or the ironical spirit of anti-romance.   Nor had they the most elementary idea of portraying character or much skill for weaving incident into a sustained narrative.   *The English Rogue* with its various continuations became an enormous serial, that went on as long as there were readers to make it worth while to rehash anecdotes and odds and ends of villainy or brutal jocularity picked up from any quarter.   The authors rummaged all the best-known Spanish novels, not excluding *Don Quixote*, and extracted miscellaneous items from Sorel's *Francion*, the *Histoire des Larrons*, and other French works.   They stole from the *Decameron* to eke out their supply of erotic adventure, a commodity not as a rule much run upon in picaresque romance ;

[1] Chandler, 155.
[2] On the first point see Chandler, i., 153; for the other, compare the two incidents of the fortune-hunter feigning to be at the point of death in order to persuade the heiress to marry him (see below, p. 119).

and they levied without restraint on the English cony-catching pamphlets and all the rest of the vagabond literature from Awdeley to Dekker.

The first and best part was by Head. It was entitled *The English Rogue described, in the Life of Meriton Latroon, a Witty Extravagant. Being a complete History of the most Eminent Cheats of Both Sexes* (1665). This carries the life of the English picaro from a mischievous boyhood down to his deliverance from prison through a reprieve and his departure from England on a course of adventure in the East Indies. Kirkman was a bookseller, who had already brought out three new editions of Head's novel when he published a sequel by himself. This second part (1668) is a hotch-potch of the tricks and escapades of the Rogue himself, his father and mother, the women with whom he is hand and glove, and some other disreputable characters. It does not take up the story where Head had left off, and is inferior to the first part in every respect. But there was no improvement when the two rivals collaborated and produced a new edition with a third and a fourth part (1671). Nevertheless, the book sold, and frequent reprints and abridgments were called for, down to the first quarter of the next century. And for half a century longer there were pirated editions and altered versions, such as *The English Rogue, or Life of Jeremy Sharp* (1776), in which there is a fruitless effort to give some kind of unity to the book by making the Rogue, here rechristened, hero of all the multifarious adventures.

Both Head and Kirkman were the authors of other books. *Other picaresque works by Head and Kirkman* Head tried his hand at charactery in *Proteus Redivivus, or the Art of Wheedling* (1675), confining himself, however, to his special field, the tricks and impositions of tradesmen, attorneys, inn-keepers, catchpoles, and others whose occupations gave them choice opportunities for the practice of over-reaching. More successful as a saleable work was his *Life and Death of Mother Shipton* (1667), which went through many editions. His *Nugae Venales: or a Complaisant Companion* (1686) was a jest-book compiled from miscellaneous sources. He also mimicked the imaginary voyage in two books that are mildly amusing : *The Floating Island : or, a New Discovery, relating the strange*

Adventure on a late Voyage, from Lambethana to Villa Franca, alias Ramallia, To the Eastward of Terra del Templo . . . *by Franck Careless, one of the Discoverers* (1673) *;* and *The Western Wonder : or, O Brazeel, an Inchanted Island discovered ; with a Relation of Two Ship-wracks in a dreadful Sea-storm in that discovery. To which is added, A Discovery of a Place, called Montecapernia* (1674). In the one, Head sails from country to country, typifying the different quarters of the metropolis, and describes the loose manners and morals of the inhabitants. The second part, devoted to Ramallia, the name of which is derived from the notorious Ram Alley, in Alsatia, is rather in the manner of Awdeley. The other book seems to be a skit on extravagant travellers' tales, and alludes to such monstrous fictions as the *Isle of Pines, A New World in the Moon,* and the like. But it also shows where Head's real interests lay, in its account of the land of goats and its brutish population. Kirkman was the author of a miscellany called *The Unlucky Citizen Experimentally Described in the Various Misfortunes of an Unlucky Londoner* (1673), a rogue's autobiography eked out with the usual complement of hackneyed tales. It is noteworthy that he translated the second part of *Don Bellianis*, and was the publisher of several other translations and adaptations of late chivalric romance.

Other works current in Bunyan's youth

So far as any vital effect on English fiction was concerned, the older generation of picaresque novels left hardly any impression ; it was the later issue, the fully-developed picaresque of Le Sage that was to be a stimulating example to Fielding and Smollett, and through them to provide a favourite motive, and often a distinct form of plot, to all the novelists who have made an adventurer or adventuress the centre of interest. Head and Kirkman were mere literary hucksters, and are of no historical importance, except as purveyors of the demoralizing books condemned by Mr Wiseman, and as an index of the low estate to which the novel dealing with the life of the common herd had sunk since the time of Nashe, Deloney, and Dekker. But the other brands of fiction in vogue when Bunyan made his unprecedented contribution to popular literature were no better, all of which have now been reviewed. The other brand, the vulgarized romance, of the two with which he was likeliest to come into contact, was the only other with any extensive circulation. The more sophisticated modern romance, French or English, like the collections of characters, which were only as yet a potential tributary and had not yet begun to flow towards the point of confluence with the main stream of fiction, had but a narrow circle of readers. The same is no doubt true of most of the translations of foreign masterpieces, certainly of Urquhart's Rabelais (1653),[1] the Queen of Navarre's *Heptameron* (1654), and Petronius (1654), though not of Scarron.

[1] The first two parts were all that appeared till 1693.

CHAPTER III

BUNYAN

*Small
influence
of current
fiction on
Bunyan's
work*
THUS the question how far Bunyan may have been influenced by
previous writers of fiction is narrowed down to few possibilities.
For the tale of rascality and wantonness he shows nothing but
repulsion. The romances did not receive his blessing because he
was too well acquainted with the late perversions in the current
chap-books. And yet he planned two of his evangelistic stories
on the lines of allegorical romance, and cast a large proportion
of the characters and incidents in the more primitive romantic
mould. It was the romances that gave him his initial idea of
what a story should be. But to try to fit his books into the history of English fiction as if they marked a progressive stage in its
development would be a mistake. They mark the first appearance of original genius in that history ; but the genius had none
of the far-reaching effects on other writers that might have been
expected. For his vivid painting of the diversified life around
him and the native art with which he makes the characters reveal
themselves in their every speech and gesture, Bunyan was indebted to no one but himself. His conception of the world as
a battle-ground of good and evil spirits, his haunting dread of
eternal retribution, and his fierce evangelistic zeal were those of
his age and sect. But in whatever century or in whatever way
he had been writing, he would have shown the same creative-
ness. If instead of being John Bunyan he had been William
Langland, his *Vision of Piers Plowman* would have been as rich
and varied in human colour as the contemporary tales of the
Canterbury pilgrims. Though he set no value on imaginative
literature as an object in itself, he was better endowed than any
Englishman before him, Chaucer and Shakespeare alone ex-
cepted, for the imaginative reproduction of the drama of life.
But as the master of an art—the unconscious master, for his

mind was centred unswervingly on obeying the divine command
and warning mankind of their imminent danger—he was less
the child of his age than either Chaucer or Shakespeare. He
owed nothing to his fellow-craftsmen. They were pigmies compared with him in understanding, and had nothing to teach
him. He had no progenitors and left no posterity. The novel
remained unaffected by his testimony to the power of simple
realism to make dead bones live, since those who should have
profited by his lessons disdained to read the homely writings of
the unlearned peasant preacher.

John Bunyan (1628-1687) was fifty years old when he gave the
world his *Pilgrim's Progress*, the first of four books in which he
told a long story in order to lead the erring into the paths of
righteousness. He was already the author of more than a score
of works, chiefly religious tracts, discussions of points of doctrine, books of meditation, and the like, with one of considerable
length, *Grace Abounding to the Chief of Sinners* (1666), in which
he had recounted his own spiritual conflicts and displayed a
power of unveiling the secrets of the heart and depicting the
experiences of a soul racked by fear and remorse which the
greatest of novelists or of dramatists could not surpass. In this
and the rest he also showed his command of a simple, unadorned,
but graphic and forcible English prose, which was to be of
invaluable service in his realistic portrayal of life and the narration either of homely incident or events of the most tremendous
significance. *The Pilgrim's Progress from This World to That
which is to come: Delivered under the Similitude of a Dream
Wherein is Discovered, The manner of his setting out, His Dangerous Journey; and Safe Arrival at the Desired Countrey* (1678),
received important augmentations in the second edition of the
same year and the third of the next. It was followed, immediately but for two tracts, by *The Life and Death of Mr Badman,
Presented to the World in a Familiar Dialogue Between Mr Wiseman and Mr Attentive* (1680), and that by *The Holy War, made
by Shaddai upon Diabolus, For the Regaining of the Metropolis of
the World, Or, the Losing and Taking Again of the Town of
Mansoul* (1682). Then, after some minor writings, Bunyan was
induced to bring out a fourth narrative complementary to the

*John
Bunyan:
his four
religious
stories*

first, which he entitled *The Pilgrim's Progress . . . The Second Part . . . Wherein is set forth the manner of the setting out of Christian's Wife and Children, their Dangerous Journey, and Safe Arrival at the Desired Country* (1684).

Bunyan, the man

There was never a Muse of Theology. Yet many books dealing with religion, even with controversy on points of doctrine, are among the classics of literature, and these of Bunyan's are by universal assent among them. Bunyan was the son of a village workman, who was too poor to allow him any but the meagrest schooling or to let him remain idle when he was old enough to lend a hand at his father's forge. He confessed, in *Grace Abounding*,[1] that he soon lost what he had learned. But defective as his education was according to conventional rules, the schooling which a hard life gave him, and the reading in a few books, including the Bible, which he gave himself, were the best possible preparation for the work he was to do. The lad's apprenticeship to his father's trade was interrupted by the demands of military service. At the age of sixteen he was called up to join the army of the Parliament;[2] and it has recently been discovered that for some three years (1644-1647) he was under the command of Sir Samuel Luke, the Puritan officer to whom Samuel Butler was tutor and secretary and whom he gibbeted in *Hudibras*.[3]

After the Royalist defeat (1647) Bunyan was sent home, and a little later married. His wife was a poor woman who had little household stuff, but possessed two books left by her father, *The Plaine Man's Pathway to Heaven*, by Arthur Dent, and the *Practice of Piety*, by Bishop Bayly. These he sometimes read, but as yet he " met with no conviction." Even as a child of nine or ten he had been afflicted by the fear of hell; but he had repressed these terrors and yielded to the gaiety and lawlessness of youth. And now, in manhood, despite the misgivings which thoughts of religion inspired, he relapsed into disordered

[1] G. A., paragraph 3.
[2] See remarks of Bunyan's editor, the Rev. John Brown, on the information afforded by the newly discovered muster-rolls of the Newport Pagnell garrison (*Cambridge Hist. of Eng. Lit.*, vii., 167). Froude, in his monograph on Bunyan in the Men of Letters series, contended against Carlyle and Macaulay that Bunyan served with the Royalist forces.   [3] *Ibid.*

courses and became noted for his daring profanity. He tried not to think of the judgment hanging over his head ; but the voice within would not be hushed, and he wavered between fits of black despondency and reckless outbreaks of the old Adam. In utter despair, he thought, since heaven was gone already, why should he not take his fill of sin?

Grace Abounding is the history of his conversion. He came after a while to read the Bible with a new understanding, and thus entered upon that journey towards the light of which his *Pilgrim's Progress* was afterwards the figurative record. Not at once did he free himself from errors and backslidings. He halted repeatedly between belief and disbelief. He found himself " as in a miry bog," that shook if he did but stir. Visions of angels were succeeded by visions of goblins and of frightful cataclysms like those of the Apocalypse. The voice of the tempter and the voice of conscience carried on an audible dialogue within him. Burdened with the consciousness of sin, he struggled out of his Slough of Despond, but still had before him his valley of the shadow, and incessant combats with fleshly lusts and spiritual doubts. He was never free from the temptation to give up the effort and forsake a road beset with so many difficulties.

" Grace Abounding," his spiritual autobiography

As he tells the story, the warring forces of good and evil grow palpable. The reader is seized and tortured by the same mental strain as the narrator. Never was moral anguish more powerfully, more appallingly, visualized. Yet whilst Bunyan was fleeing from God as from the face of a dreadful judge, convinced that he was guilty of the sin against the Holy Ghost, he suddenly heard a different voice, " as if there had rushed in at the window the noise of wind upon me, but very pleasant." Then, in a moment, his whole spiritual life was spread out before him, and he was shown that he had not wittingly offended.

This made a strange seizure upon my spirit ; it brought light with it, and commanded a silence in my heart of all those tumultuous thoughts that did before use, like masterless hellhounds, to roar and bellow and make a hideous noise within me. . . . But as to my determining about this strange dispensation, what it was, I know not ; or from whence it came, I know not ; I have not yet in twenty years time been able to make a judgment of it; " I thought then what here I should be loath to speak." But verily that sudden rushing wind was as if an angel had come upon me, but both it and the salvation I will leave unto the day of judgment ; only this I say, it commanded a great calm in my soul ; it persuaded me there might be hope ; it showed me, as I thought, what the sin unpardonable was, and that my soul had yet the blessed privilege to flee to Jesus Christ for mercy. . . . This lasted in the favour of it for about three or four days, and then I began to mistrust and to despair again.[1]

His imprisonment

Having found the truth and joined a free congregation in Bedford, Bunyan was soon induced to undertake the office of preacher in the town and the neighbouring villages. His teaching was based on the New Testament and the events therein recorded on which man's hope of redemption is based. The Quakers, who were very active at this time, reproved him for ignoring the inner revelation, the light that is to be discerned in one's own soul. They challenged him in the presence of his congregation. This was the occasion of Bunyan's first book, *Some Gospel Truths opened* (1656), and of a second written in reply to an attempt to refute him. He soon had leisure for further works. The Conventicle Act of 1593 was put in force again at the Restoration, and Bunyan was one of the earliest to be arrested as an unauthorized preacher. He was thrown into Bedford Gaol ; and as he steadily refused to give an undertaking not to offend again, there he remained for twelve years (1660-1672). During the first half of that period, he wrote nine books, including *The Holy City, or the New Jerusalem* (1665), which foreshadows the culminating vision of *The Pilgrim's Progress*, and *Grace Abounding* (1666). During the latter part of his imprisonment he wrote very little, but his pen as well as his voice grew busy again when the Declaration of Indulgence gave him his freedom.

He writes "The Pilgrim's Progress"

When the Indulgence was revoked (1675), Bunyan was again imprisoned, this time in the small gaol on Bedford Bridge. The second captivity lasted only six months, but it is memorable as the period during which he wrote the first part of *The Pilgrim's*

[1] *G. A.*, 174.

Progress.[1] He began it, he says, not with any intention of writing and publishing a book, but to divert his mind from worser thoughts. It was later on that he realized what a useful guide the story would be to the Christain life.[2] At first

> I only thought to make
> I knew not what : nor did I undertake
> Thereby to please my neighbour : no, not I :
> I did it my own self to gratify.

As he meditated on the way of the saints, he fell suddenly into an allegory

> About their journey, and the way to glory.

And as he set down twenty things that came into his mind, twenty more came crowding in,

> And they again began to multiply,
> Like sparks that from the coals of fire do fly.[3]

Bunyan's was one of those minds that think always in concrete images and shun abstractions. The mental history recounted in *Grace Abounding* is enough to prove this. In some early chapters of that book he tells how the little community of people at Bedford who had received the light seemed to him to be on the sunny side of a mountain ; and he saw a wall encompassing the mountain, outside which he was shivering in frost, snow, and darkness. Searching for a way through, he at length found a straight and narrow passage, and by great striving got to the other side. And the vision, by an instinctive turn of his mind, becomes an allegory. The mountain is the church of the living

" The Author's Apology for his Book "

[1] Perhaps he was released before he had quite finished the book. That would explain the break in the story after the visit to the Delectable Mountains, where Bunyan says, "So I awoke from my dream." When he resumes, he says, "And I slept and dreamed again, and saw the same two pilgrims going down the mountains along the highway."
[2] Sir Charles Firth has pointed out (*John Bunyan*, English Association Leaflet, No. 19, 1911) that Bunyan was writing his pamphlet *The Strait Gate, or the great difficulty of going to Heaven* (1676) just before he began *The Pilgrim's Progress*. His characterization of the different kinds of Christian who would fail to reach the kingdom of Heaven would easily have prompted the idea of the road and its many obstacles and dangers.
[3] P. P.,—"The Author's Apology for his Book."

God ; the wall is the world ; and the gap he thought was Jesus Christ, "who is the way to God the Father."[1] There had been allegories of the spiritual life already. Ingelo's *Bentivolio and Urania* was a comparatively recent book. Guillaume de Guileville's *Pélerinage de l'Homme* had been translated by Lydgate more than two centuries before. Spenser's *Faerie Queene* was an allegory of the warfare of the soul and the victory of truth and holiness. But Spenser's idealisms were worlds apart from Bunyan's men and women of flesh and blood. There was a closer kinship in Langland, whose allegory, however, in *Piers Plowman* runs on totally different lines from the scheme of *The Pilgrim's Progress*. But there is no evidence that Bunyan had read any of these works, nor need it be supposed that he was in any way indebted to them, beyond being aware that allegory was an excellent mode of presenting his conceptions. A pilgrimage is the obvious simile for the course of man's life from birth to eternity, especially in conjunction with the ideas of original sin, salvation by grace, and eternal bliss or damnation as the final lot of all men.[2] The Bible itself may have yielded Bunyan the germ of his idea.[3]

" *The Pilgrim's Progress* "

But the success of an allegorical story depends less upon its ingenuity or appropriateness than upon elements that transcend mere allegory. It is, in the first place, the dramatic interest of the story, the fear and suspense holding us ; and, secondly, the strength and firmness of the portraiture, whether of individuals or of crowds, that make this the most enthralling piece of narrative fiction yet produced in English. From the moment when Bunyan in his dream sees his man " clothed with rags, standing in a certain place, with his face from his own house, a book in his hand, and a great burden upon his back," till at the end of the journey Christian and his comrade pass the river of

---

[1] *G. A.*, 53-55.

[2] Richard Heath (see " The Archetype of the ' Pilgrim's Progress,' " *Contemporary Review*, Oct. 1896) thought Bunyan must have derived the idea, and even the details, of his pilgrimage from the experiences of the wandering and persecuted Anabaptists in Germany, Switzerland, etc. He must have come into contact with some of the Anabaptists in England.

[3] *E.g.*, Heb. xi. 13-16 :—" They were strangers and pilgrims on the earth. For they that say such things, declare plainly that they seek a country . . . they desire a better country, that is, an heavenly : wherefore God is not ashamed to be called their God : for he hath prepared for them a city."

death and are led by the shining ones up to the celestial city, our absorption never flags. Both the human and the supernatural personages are live beings, not types or abstractions or idealisms. Christian is a peasant like Bunyan, with the idiosyncrasies of his begetter, the agonies of conscience, the alternations of hope and misgiving, the demure humour. Pliable, Obstinate, Mr Worldly Wiseman, Mr Talkative, Mr Facing-both-ways, are such persons as he had met with in Bedford and the countrysides where he worked and preached. They answer to their names, but their names do not sum up entirely their quirks and foibles. Mr Greatheart, Giant Grim and Giant Despair, Apollyon, the ladies of the House Beautiful, are not mere shadows, relics of fable and romance read in his childhood ; they too are characters with sufficient individuality. And Bunyan's thumbnail sketches of the witnesses and jurymen at the trial in Vanity Fair are likewise a minor triumph of rapid individualization.

The child reads *The Pilgrim's Progress*, with its sequel, as a tale of adventure, of brave fighters, knights in armour, ogres, dragons, thrilling perils, and hairbreadth escapes. The mature reader feels the deeper spell, the inner significance ; he cannot but identify himself with Christian and his fortunes. It is no longer romance, but the drama of human life on which he gazes, a rapt spectator. Tragic issues are being decided ; but, as in life, there is a comic aspect to many of the incidents. Bunyan's sense of humour comes out best in the casual rencounters met with by Christian on his journey. He and Faithful, for instance, fall in with Talkative, " a tall man, and something more comely at a distance than at hand." Says he to Faithful :—

Life-like portraiture and dialogue

" I will talk of things heavenly, or things earthly ; things moral, or things evangelical ; things past, or things to come ; things foreign, or things at home ; things more essential, or things circumstantial ; provided that all be done to our profit."

Now did Faithful begin to wonder ; and stepping to Christian (for he walked all this while by himself), he said to him, but softly, " What a brave companion have we got ! Surely this man will make a very excellent pilgrim."

At this Christian modestly smiled and said, " This man, with whom you are so taken, will beguile, with that tongue of his, twenty of them that know him not."

" Do you know him then ? "

" Know him ! Yes, better than he knows himself."

" Pray, what is he ? "

" His name is Talkative ; he dwelleth in our town. I wonder that you should be a stranger to him, only that I consider that our town is large."

" Whose son is he, and whereabout does he dwell ? "

" He is the son of one Say-well ; he dwelt in Prating Row ; and is known of all that are acquainted with him by the name of Talkative of Prating Row ; and notwithstanding his fine tongue, he is but a sorry fellow."

" Well, he seems to be a very pretty man."

" That is, to them who have not thorough acquaintance with him ; for he is best abroad ; near home, he is ugly enough. Your saying that he is a pretty man, brings to my mind what I have observed in the work of the painter, whose pictures show best at a distance, but, very near, more unpleasing."

This is the most lifelike dialogue that we have hitherto come across in our own itinerary ; that it does not mark an epoch in the history of fiction is due to the obstinate deafness of the professional writers, all of them citizens of the town called Vanity.

Satire of his age   The comic touches turn to strokes of satire in the account of Vanity Fair, which is a microcosm, not merely of the frivolous English world under Charles II., but of Europe at large, where, except among the small minority whose religion was earnest and their conduct strict, indifference and licentiousness ruled, and the baubles of Rome were the chief merchandise. Brilliant as a swift succession of scowling, fawning, or sneering faces, the trial scene is equally telling as an indictment of judicial tyranny and of the superstition, hypocrisy, and malice that were its ignoble ministers. The satire is more of the nature of a sermon in the dialogue with Mr By-ends.

So I saw that quickly after they were got out of the fair, they overtook one that was going before them, whose name was By-ends : so they said to him, What countryman, sir ? and

how far go you this way ? He told them that he came from
the town of Fair-speech, and he was going to the Celestial
City ; but told them not his name.

From Fair-speech ! said Christian. Is there any that be
good live there ?

By-ends. Yes, said By-ends, I hope.

Chr. Pray, sir, what may I call you ? said Christian.

By-ends. I am a stranger to you and you to me : if you be
going this way, I shall be glad of your company ? if not I must
be content.

Chr. This town of Fair-speech, I have heard of it, and, as I
remember, they say it is a wealthy place.

By-ends. Yes, I will assure you that it is ; and I have very
many rich kindred there.

Chr. Pray, who are your kindred there, if a man may be so
bold?

By-ends. [Almost the whole town ; and, in particular, my
Lord Turn-about, my Lord Time-server, my Lord Fair-speech
(from whose ancestors that town first took its name); also Mr
Smooth-man, Mr Facing-both-ways, Mr Anything ; and the
parson of our parish, Mr Two-tongues, was my mother's own
brother by father's side], to tell you truth, I am a gentleman of
good quality ; yet my great-grandfather was but a water-man,
looking one way and rowing another, and I got most of my
estate by the same occupation.

Chr. Are you a married man ?

By-ends. Yes, and my wife is a very virtuous woman, the
daughter of a virtuous woman ; she was my Lady Feigning's
daughter, therefore she came of a very honourable family,
and is arrived to such a pitch of breeding, that she knows
how to carry it to all, even to prince and peasant. It is
true, we somewhat differ in religion from those of the stricter
sort—yet but in two small points : First, we never strive
against wind and tide. Secondly, we are always most zealous
when Religion goes in his silver slippers ; we love much to
walk with him in the street, if the sun shines and the people
applaud it.

Then Christian stepped a little to-side to his fellow, Hopeful,
saying, It runs in my mind that this is one By-ends, of Fair-
speech ; and if it be he, we have as very a knave in our company
as dwelleth in all these parts. Then said Hopeful, Ask him ;
methinks he should not be ashamed of his name. So Christian
came up with him again, and said, Sir, you talk as if you knew
something more than all the world doth ; and if I take not my

mark amiss, I deem I have half a guess of you.   Is not your name
Mr By-ends, of Fair-speech ?

By-ends. That is not my name ; but indeed it is a nickname
that is given me by some that cannot abide me, and I must be
content to bear it as a reproach, as other good men have borne
theirs before me.

Chr. But did you never give an occasion to men to call you
by this name ?

By-ends. Never, never ! The worst that ever I did to give
them an occasion to give me this name was that I had always
the luck to jump in my judgment with the present way of the
times, whatever it was, and my chance was to get thereby : but
if things are thus cast upon me, let me count them a blessing ;
but let not the malicious load me, therefore, with reproach.

Chr. I thought, indeed, that you was the man that I had
heard of ; and to tell you what I think, I fear this name belongs
to you more properly than you are willing we should think it
doth.

By-ends. Well, if you will thus imagine, I cannot help it ; you
shall find me a fair company-keeper, if you will still admit me
your associate.

Chr. If you will go with us, you must go against wind and
tide ; the which, I perceive, is against your opinion.   You must
also own Religion in his rags, as well as when in his silver slippers ;
and stand by him, too, when bound in irons as well as when he
walketh the streets with applause.

By-ends. You must not impose nor lord it over my faith ;
leave me to my liberty, and let me go with you.

Chr. Not a step further, unless you will do in what I pro-
pound as we.

Then said By-ends, I shall never desert my old principles,
since they are harmless and profitable.   If I may not go with you,
I must do as I did before you overtook me, even go by myself,
until some overtake me that will be glad of my company.[1]

In this and other incidents, such as Christian's talk with his
wife before he sets out, the remonstrance of Mr Worldly Wiseman, and Christian's discourse in the palace called Beautiful,
Bunyan added some of his finest touches to the second and third
editions. He wrote the book, he said, to please himself ; but
that he quickly realized its practical value, and accordingly took

[1] *Pilgrim's Progress*, Pt. I., 1895, pp. 137-141.

pains to perfect the story and annotate it with scriptural references, there can be no doubt. His earnestness of purpose and
the intensity of his emotion was a help, not a snare ; it detracted
nothing from the literary quality of the book. It gave vigour
and actuality to the rapid sketches of character : it made
Bunyan see the figures he evoked as individuals in stern jeopardy,
and not merely as examples of human virtues or shortcomings.
It gave precision and a biblical force to his descriptions of
scenery. The hill Difficulty, the gloomy valley, and the distant
view of the Delectable Mountains are imaged in our memories
as clearly as any hills and vales our bodily eyes have seen.[1]
Without any literary ambition, with no thought of fine writing,
out of the innate conscientiousness of a good workman, he
attained the highest results with the homeliest materials. Being
a clear-eyed observer and heart and soul a lover of his fellow-
creatures, he produced a masterpiece of realistic fiction without
knowing it.

The second part of *The Pilgrim's Progress* was the fourth and
last of Bunyan's religious stories. This account of Christiana's
pilgrimage falls far short of her husband's story in power and
beauty. Neither the transfiguring imagination nor the convincing truth of Bunyan's first narrative is visible here. He
allowed too much play to his reminiscences of the old-fashioned

*Second
part of
" The
Pilgrim's
Pro-
gress "*

[1] I once listened to an extremely learned paper read to a society of anti-
quaries by an enthusiast who claimed to have discovered the actual route
which suggested the main features of Christian's journey. It was a curious
proof, at any rate, of the spell Bunyan's scene-painting casts on the reader.
Bunyan, it was stated, often visited the town of Guildford, and travelled the
road running east beside the North Downs, in fact, the old Pilgrims' Way.
The marshy ground outside Guildford suggested the Slough of Despond, the
hill Difficulty was the steep ridge crowned by the old church of St Martha.
Wotton Hall was the palace called Beautiful (usually identified as Houghton
House, Ampthill, Bedfordshire). In the distance can be seen the Delectable
Mountains, to wit, the Leith Hill range. In Bunyan's time, the furnaces that
once existed in this valley may have been in full blast. Close to the hammer-
pond at Friday Street was one, which would mark the fiery and smoky spot
where Bunyan put his back-way to hell. The flame, smoke, and noise,
especially after nightfall, were presumed to have inspired the grim vision of
the Valley of the Shadow. Nay, it was even contended that a fight Bunyan
may have had with a ruffianly smith gave him the idea of the combat with
Apollyon. Dowding Castle is certainly shown on the Ordnance Survey map
only a mile or two off the road, and is another of the numerous features said
to correspond with those described in *The Pilgrim's Progress*. The case was
elaborated in all seriousness, with the support of maps, views, and other
evidence that was obviously the result of years of ardent research.

tale of heroic adventure, with its Grail knight, Mr Greatheart, its giants, savage beasts, and celestial champions. It appeals to children. Mr Greatheart is a favourite character of one's boyhood.[1] And it was read with as much delight by hosts of uncritical folk as the original story. That had already gone into many editions, and been translated into a number of foreign languages, as Bunyan notices with satisfaction in the versified preface to the second part. Though some have made light of *The Pilgrim's Progress* as mere romance, he refuses to be put out. He has realized the potency of allegory.

> I also know a dark similitude
> Will on the fancy more itself intrude,
> And will stick faster in the heart and head,
> Than things from similes not borrowèd.

The Life and Death of Mr Badman

His next story, however, was not allegorical, but undisguisedly didactic ; it took the rather clumsy form of a narrative by one of the speakers in a long conversation.[2] Having shown

[1] The declension may be gauged by comparing such a passage as the meeting with Mr Talkative and the amusing incident of the purge administered to Christiana's little boy suffering from the gripes of conscience. This is manifestly a lesson for children—or those of childlike mind :—
So he made him a purge, but it was too weak ; it was said it was made of the blood of a goat, the ashes of a heifer, and with some of the juice of hyssop, etc. (Heb. x. 1-4). When Mr Skill had seen that that purge was too weak, he made him one to the purpose ; it was made ex carne et sanguine Christi (John vi. 54-57 ; Heb. ix. 14) (you know physicians give strange medicines to their patients) ; and it was made up into pills, with a promise or two, and a proportionable quantity of salt (Mark ix. 49). Now he was to take them three at a time fasting, in half a quarter of a pint of the tears of repentance (Zech. xii. 30).
When this potion was prepared and brought to the boy, he was loath to take it, though torn with the gripes as if he should be pulled in pieces. Come, come, said the physician, you must take it. It goes against my stomach, said the boy. I must have you take it, said his mother. I shall vomit it up again, said the boy. Pray, sir, said Christiana to Mr Skill, how does it taste? It has no ill taste, said the doctor ; and with that she touched one of the pills with the tip of her tongue. O Matthew, said she, this potion is sweeter than honey. If thou lovest thy mother, if thou lovest thy brothers, if thou lovest Mercy, if thou lovest thy life, take it. So, with much ado, after a short prayer for the blessing of God upon it, he took it, and it wrought kindly with him. It caused him to purge ; it caused him to sleep and rest quietly ; it put him into a fine heat and breathing sweat, and did quite rid him of his gripes. So in a little time he got up, and walked about with a staff, and would go from room to room, and talk with Prudence, Piety, and Charity, of his distemper, and how he was healed (*The Pilgrim's Progress*, Part II., 1887, pp. 297-298).
[2] The form was derived from one of the books belonging to his wife, and mentioned by Bunyan in *Grace Abounding* (see supra, p. 52), viz.: *The*

the Christian fighting his way out of a world of iniquity and
at last winning salvation, Bunyan now painted the obverse, the
dreadful career of the man who loves iniquity, and enslaved by
the lusts of the flesh sinks deeper and deeper, until, with heart
harder than any stone, he dies impenitent, losing his soul even
before he is quit of the body. Mr Badman's history is related
by Mr Wiseman, Mr Attentive listening and making shrewd
comments. But the narrator often takes up the other's points,
and the story comes to a standstill whilst they discuss questions
of doctrine and its applications. Here, for instance, is a passage
in which, from Mr Attentive's remarks on the theory of
original sin, Mr Wiseman proceeds to develop the view of
Bunyan's co-religionists that sinners alone are capable of
salvation :—

Wise. I will endeavour to answer your desires, and first, I
will tell you, that from a Child he was very bad : his very
beginning was ominous, and presaged that no good end was,
in likelihood, to follow thereupon. There were several sins
that he was given to, when but a little one, that manifested him
to be notoriously infected with Original corruption ; for I dare-
say he learned none of them of his Father or Mother ; nor was
he admitted to go much abroad among other children, that
were vile, to learn to sin of them : Nay, contrariwise, if at any
time he did get abroad amongst others, he would be as the
Inventor of bad words, and an example in bad actions. To
them all he used to be, as we say, the ring-leader, and Master-
sinner from a Child.

Atten. This was a bad beginning indeed, and did demonstrate
that he was, as you say, very much polluted with Original
Corruption. For to speak my mind freely, I do confess, that
it is mine opinion, that Children come polluted with sin into
the World, and that ofttimes the sins of their youth, especially
while they are very young, are rather by virtue of Indwelling
sin, than by examples that are set before them by others. Not
but that they learn to sin by example too, but Example is not

Plaine Man's Pathway to Heaven, by Arthur Dent (11th ed., 1609). In
Dent, Theologus and Philagathus ; in Bunyan, Mr Wiseman and Mr
Attentive spend a long day in a moral discussion ; but Dent has no story
to tell (see introductory "Note" to *Mr Badman*, ed. J. Brown, 1905, vi.,
and "Bunyan's *Mr Badman*," by J. B. Wharey (*Mod. Lang. Notes*, xxxvi., 1921,
pp. 65-79).

the root, but rather the Temptation unto wickedness. The root is sin within ; for from within, out of the heart of man proceedeth sin.

Wise. I am glad to hear that you are of this opinion, and to confirm what you have said by a few hints from the Word. Man in his birth is compared to an Ass (an unclean Beast), and to a wretched Infant in its blood : besides, all the first-born of old that were offered unto the Lord, were to be redeemed at the age of a month, and that was before they were sinners by imitation. The Scripture also affirmeth, that by the sin of one, Judgment came upon all ; and renders this reason, for that all *have* sinned : nor is that objection worth a rush, That Christ by his death hath taken away Original Sin. First, Because it is Scriptureless. Secondly, Because it makes them incapable of Salvation by Christ ; for none but those that in their own Persons are sinners, are to have Salvation by Him. Many other things might be added, but between persons so well agreed as you and I are, these may suffice at present ; but when an Antagonist comes to deal with us about this matter, then we have for him often other strong Arguments if he be an Antagonist worth the taking notice of.[1]

Outline of the Story

The Life and Death of Mr Badman is the biography of a selfish, brutal, dishonest tradesman, such a one as Bunyan must have known in Bedford or some other provincial town. From the outset, he shows an evil disposition, and with hypocritical cunning or daredevil sullenness he resists every attempt to reclaim him. As a youth, he is a byword for profligacy and blackguardism. Set up in business by his father, he is brought by dissipation and extravagance to the brink of ruin. Then he makes up to a religious woman who has money, and pretending to be repentant induces her to become his wife, in the fond belief that she will complete his reformation. Once master of her fortune, he mocks at his recent professions, and neglects his

Parallel with Dekker's " Politick Bankruptisme,"

poor dupe to run after loose women. The money has set him up again, and he becomes the head of a large and prosperous business. But self-indulgence and rash speculation bring him once more to the verge of disaster. In this emergency he falls back upon the device stigmatized by Dekker in the passage on

[1] *The Life and Death of Mr Badman*, ed. John Brown, 1905, pp. 20-21.

" Politick Bankruptisme," in *The Seven Deadly Sinnes of London*.[1]
Mr Wiseman describes how it was done :—

Wise. Hold you there ; some of Mr Badman's sins were
costly, as his drinking, and whoring, and keeping other bad
company ; though he was a man that had ways too many to
get money, as well as ways too many to spend it.

Atten. Had he then such a good Trade, for all he was such a
bad man ? or was his Calling so gainfull to him, as alwayes to
keep his Purses belly full, though he was himself a great spender ?

Wise. No : It was not his Trade that did it, though he had
a pretty trade too. He had another way to get Money, and
that by hatfulls and pocketfulls at a time.

Atten. Why, I trow he was no Highway man was he ?

Wise. I will be sparing in my speech as to that, though some
have muttered as if he could ride out now and then, about
no body but himself knew what, over night, and come home all
dirty and weary next morning. But that is not the thing I
aim at.

Atten. Pray let me know it, if you think it convenient that
I should.

Wise. I will tell you : It was this, he had an art to Break,
and get hatfulls of money by breaking.

Atten. But what do you mean by Mr Badmans Breaking ?
you speak mystically, do you not ?

Wise. No, no, I speak plainly. Or, if you will have it in
plainer language, 'tis this : When Mr Badman had swaggered
and whored away most of his wife's portion, he began to feel
that he could not much longer stand upon his legs in this course
of life, and keep up his Trade and Repute (such as he had) in
the world ; but by the new Engine of Breaking. Wherefore,
upon a time, he gives a great, and sudden rush into several mens
debts, to the value of about four or five thousand pound, driving
at the same time a very great trade, by selling many things for
less than they cost him, to get him custom, therewith to blind
his Creditors eyes. His Creditors, therefore feeling that he
had a great employ, and dreaming that it must needs at length
turn to a very good account to them, trusted him freely without
mistrust, and so did others too, to the value of what was mentioned before. Well, when Mr Badman had well feathered
his Nest with other mens goods and money, after a little time
he breaks. And by and by it is noysed abroad that Mr Badman

1 Vol. ii., 212-213.

had shut up Shop, was gone, and could trade no longer. Now, by that time his breaking was come to his Creditors ears, he had by Craft and Knavery made so sure of what he had, that his Creditors could not touch a penny. Well, when he had done, he sends his mournfull, sugered letters to his Creditors, to let them understand what had happened unto him, and desired them not to be severe with him ; for he bore towards all men an honest mind, and would pay so far as he was able. Now he sends his letters by a man confederate with him, who could make both the worst, and best of Mr Badmans case : The best for Mr Badman, and the worst for his Creditors. So when he comes to them, he both bemoans them, and condoles Mr Badmans condition : Telling of them, that without a speedy bringing of things to a conclusion, Mr Badman would be able to make them no satisfaction, but at present he both could, and would, and that to the utmost of his power : and to that end, he desired that they would come over to him. Well, his Creditors appoint him a time and come over ; and he, meanwhile, authorizes another to treat with them, but will not be seen himself, unless it was on a Sunday, lest they should snap him with a Writ. So his deputed friend treats with them about their concern with Mr Badman, first telling them of the great care that Mr Badman took to satisfy them and all men for what-soever he ought, as far as in him lay, and, how little he thought a while since to be in this low condition. He pleaded also the greatness of his Charge, the greatness of Taxes, the Badness of the times, and the great Losses that he had by many of his customers, some of which died in his debt, others were run away, and for many that were alive, he never expected a farth(i)ng from them. Yet nevertheless he would shew himself an honest man, and would pay as far as he was able ; and if they were willing to come to terms, he would make a composition with them, (for he was not able to pay them all). The Creditors asked what he would give ? 'Twas replied, Half a crown in the pound. At this they began to huff, and he to renew his complaint and entreaty ; but the Creditors would not hear, and so for that time their meeting without success broke up. But after his Creditors were in cool blood, and admitting of second thoughts, and fearing lest delays should make them lose all, they admit of a second debate, come to-gether again, and by many words and great ado, they obtained five shillings in the pound. So the money was produced, Releases and Discharges drawn, signed, and sealed, Books crossed, and all things confirmed ; and then Mr Badman can put his head out a dores again, and be a better man than when he shut up Shop, by several thousands of pounds.

Atten. And did he do thus indeed ?

Wise. Yes, once, and again. I think he brake twice or thrice.

Atten. And did he do it before he had need to do it ?

Wise. Need! What do you mean by need ? there is no need at any time for a man to play the knave. He did it of a wicked mind, to defraud and beguile his Creditors : he had wherewithall of his Father, and also by his Wife, to have lived upon, with lawfull labour, like an honest man. He had also when he made this wicked break (though he had been a profuse and prodigal spender) to have paid his creditors their own to a farthing. But had he done so, he had not done like himself, like Mr Badman ; had he, I say, dealt like an honest man, he had then gone out of Mr Badman's road. He did it therefore, of a dishonest mind, and to a wicked end ; to wit, that he might have wherewithall, howsoever unlawfully gotten, to follow his Cups and Queans, and to live in the full swing of his lusts, even as he did before.

Atten. Why this was a meer Cheat.

Wise. It was a cheat indeed. This way of breaking, it is nothing else but a more neat way of Thieving, of picking of pockets, of breaking open of shops, and of taking from men what one has nothing to do with. But though it seem easie, it is hard to learn, no man that has conscience to God or man, can ever be his Crafts Master in this Hellish art.

Atten. Oh! Sirs! what a wicked man was this ?

Wise. A wicked man indeed. By this art he could tell how to make men send their goods to his shop, and then be glad to take a penny for that which he had promised before it came thither, to give them a Groat ; I say, he could make them glad to take a Crown for a pounds worth, and a thousand for that for which he had promised before to give them four thousand pounds.

Atten. This argueth that Mr Badman had but little conscience.

Wise. This argued that Mr Badman had No Conscience at all ; for Conscience, the least spark of a good Conscience cannot endure this.[1]

Mr Badman's conscience had become gangrened and insen- *The con-* sible, yet he was not beyond the reach of fears for his soul. One *clusion*

---

[1] *The Life and Death of Mr Badman*, ed. John Brown, pp. 92-96.

night, riding home drunk, he fell and broke his leg. He thought his last hour had come, and for a while suffered agonies of dread. But as soon as he was about again he relapsed into his old ways, and broke his wife's heart with the disappointment. Then he was fool enough to marry again, and the second wife proved a match for him in wickedness and brutality. For sixteen years their life was a hell of incessant quarrelling and fighting, rendered still more wretched by the loss of his wealth. And now the end is in sight. As Froude pointed out,[1] Bunyan was too good an artist to make his example of thoroughpaced wickedness fall suddenly from the height of prosperity into the disasters he so well deserved. He painted life as it is, and visited upon Mr Badman's head the retribution that actually does accompany resolute misdoing, the final and irredeemable loss of the soul. The unbeliever in the doctrine of eternal punishment reads the account of the sinner's last moments with the same horror and the same conviction that justice has been performed as the Calvinists of Bunyan's own time read it. Here once more Bunyan wrote better than he knew, and the story satisfies in full the more modern idea of poetic justice : sentence is delivered truly and inexorably in the mind of every sensitive reader in which the drama is played out. Each reader feels that there is nothing but squalor and abomination in such a life and such a death. In the end the scales are evenly balanced. Bunyan, however, true to his beliefs, maintains throughout the ghastly parallel : the good man attains eternal bliss, the evil man eternal woe.

Atten. I do fully acquiesce with you in this. But, Sir, since you have charged him with dying impenitent, pray let me see how you will prove it : not that I altogether doubt it, because you have affirmed it, but yet I love to have proof for what men say in such weighty matters.

Wise. When I said, he died without repentance, I meant, so far as those that knew him, could judge, when they compared his Life, the word, and his Death together.

Atten. Well said, they went the right way to find out whether he had, that is, did manifest that he had repentance or no. Now then shew me how they did prove he had none ?

[1] *John Bunyan* (Eng. Men of Letters), 1880, c. 7.

Wise. So I will : And first, this was urged to prove it. He had not in all the time of his sickness, a sight and sense of his sins, but was as secure, and as much at quiet, as if he had never sinned in all his life.

Atten. I must needs confess that this is a sign he had none. For how can a man repent of that of which he hath neither sight nor sense ? But 'tis strange that he had neither sight nor sense of sin now, when he had such a sight and sence of his evil before : I mean when he was sick before.

Wise. He was, as I said, as secure now, as if he had been as sinless as an angel : though all men knew what a sinner he was, for he carried his sins in his forehead. His debauched Life was read and known of all men ; but his reputation was read and known of no man ; for, as I said, he had none. And for ought I know, the reason he had no sense of his sins now, was because he profited not by that sence that he had of them before. He liked not to retain that knowledge of God then, that caused his sins to come to remembrance : Therefore God gave him up now to a reprobate mind, to hardness and stupidity of Spirit ; and so was that scripture fulfilled upon him, He hath blinded their eyes. And that, Let their eyes be darkned that they may not see. Oh ! for a man to live in sin, and to go out of the world without repentance for it, is the saddest judgment that can overtake a man.[1]

It is entirely off the mark to compare this powerful didactic work with picaresque fiction.[2] It is radically different. The essence of the rogue-story is light-hearted though sour and biting comedy, even if an Alemán interlards the comedy with incongruous sermons. The rogue is a hero, however rascally a hero. Usually he tells his own story ; but whether he does so or not, he frankly rejoices in the sport that he gets out of such a sorry thing as life. But this grim recital of Mr Wiseman's is formidably serious ; it is a stern morality-play devoid of comic relief. Some comparison may be allowed with the denunciatory pieces of Nashe and Dekker, but with the large proviso that they were journeymen of letters writing for display on a chosen theme, and moralizing for readers who enjoyed seeing the delinquencies of the age castigated in violent terms ; whilst

Mr Badman not a picaresque story

---

[1] *Mr Badman*, pp. 158-159.   [2] See, *e.g.*, Chandler, i., 225-226.

Bunyan from beginning to end was in mortal agony for those whom he saw dancing on the lava-crust of hell-fire.

The Holy War (1682) is a much more elaborate and intricate allegory than either the first or the second part of *The Pilgrim's Progress*, and extends almost to the length of the two put together. In Bunyan's first story, the metaphor of a pilgrimage made the battle of life, and its moral and spiritual crises, more intelligible to a plain mind. Not so *The Holy War*, which is an ingenious fable rendering the simple more complicated. Bunyan had not the metaphysical poet's excuse for intellectual subtleties, that he was aiming to explain the inexplicable, for the clarity of his religious convictions was the reverse of mystical. He was led astray by the success of his first allegorical story, and perhaps by the liking for allegory which he found in his readers. Milton in *Paradise Lost* and *Paradise Regained* had recounted the fall of man and the redemption. Bunyan takes even a longer span of history, for he reaches back to the beginning of things, and leaves us peering with apprehension into the future. Like Milton, he was hampered by the need to accommodate his story to a fixed framework ; the dramatic unfolding of character was rigidly circumscribed. Motives had to be provided to yield given results. And, like Milton, he committed the impropriety of showing the Almighty initiating measures that are destined to be abortive, and deliberating about the manner of attaining results that are predetermined and foreseen. But here again, as in *The Pilgrim's Progress*, Bunyan the humanist was at his best in the casual incidents and the touches of nature that were not prescribed by the allegorical scheme.

The events take place in the large and spacious country of Universe, where lies a fair and delicate town called Mansoul, built by Shaddai for his own delight. It was ordained that the walls of Mansoul could never be broken down except by consent of the townsmen. So likewise the five gates, named after the five senses, might never be forced but by the will of those within. Upon a time, a mighty giant Diabolus, formerly a servant of Shaddai but now banished for treason and rebellion, conspires to revenge himself by seizing and corrupting Mansoul. By cunning overtures he persuades certain influential citizens to admit

"The Holy War"

Outline of the story

him, and he speedily makes himself master of the place, although the mayor, Lord Understanding, and the recorder Mr Conscience, are not slain but only imprisoned and so prevented from stirring up opposition to the Diabolonians. New officers are appointed, Lord Willbewill becoming governor, with Mr Mind as clerk and Mr Vile-Affection as deputy ; Lord Lustings is the new mayor ; Mr Forget-Good recorder; and Mr Incredulity, Mr Atheist, and others of like stamp, thirteen in all, are made chief burgesses and aldermen.[1]

When the intelligence is brought to Shaddai, a council is summoned in heaven, and the divine purposes are declared. It is determined to send four captains to recover the city : their names are Boanerges, Captain Conviction, Captain Judgment, and Captain Execution. At the head of forty thousand troops they advance against Mansoul and summon it to surrender. There are dissensions within the city, some being desirous of making terms. Bunyan himself, no doubt, had had experience during the Civil War of disaffected and wavering persons who made it difficult to keep a united front. *The Holy War* is the history of a Great Rebellion. But Diabolus checks these outbreaks of loyalism ; and, after much fighting, described with the vivid particulars of one who knew something about skirmishes and sieges himself, Captain Boanerges and his rother-officers report that they are unsuccessful, and petition t..e King to send more forces, under a leader whom the people of Mansoul may both love and fear.

In all this, of course, Bunyan is expounding the doctrine of his party. He has a holy war of his own to carry on, against Rome, against the temporizing Anglican Church, and other propagandists of error. By this initial failure he implied that the Old Covenant was of no avail. Man cannot be saved by his own unaided efforts. Redemption is through faith, not works. Wherefore Shaddai now sends his only son Emmanuel, at the head of a still more powerful army, to reoccupy Mansoul. He invests the

---

[1] Sir Charles Firth has pointed out that this remodelling of the magistracy of Mansoul was probably suggested by the Tory attack on the charters of corporate towns at the end of the reign of Charles II., when Whigs and Nonconformists were removed from the corporation of Bedford and other towns and tools of the court put in their place (*John Bunyan*, 107).

place, and offers terms to the inhabitants ; with Diabolus he will hold no parley. Bunyan's adroitness in controversy is well seen in Emmanuel's dialogue with Mr Loath-to-stoop, who tries to negotiate a compromise, and is peremptorily informed that Diabolus must be expelled from Mansoul and no communication whatever allowed with him in future. Mr Loath-to-stoop remonstrates :—

But, great Sir, since my master hath many friends, and those that are dear to him, in Mansoul, may he not, if he should depart from them, even of his bounty and good nature, bestow upon them, as he sees fit, some tokens of his love and kindness that he had for them, to the end that Mansoul, when he is gone, may look upon such tokens of kindness once received from their old friend, and remember him who was once their king, and the merry times that they sometimes enjoyed one with another, while he and they lived in peace together ? [1]

God is on the side of the Puritans, and strictly forbids that " the least scrap, shred, or dust " of the old worship shall be left behind.

The citadel is seized, Diabolus captured and expelled ; those citizens who have thrown in their lot with the usurper, whether of choice or compulsion, await the conqueror's sentence. Petition after petition is sent to Emmanuel without effect. He will not be appeased but by unconditional surrender.

This petition, when drawn up, was designed to be sent to the Prince as the first ; but who should carry it ?—that was the question. Some said, " Let him do it that went with the first " ; but others thought not good to do that, and that because he sped no better. Now, there was an old man in the town, and his name was Mr Good-deed ; a man that bore only the name, but had nothing of the nature of the thing. Now, some were for sending of him ; but the Recorder was by no means for that ; " for," said he, " we now stand in need of, and are pleading for mercy : wherefore to send our petition by a man of this name, will seem to cross the petition itself. Should we make Mr Good-deed our messenger when our petition cries for mercy ?

" Besides," quoth the old gentleman, " should the Prince now,

[1] *The Holy War*, ed. J. Brown, 1905, 261.

as he receives the petition, ask him and say, 'What is thy name?'—as no body knows but he will,—and he should say, 'Old Good-deed,' what, think you, would Emmanuel say but this? 'Ay! is old Good-deed yet alive in Mansoul? then let old Good-deed save you from your distresses.' And if he says so, I am sure we are lost; nor can a thousand of old Good-deeds save Mansoul."

After the Recorder had given in his reasons why old Good-deed should not go with this petition to Emmanuel, the rest of the prisoners and chief of Mansoul opposed it also, and so old Good-deed was laid aside, and they agreed to send Mr Desires-awake again. So they sent for him, and desired him that he would a second time go with their petition to the Prince, and he readily told them he would. But they bid him that in anywise he should take heed that in no word or carriage he gave offence to the Prince: " for by doing so, for ought we can tell, you may bring Mansoul into utter destruction," said they.

Now, Mr Desires-awake, when he saw that he must go of this errand, besought that they would grant that Mr Wet-eyes might go with him. Now this Wet-eyes was a near neighbour of Mr Desires, a poor man, a man of a broken spirit, yet one that could speak well to a petition; so they granted that he should go with him. Wherefore, they address themselves to their business: Mr Desires put a rope upon his head, and Mr Wet-eyes went with his hands wringing together. Thus they went to the Prince's pavilion.[1]

Here the hand that threw into clear definition each individual of the crowd in Vanity Fair is as cunning as ever, though now the task is more complicated, to combine theology with character-drawing. There is an excess of psychological and ethical hair-splitting in *The Holy War*; but the artist in Bunyan brings the abstractions to life. Old Good-deed, Mr Desires, and Mr Wet-Eyes have all failed; Mr Inquisitive now pushes himself forward.

Combination of theology and character-drawing

Now, there was in the company a notable, sharp-witted fellow, a mean man of estate, and his name was old Inquisitive. This man asked the petitioners if they had told out every whit of what Emmanuel said, and they answered, " Verily, no." Then said Inquisitive, " I thought so, indeed; pray, what was it more that he said unto you?" Then they paused a while

[1] *The Holy War*, ed. John Brown, 280-281.

but at last they brought out all, saying, " The Prince bade us bid Captain Boanerges and Captain Conviction bring the prisoners down to him to-morrow ; and that Captain Judgement and Captain Execution should take charge of the castle and town till they should hear further from him." They said also, that when the Prince had commanded them thus to do, he immediately turned his back upon them, and went into his royal pavilion.

But, oh! how this return, and especially this last clause of it, that the prisoners must go out to the Prince into the camp, brake all their loins in pieces ! Wherefore, with one voice they set up a cry that reached up to the heavens. This done, each of the three prepared himself to die (and the Recorder said unto them, " This was the thing that I feared ") ; for they concluded that to-morrow, by that the sun went down, they should be tumbled out of the world. The whole town also counted of no other, but that, in their time and order, they must all drink of the same cup. Wherefore the town of Mansoul spent that night in mourning, in sackcloth and ashes. The prisoners, also, when the time was come for them to go down before the Prince, dressed themselves in mourning attire, with ropes upon their heads. The whole town of Mansoul also showed themselves upon the wall, all clad in mourning weeds, if, perhaps, the Prince with the sight thereof might be moved with compassion. But, oh! how the busybodies that were in the town of Mansoul did now concern themselves ! They did run here and there through the streets of the town by companies, crying out as they run in tumultuous wise, one after one manner, and another the quite contrary, to the almost utter distraction of Mansoul.[1]

The trial scene

Having thrown themselves unreservedly on the mercy of Emmanuel, the Mansoulians are pardoned, the government of the town is reconstituted, and the people are entertained by a grand review of the celestial troops. Justice remains to be done on the more obdurate Diabolonians. This scene is not inferior to that of the trial at Vanity Fair. Mr Forget-Good stands at the bar, and pleads age and frailty of brain. Hate-lies, Know-all, and Tell-true appear against him.[2]

[1] *The Holy War*, ed. John Brown, 285-286.
[2] Sir Charles Firth calls attention to the frequency of the literary device of a trial in polemical and other works of this period. Richard Bernard's moralistic story, *The Isle of Man : Or The Legall Proceeding in Man-shire against*

BUNYAN

Hate. My lord, I have heard this Forget-Good say, that he could never abide to think of goodness, no, not for a quarter of an hour.

Clerk. Where did you hear him say so ?

Hate. In All-base-lane, at a house next door to the sign of the Conscience seared with an hot iron.

Clerk. Mr Know-all, what can you say for our Lord the King against the prisoner at the Bar ?

Know. My lord, I know this man well. He is a Diabolonian, the son of a Diabolonian : his father's name was Love-naught ; and for him, I have often heard him say, that he counted the very thoughts of goodness the most burdensome thing in the world.

Clerk. Where have you heard him say these words ?

Know. In Flesh-lane, right opposite to the Church.[1]

Next comes the defeatist, Mr False-peace, who is admirably characterized :—

"Mr False-peace, thou art here indicted by the name of False-peace (an intruder upon the town of Mansoul) for that thou didst most wickedly and satanically bring, hold, and keep the town of Mansoul, both in her apostasy and in her hellish rebellion, in a false, groundless, and dangerous peace, and damnable security, to the dishonour of the King, the transgression of his law, and the great damage of the town of Mansoul. What sayest thou ? Art thou guilty of this indictment, or not ? "

Then said Mr False-peace, "Gentlemen, and you now appointed to be my judges, I acknowledge that my name is Mr Peace ; but that my name is False-peace I utterly deny. If your honours shall please to send for any that do intimately know me, or for the midwife that laid my mother of me, or for the gossips that were at my christening, they will, any or all of them, prove that my name is not False-peace, but Peace. Wherefore I cannot plead to this indictment, forasmuch as my name is not inserted therein ; and as is my true name, so are also my conditions. I was always a man that loved to live at quiet, and what I loved myself, that I thought others might love also.

Sinne. Wherein by way of a continued Allegorie, the chiefe Malefactors disturbing both Church and Common Wealth, are detected and attached (1627), has remarkable resemblances, of a crude sort, to Bunyan's trial-scenes here and in *The Pilgrim's Progress (John Bunyan,* 21-22).

[1] *The Holy War,* ed. John Brown, 306.

Wherefore, when I saw any of my neighbours to labour under a disquieted mind, I endeavoured to help them what I could ; and instances of this good temper of mine many could I give." [1]

Evidences of identification are called. Mr Search-truth and Mr Vouch-truth attest that the prisoner's name is False-Peace.

Search. My lord, I know and have known this man from a child, and can attest that his name is False-peace. I knew his father ; his name was Mr Flatter : and his mother, before she was married, was called by the name of Mrs Sooth-up : and these two, when they came together, lived not long without this son ; and when he was born, they called his name False-peace. I was his playfellow, only I was somewhat older than he ; and when his mother did use to call him home from his play, she used to say, " Falsepeace, Falsepeace, come home quick, or I'll fetch you." Yea, I knew him when he sucked ; and though I was then but little, yet I can remember, that when his mother did use to sit at the door with him, or did play with him in her arms, she would call him, twenty times together, " My little Falsepeace ! my pretty Falsepeace ! " and, " Oh ! my sweet rogue, Falsepeace ! " and again, " Oh ! my little bird, False-peace ! " and " How do I love my child ! " The gossips also know it is thus, though he has had the face to deny it in open court.

Then Mr Vouch-truth was called upon to speak what he knew of him. So they sware him.

Then said Mr Vouch-truth, " My lord, all that the former witness hath said is true. His name is Falsepeace, the son of Mr Flatter and of Mrs Sooth-up, his mother : and I have in former times seen him angry with those that have called him anything else but Falsepeace, for he would say that such did mock and nickname him ; but this was in the time when Mr Falsepeace was a great man, and when the Diabolonians were the brave men in Mansoul." [2]

Conclusion of " The Holy War "

Bunyan does not end his story with the deliverance and regeneration of Mansoul. *The Holy War* is at once a history of man's redemption and, in part at least, an allegory of the Reformation. Such hits as that quoted at the Anglican compromise are evidence of this. Bunyan commenced with an allegory in which the human soul is symbolized by a beleaguered town, and the active figures are personified virtues, vices, mental faculties,

[1] *The Holy War*, ed. John Brown, 307.　　　　[2] *Ibid.*, 308-309.

and moral attitudes. But unconsciously he swerved from the
history of man's soul to the spiritual history of all mankind.
That history is still incomplete : the drama of redemption has
to be played out over and over again in every individual born.
The end is still in the future. Hence Bunyan, after the over-
throw of the Diabolonians, had to show the war still going on.
Incredulity escapes to the enemy. Mr Carnal Security, Mr
Profane, and others are easily seduced and become agents of
Diabolus. The infernal host is again under arms, and led by
Lord Beelzebub, Lord Lucifer, Lord Apollyon, and Lord Belial,
approach, with pennons streaming and hell's own drum roaring,
like an army of Cavaliers and Malignants. With foes without and
rebels and traitors within, the town of Mansoul falls again into
fearful jeopardy. Divine intervention is required anew. For the
soul of man is always subject to the assaults of the tempter ;
there will be war without and sedition and weakness within to
the very last. Bunyan closes his narrative with an exhortation
from Emmanuel, and the watchword, " Hold fast, till I come."

To recapitulate, Bunyan presented character intensively in *Bunyan's*
Christian and Mr Badman, and in all its variety in the figures *achieve-*
that throng the pages of *The Pilgrim's Progress* and *The Holy* *ment in*
War. Hitherto, English fiction had hardly penetrated beyond *fiction*
the outward husk ; but he exhibited the pangs and contritions,
the fears and ecstasies of the mind and soul, as he himself had
experienced them ; and, in the history of Mr Badman, traced
the entire development of a character from the cradle to the
grave. He drew life in its broad outlines and he painted manners
and idiosyncrasies with a sureness and precision never before
attained. Further, he excelled at the art of telling a story in a
way that held the reader subdued. The dramatic interest never
halts ; it is sustained on the steady onward march as at the
moment of suspense and crisis. No predecessor had so pictured
scenery as to make it an integral element of the story, giving
depth and atmosphere. His dialogue, also, is the current language of men, the true vernacular, but skilfully and felicitously
employed to carry the story forward and at the same time to
bring out the spiritual meaning. And all this was not acquired
by study of what other craftsmen had done ; if he had had more

learning, and if he had tried to write as others were writing, not less intent than he on exciting the interest of every potential reader, his books would have been something very different. His skill, his insight, his sureness of touch were due to the simplicity and directness with which he set down the things that possessed his mind. After all, his theme was always one and the same— the momentous, all-engrossing problem that ever haunted his imagination. A rich and ripe and sane experience enabled him to deal with that theme in three several stories. The idea of two of these, *The Pilgrim's Progress* and the *Life of Mr Badman*, came to him in the most natural way ; the other, which is decidedly the least successful, was probably the result of much laborious effort.

CHAPTER IV

MRS BEHN AND SOME ENGLISH
ANTI-ROMANCES

ONCE more fiction had made a great stride forward in range and technical mastery through efforts directed elsewhere, although the effect this time was not to accelerate a general advance. Genius, now as in other instances, did less for that end than was to be accomplished by mere energy and ordinary intelligence, as the next writer to be considered aptly testifies. Mrs Aphra Behn had only a mediocre allowance of talent; but she made herself the servant of her time as Bunyan was free of it. Obliged by circumstances to write for bread, she cheerfully and attentively accepted the tastes and attitudes of her day; she learned what there was to learn from other writers, and handed it on with all the improvements gained in her own practice.

Extremely little is known for certain about her, although till a comparatively recent date it was supposed that we possessed an authentic memoir, supplemented with other particulars that she had inserted in good faith in her novels. When, however, one statement was checked by another and the test of historical chronology applied, it was found that the memoir and the scraps of supposed autobiography were full of impossibilities, and that even what was credible had nothing to show that it was fact.[1] According to the memoir,[2] she was born a gentlewoman, of a Canterbury family named Johnson, and as a young girl sailed with her parents and the other children to the West Indies, her father having been appointed lieutenant-governor of Surinam,

Mrs Aphra Behn

---

[1] Ernest Bernbaum: "Mrs Behn's Biography a Fiction" (*Mod. Lang. Association of America*, xxviii., pp. 432-453). Professor Bernbaum's conclusions are contested by Mr Montague Summers, "Memoir of Mrs Behn" (*Works of Aphra Behn*, 1915, i., pp. xv-lxi).

[2] *History of the Life and Memoirs of Mrs Aphra Behn, written by one of the Fair Sex* (1696), probably by Charles Gildon, who had prefixed a shorter account to her play, *The Younger Brother* (1689).

but dying on the voyage out. Whilst living in that colony, so she avers in *Oroonoko*, and the memoir repeats it, she saw with her own eyes the occurrences forming the gist of the romance. Then she came back to London, married a wealthy Dutch merchant, and after his death was sent by the English government as a secret agent to Holland, where she had various amorous adventures, but deserves credit for having warned the English authorities of De Witt's intended raid on the Medway. Her information was, however, contemptuously ignored, her services were unrewarded, and coming home destitute she was obliged to earn her living by her pen.

Her bio-graphy probably fictitious

These introductory chapters to her literary career seem to be largely apocryphal, and to have been made up entirely out of gossip or of statements in *Oroonoko* and other stories which were inserted to give an air of circumstance and more convincing truth to the main incidents. Aphra's maiden name was not Johnson but Amis,[1] and she was born at Wye, in Kent, where her baptismal entry is preserved. According to a note written by Lady Winchilsea opposite an allusion to Mrs Behn in one of her poems, Aphra's father was a barber. Whether this be true or he were of sufficient gentility to be made governor of an English colony, it is strange that no official record can be found of his appointment, though the other chief personages connected with Surinam at that period who are mentioned in *Oroonoko* can be identified in the State Papers.[2] Moreover, to fit into the outline of her supposed biography, the events in Surinam must have taken place at a date before the Restoration, as she was a girl of eighteen when she returned to England. This would be about 1658 ; yet her biographer states that she gave Charles II. " so pleasant and rational an account of his affairs there, and particularly of the misfortunes of Oroonoko, that he desired her to deliver them publicly to the world." This chronological hitch might perhaps be due to carelessness. But if the date indicated by the names of the English officers stationed in Surinam be taken, other difficulties arise. This would be the period 1665-1666,

---

[1] Summers, xvi-xviii.
[2] E. Bernbaum : " Mrs Behn's Oroonoko " (*Anniversary Papers by Colleagues and Pupils of G. L. Kittredge*, Boston, 1913, pp. 419-433).

which agrees with Mrs Behn's statement that immediately after the death of Oroonoko the colony was taken by the Dutch. The Dutch took the colony in March 1667.[1] Aphra returned home, at the earliest in December 1665, and probably later, if she ever was in Surinam at all. According to the State Papers her sojourn in Holland was from August 1666 to the following December or possibly January. Between her return from the West Indies and her departure for the Low Countries we have to imagine time for all that her biographer says happened to her—the interview with Charles II., her marriage to the alleged Mr Behn, her widowhood. Her mission in Holland was to watch the doings of certain English malcontents, and for this purpose she was to get into communication with a William Scott, son of one of the regicides, and induce him to turn spy. In their cipher correspondence, Scott was Celadon and Mrs Behn Astrea. Scott proved to be willing, but impecunious, and Astrea's letters to the Secretary of State are chiefly devoted to urgent requests for money. Before long Scott was imprisoned for debt, and Mrs Behn found herself penniless. She borrowed enough money to return home, but there are extant three petitions to the king, through Killigrew, her friend at court, begging for payment of the money due. Before it was paid, if paid it ever was, she was herself in a debtors' prison. All that is related in the memoirs about Astrea's negotiations with the Dutchman Vander Albert, who fell in love with her and from whom she wormed out valuable secrets, is evidently fiction. She could not have given timely warning of the imminent raid, as she had left the country several months before this design was authorized by the States General.[2]

" The rest of her life was entirely dedicated to pleasure and poetry," says the memoir. She seems to have written the original draft of a tragi-comedy, *The Young King*, when she was a mere girl, fresh from reading La Calprenède's romance *Cléopâtre*. From one episode she drew her plot, the love-story of the Scythian king Alcamène. But it was not till 1679 that Mrs Behn

Aphra Behn's plays

[1] E. Bernbaum: "Mrs Behn's 'Oroonoko'" (*Anniversary Papers by Colleagues and Pupils of G. L. Kittredge*, Boston, 1913, p. 422).
[2] Bernbaum: *Mrs Behn's Biography a Fiction*, 441.

saw this on the stage, after it had been revised and perhaps recast. By that time she was an established playwright. Her first play to be acted was *The Forc'd Marriage ; or, the Jealous Bridegroom* (1670), a tragi-comedy in blank verse. It was followed by *The Amorous Prince* (1671), and that by a comedy, *The Dutch Lover* (1673).[1] There is no need here for a full list of her plays. *Abdelazar ; or, the Moor's Revenge* (1676) was a ranting melodrama masquerading as tragedy. It is remarkable for its reminiscences of the Elizabethans, the bombast and horrors of Marlowe and Kyd, on the one hand, and some admirable lyrics, on the other. But though she could write two such pieces as " Make haste, Amyntas, come away ! " and " Love in fantastic triumph sat," her true vein was comedy. Her best play is *The Rover* (1677), to which she composed a sequel (1681). It presents, in frank defiance of any moral considerations, the merry doings of a band of exiled Royalists in a foreign city :—

> The banisht Cavaliers ! a Roving Blade !
> A popish Carnival ! a Masquerade !
> The Devil's in't if this will please the Nation,
> In this our blessed Times of Reformation,
> When Conventicling is so much in Fashion.
> And yet——

Thus the epilogue,[2] alluding to the standing feud between the popular party, led by Shaftesbury, champion of Nonconformity, and the court party, who no doubt applauded such sentiments as her definitions of conscience and constancy :—

> " Conscience : a cheap pretence to cozen fools withal ; "
> " Constancy, that current coin for fools."

The following year was signalized by the discovery of the alleged Popish Plot, by Titus Oates, whom she caricatured at

---

[1] Why Professor Bernbaum should gibe at me for saying of Mrs Behn that in this play "She drew upon her Dutch experiences in describing the boorish Haunce von (*sic*) Ezel," I am not gifted enough to see. Dr Bernbaum has discovered some errors in the traditional account of Mrs Behn's stay in Holland ; but though the dates are wrong, she admittedly had been there, and being an intelligent woman no doubt made some observations of manners and characters. If she did not use these in her picture of Van Ezel, what did she use ?

[2] *Works*, ed. Montague Summers, i., 105.

full length in *The City Heiress ; or, Sir Timothy Treatall*. She attacked the Whigs again in *The Roundheads ; or, the Good Old Cause* (1682), a scurrilous lampoon on the Commonwealth. Contemporary with this poor abuse was the wittier and more provocative comedy, *The City Heiress*, based on Middleton's *A Mad World, my Masters*. Sir Timothy, the general butt of the satire, is meant for Shaftesbury himself, Dryden's " false Achitophel," and the political meaning is underlined throughout.

Between now and her death in 1689, amidst a good deal of other writing, including a notable translation, or rather a popular adaptation, of Fontenelle's dialogue on *The Plurality of Worlds*, to which she prefixed a significant " Essay on Translated Prose," she composed her various works of fiction. The first, *Love Letters between a Nobleman and his Sister* (1683), appeared the year after the second part of *The Pilgrim's Progress*. It comprised three series of letters, sometimes entitled *The Amours of Philander and Sylvia*, purporting to have been exchanged between a young French nobleman, in the time of the Huguenot rebellion in Paris, and his wife's sister, who elopes with him to St Denis, is married as a matter of form to one of his creatures, and when he is taken prisoner on the failure of the rebellion and escapes, goes and lives with him. But the whole story is a fraudulent attempt to exploit a contemporary scandal that had excited a great sensation in London in 1682. Philander is really the notorious Forde, Lord Grey, afterwards Earl of Tankerville ; and Sylvia, his sister-in-law, Lady Henrietta Berkeley. Lord Grey was implicated in the Rye House Plot, and played a contemptible part in the Monmouth Rebellion. He was tried in 1682, and convicted of conspiracy to carry off his mistress. It was as an intimate version of this affair that the love-letters made their mark. But in their composition Mrs Behn followed a famous model. Five years earlier there had been published an anonymous translation of the celebrated *Portuguese Letters*,[1] under the title of *Five Love-Letters from a*

Letters in the manner of a Portuguese nun

---

[1] They had appeared first as *Les Lettres portugaises, traduites en français* (1669), and were long believed to be genuine love-letters written by a nun, Marianna Alcoforado, in the convent of Beja, to a French soldier, identified as the Count de Chamilly or the Chevalier de Clermont. All these identifications,

Nun to a Cavalier (1678). The translator was Sir Roger L'Estrange, as the edition of 1686 acknowledged. These letters of a deserted nun to a lover who had forsaken her seem to breathe the true accents of desperate passion ; they laugh to scorn all conventional reserves and dwell fondly on past ecstasies and present anguish.

This was something very different from the bloodless sentimentalism of the later romances, which had never met with much response in England, except from a few exquisites or young ladies brought up in ignorance of the world. English romanticism was but a masquerade, a specious disguise for the licentiousness of those who had nothing to do but follow pleasure ; and to the animal passions which it falsely idealized the emotional exaltation of the Portuguese nun gave a further stimulus and something like a poetic lustre. Mrs Behn's fifty-two letters are written in the same style of feverish self-abandonment, with a spice of sheer pruriency which was, unfortunately, to be the special condiment of her many imitators, particularly Mrs Manley and Mrs Haywood. The letters of the Portuguese nun were reissued many times, sometimes with replies from the Cavalier ; they were turned into verse, and gave an impetus to fiction in the epistolary form which even in these modern days shows itself now and again as active as ever.

Mrs Behn's own personal letters, especially the burlesque series supposed to have passed between one of her admirers and herself, read more like rough sketches for fiction than genuine correspondence. A set of eight " Love Letters to a Gentleman " is appended to her biography; the gentleman is called Lycidus, and is not to be confused with the hero of another erotic book, *Lycidus : or the Lover in Fashion. Being an Account from Lycidus to Lysander, of his Voyage from the Island of Love* (1688). In this she freely paraphrased in prose and verse the Abbé Tallemant des Réaux' *Voyage de l'Isle d'Amour*. Lycidus relates his happy sojourn with Sylvia, a denizen of the amorous isle, and how she

however, were conjectural, and it appears that the *Letters* were composed by a literary man named Guilleraques for the publisher Claude Barbin. See Green, F. C., " Who was the author of the *Lettres Portugaises ?* " (*Mod. Lang. Review*, xxi., 1926, pp. 159-167). *The Letters of a Portuguese Nun*, translated by Edgar Prestage (Portland, Me.. 1900) is the modern version.

was turned against him by an ugly and peevish woman, Indifference, who brought her to the Lake of Disgust. But he is recompensed by further love-adventures in the course of his travels to places called " Amusement," " Favors," and " Irresolution," and we leave him in a blissful state of hesitation between two rival charmers, Bellinda and Bellimante.

Three short stories, *The Adventure of the Black Lady*, *The Court of the King of Bantam*, and *The Unfortunate Happy Lady, a True History*, were probably written about this time, though not published till 1697, eight years after the writer's death. Mrs Behn called her stories " histories " or " novels," the latter term, now coming into use, indicating that she patterned them on the *novella*. The scene of all three is London, and, apart from the phrase applied to the third, there are signs that she was desirous of passing them off as true histories. The first, lame as a story, has the look of a bit of life only a little dressed up. Definite localities, Soho, " The Rose " in Covent Garden, the Exchange, Bridges Street, and Locket's, the ordinary at Charing Cross, are mentioned. It is about a lady, Bellamora, who comes up to town in pursuit of a fickle lover, and fortunately for herself stumbles upon a landlady who turns out a good Samaritan, and who prevails upon Fondlove, in the nick of time, to make the little brunette an honest woman. *The King of Bantam* is said to have been written for a wager to show that Mrs Behn could tell a tale in the manner of Scarron. The abrupt opening, the frisky style, and the elaborate practical joke, even if they do not quite hit the mark, are a notable attempt to avoid the clumsiness and surplusage of most English story-telling. The King is a purse-proud, amorous cit, who is hoaxed into parting with his money, which enables his impecunious young rival to marry the lady whom he had expected to play Danaë to his Jupiter.

Much more piquant and more like a true *novella* is the third, *The Unfortunate Happy Lady*, which like the others is averred to be true in fact though the names are changed. She says that it " was attested to me by one who liv'd in the family, and from whom I had the whole truth of the story." It is a romance telescoped into an inadequate number of pages. A debauched

Her histories and novels

" The Unfortunate Happy Lady "

young Cavalier basely hands his innocent sister over to a brothel-keeper, in order to repair his ruined fortunes by embezzling her portion. Like St Agnes in the legend, she is rescued by a young merchant,[1] and he is about to marry her, when business takes him on a journey to the East Indies. In regular romantic style, he is shipwrecked and reported dead, and in due time the lady, resigned to her loss, obeys the wish of her dying bene-factress and becomes the wife of her lover's rich old uncle. She nurses his old age ; but he soon dies, leaving her a wealthy widow. Then the long-lost wanderer comes back, a penniless vagabond, and receives the reward of constancy. The repulsive-ness of the opening incidents is redeemed by the fine feeling with which the unfortunate happy lady is drawn ; but it is too much when she forgives the vile brother and magnanimously gives him back his fortune with a beautiful heiress to boot.

Transla-tions from Bonne-corse

The chronology of Mrs Behn's novels is very obscure, and the order is to a large extent guess-work. Probably the next to appear was a translation, *La Montre : Or the Lover's Watch* (1686). The sentimental dalliance of Damon and Iris, a pair of elegant lovers, is carried on in sugary prose and stilted verse through three books, *The Lover's Watch, or the Art of Making Love, The Case for the Watch*, and *The Lady's Looking-Glass to dress herself by, or the Art of Charming*, all amorously adapted from *La Montre* (1666) and a sequel, *La Boëte et Le Miroir* (1671), of Balthasar de Bonnecorse, the mock-heroic poet. Between this and *Oroonoko* and *The Fair Jilt* were probably written four novelettes, *The Unfortunate Bride, The Wandering Beauty, The Dumb Virgin*, and *The Unhappy Mistake*, which did not appear in print till later dates.[2] These and *The Lucky Mis-take* (1689) are brisk stories of intrigue, compact of incident, in which Mrs Behn's stage experience or her desire to outrival the *novella* succeeds, more or less, in weaving the threads into a plot. By one device or another, she endeavours also to convey the impression that the tales are true.

The Unfortunate Bride ; or, the Blind Lady a Beauty, is a

---

[1] The same situation occurs to Theodora in Robert Boyle's laborious and much-praised romance, *The Martyrdom of Theodora, And of Didymus* (1687).
[2] Printed in her *Works*, ed. Montague Summers, 1915, v.

more than usually affected history of two gushing young lovers, who are separated by the snares of an amorous widow. It all ends in a feeble and inconsequent tragedy. But *The Dumb Virgin ; or, The Force of Imagination*, has real power, and is Mrs Behn's nearest approach to Bandello. The theme of incest was one very congenial to the Bishop of Agen. Aphra had toyed with it already in her comedy *The Dutch Lover*; here she is serious. The son of a Venetian senator, castaway as a child, returns in manhood and becomes fatally though unwittingly enamoured of his own sister, and accidentally kills his father. The trouble taken to make the story out to be true is remarkable. The narrator states that the lady's sister knew English, and that she had had the happiness of many hours' conversation with her. The ill-fated hero was supposed to be an Englishman, and she was taken by one of the sisters to a masquerade in the hope of seeing him. Finally, when he is at the point of death, he gasps out that his name is not Dangerfield " but Cla—" and there his voice failed him, nor could she ever learn what was the name under which he had previously had a distinguished career.

" The Unfortunate Bride "

The only voucher she gives, however, for the truth of the succeeding story, *The Wandering Beauty*, is that it was imparted to her when she was a child of twelve by a lady closely concerned in the events ; but the persons and places are carefully particularized. This is about a young lady who runs away from home to escape being married to an aged friend of her parents, becomes a domestic servant in a distant county, and there captivates a young gentleman, Sir Lucius Lovewell, who marries her in spite of her humble station. Afterwards, she makes him acquainted with her family, who to his surprise prove to be as good as he. Snobbery makes its appearance here, in the person of the clergyman who falls in love with Peregrina, but cannot bring himself to the point of wedding with a girl having nothing to show for her parentage. It is gall and wormwood when he has to officiate at her wedding with a person of quality who marries her for her beauty and virtue. In *The Unhappy Mistake ; or, the Impious Vow Punish'd*, the plot hinges on the hackneyed self-deception of a lover who sees his mistress in the arms of another man, and without waiting to find out that it is her

" The Wandering Beauty "

brother wounds him apparently to death in a duel. The ensuing adventures, which of course end happily, are rather
tedious, and the plot-work is clumsy. In the course of them,
Mrs Behn tries her hand at dialect, but is not more skilful
than Deloney, in *Jack of Newbury*.[1] Her dialogue in general
is by no means so unforced, and at the same time so pithy and
humorous, as his.

"*The Fair Jilt*"   In 1688 three of her best stories came out in a single volume,
entitled *Three Histories : Oroonoko, or, The Royal Slave, The
Fair Jilt, or Tarquin and Miranda, and Agnes de Castro, or The
Force of Generous Blood*. Of these, *The Fair Jilt* was probably the
first written. In it and in *Oroonoko* Defoe's trick of authenticat-
ing fiction by claiming to give the report of an eye-witness is
anticipated, with similar consequences : many fictitious statements were accepted in good faith, and it is difficult even now
to unravel the true from the invented. A number of these
statements appeared so positive that they were admitted into
the traditional biography, until recent criticism began to ask
awkward questions. She says, in *The Fair Jilt*:—

I do not pretend here to entertain you with a feigned story,
or anything pieced together with romantic accidents ; but
every circumstance, to a tittle, is truth. To a great part of
the main I myself was an eye-witness ; and what I did not see,
I was confirmed of by actors in the intrigue, holy men, of the
order of St Francis. But for the sake of some of her relations,
I shall give my Fair Jilt a feigned name, that of Miranda ; but
my hero must retain his own, it being too illustrious to be
concealed.[2]

Miranda is a young lady of Antwerp who has taken the

1 See vol. ii., pp. 175-176.
2 *Novels*, ed. E. A. Baker, 85. Professor Bernbaum founds his case for the
inauthenticity of *The Fair Jilt* on the circumstance that the events related
must have covered at least a year, whilst Mrs Behn was in Antwerp only five
or six months at most. He overlooks her remark that she obtained some of
her facts from other people. Her statement might conceivably be true ; but
other considerations are against it, especially when this question and that of
Oroonoko are taken together. *The Fair Jilt* reads like a Behnesque version of
The Countess of Celant. And who is Prince Tarquin—the name " too illustrious
to be concealed " ? The annals of illustrious personages know him not. No,
the story is, on the face of it, a highly artificial and highly characteristic
essay on the power of love to drive men mad, and there is no need for a
comparison of dates to show up its glaring improbability.

temporary vows of a Béguine, but is so far from acquiescing in the restraints thus avouched that she makes violent love to a handsome young friar. She manages to secure him as her confessor, and when he remains adamant to her seductions, plays the part of Potiphar's wife and gets him sentenced to death for attempting her chastity. Then the German prince called Tarquin becomes infatuated with her beauty. He is held up as the complete exponent of the illimitable power of love. " As Love," says the exordium, " is the most noble and divine passion of the soul, so it is that to which we may justly attribute all the real satisfactions of life ; and without it man is unfinish'd and unhappy." Tarquin becomes an absolute slave to the enchantress ; his entire obedience to her criminal schemes is offered as a glorious witness to the romantic creed. He and Miranda lead a life of glittering extravagance, which they keep up by embezzling the fortune of her sister Alcidiana. But when they conspire to put the sister out of the way, they are detected, brought to trial, and sentenced. Tarquin by a supposed slip of the headsman escapes death, and Alcidiana, " extremely afflicted for having been the prosecutor of this great man," begs and obtains his pardon. Even the more guilty " unfortunate " is at length set free, and after due penitence reaches " as perfect a state of happiness as this troublesome world can afford."

But it is in *Oroonoko, or the Royal Slave*, that the three chief tendencies at work in Mrs Behn's fiction are most clearly distinguishable. A pupil in the school of La Calprenède and other writers of sentimental romance, and herself an adept at heroic drama, she saw the world through romantic spectacles. Used to devising effective scenes, climaxes, and curtains, she took naturally to the form of the " novel," the modernized *novella*, a form which is incipient drama and always seems to be knocking at the door of the stage. When Aphra told a story of events lasting several years, as for instance in *The Unfortunate Happy Lady*, her cleverness is all in the passages where everything is brought to a focus. But her stories had been characterized by a bareness, a lack of circumstance and atmosphere, which she was now to remedy in *Oroonoko*, by taking the more leisurely pace allowed by romance and by furnishing the drama with an

" Oroonoko "

elaborate setting. Thirdly and lastly, she knew what the majority of her readers preferred. They revelled in the sensational and the far-fetched, but they were not excited by anything that they knew to be mere invention. For truth of art they had little respect ; but none so greedy of the facts which are stranger than fiction. Hence Mrs Behn could be sparing of safeguards against violating probability, so long as she was prepared to take her oath that the crucial incidents had happened before her own eyes, and that the other facts rested on good authority.

Mrs Behn's assertions that her stories were true

These corroborative statements can now be assessed at their proper value. They are of a piece with assertions that have been accepted as veracious in some of her other stories. It has not been actually disproved that Mrs Behn had ever been in Surinam, although it is now impossible to believe that she went there as the daughter of a governor designate. But it is more reasonable to suppose that, having heard or invented the romantic story of the royal slave,[1] she proceeded, after her wont, to substantiate it and add local colour—the two things hang together—by laying the scene in an English colony, by reading up the latest description of the localities, and introducing the names of those persons who she could learn from the public prints were in authority there at the time alleged. This is the course which the most formidable critic of the now obsolete view of Mrs Behn shows that she must have actually adopted.[2] Just as Defoe was to read and digest the travel-books of Dampier, Hakluyt and Purchas, Mandelslo, Knox, and the rest, before describing the wonderful voyages of Robinson Crusoe and Captain Singleton, so Mrs Behn, albeit with less care and intelligence, perused George Warren's *Impartial Description of Surinam* (1667) before writing *Oroonoko*. Where her account of the country is tolerably

---

[1] She said of *Oroonoko*, in the Epistle Dedicatory to Lord Maitland : "The Royal slave I had the honour to know in my travels to the other world ; and though I had none above me in that country, yet I wanted power to preserve this great man. If there be anything that seems romantic, I beseech your Lordship to consider, these countries do, in all things, so far differ from ours, that they produce unconceivable wonders ; at least they appear só to us, because new and strange. What I have mentioned I have taken care should be truth, let the critical reader judge as he pleases." This declaration must be weighed against the doubts here expressed of the story's *bona fides*.
[2] Bernbaum : *Mrs Behn's " Oroonoko."*

correct, the details can be traced to the pages of Warren ; where, as often, she goes wide of the mark, one sees what was the average ill-informed woman's idea of a tropical country. The persons whom she mentions as prominent in the colony were men whose names came before the public at the time of the wars with the Dutch. But her account of what she declares she observed with her own eyes, of the government, of the colonial troops, and of life and affairs in general in Surinam, has been shown to be full of blunders and misunderstandings, of the sort of errors, in short, that a hasty person getting up the subject from reading and hearsay would be liable to commit. Mrs Behn's is not, then, the realism that depicts with vividness, even if with some licence, things actually seen ; but she is one of the pioneers of the realism that collects materials and uses them to give circumstance and an air of actuality to an imaginary action. Nearly half a century before Defoe, with much less ability, knowledge, and thoroughness, she put in practice the method of authentication of which he and the author of *Salammbô* have been the supreme masters, with the result that her deposition was accepted, with hardly a whisper of doubt, for over two centuries. She was not, however, the originator of that method. It had long been one of the ordinary devices of utopian romancers and the chroniclers of imaginary voyages. Bishop Francis Godwin, for instance, had employed it with remarkable adroitness in *The Man in the Moone* (1638), and, more trickily, Head and Kirkman had so endeavoured to make good their story of the picaro's further adventures in *The English Rogue*.[1]

In her previous " novels " and " histories," Mrs Behn had been working with indifferent success towards a more dramatic structure. She attained this fairly well in *The Fair Jilt*, in *Oroonoko*, and in *Agnes de Castro*. In *Oroonoko*,[2] also, though the local colour is inaccurate, she managed to invest the dramatic events with scenery and atmosphere that give solidity and perspective. Her plot is, in basis, one belonging to a stock type,

" Oroonoko " an heroic romance

---

[1] Cross calls this the beginning of the transformation of the rogue story into the story of adventure as it was soon to appear in Defoe (*Development of the English Novel*, 20).

[2] The first separate edition (1688) is titled *Oroonoko ; or, the Royal Slave. A True History.*

that of two lovers reft asunder by adversity and unexpectedly brought together again after many days. But she superadds a tragic reversal of fortune. Greed and cruelty renew their persecution, and the faithful pair seek a voluntary death as a protest against tyranny and injustice. This is an excellent subject for heroic drama ; the story was, in fact, twice dramatized by other hands.[1] *Oroonoko* must evidently be put with the heroic romances.

Her innovation was to make the hero and his mistress natives of Africa and victims of the slave trade. Oroonoko and Imoinda, however, have no recognizable marks of the Negro, except in their imputed colour. They are in all essentials the faultless hero and peerless heroine of romantic tradition. Oroonoko, whose name is apparently derived from Oroondates and given an ending that would sound American,[2] is the usual paragon of virtue, chivalrous feeling, and martial prowess. And like his prototypes of a different race, he is a man of intellect and refinement : " He had nothing of barbarity in his nature, but in all points addressed himself as if his education had been in some European court." " He knew almost as much as if he had read much : he had heard of and admired the Romans : he had heard of the late civil wars in England, and the deplorable death of our great monarch ; and would discourse of it with all the sense and abhorrence of the injustice imaginable." This admirable being loves the beautiful Imoinda. But when they are on the brink of happiness, the aged king demands her for his harem. Imoinda acts the part of Abishag the Shunamite, and her lover that of Adonijah. The vengeful monarch discovers their attachment, and sells Imoinda into slavery. Oroonoko, like the indignant lover in a French romance, flees to the army, but soon afterwards is decoyed aboard a ship, treacherously carried off, and sold as a slave in Surinam. Imoinda has preceded him. She is famous throughout the colony as the beautiful slave, as chaste as she is beautiful. The lovers recognize each other, in a

[1] Southerne's *Oroonoko* (1696) and William Walker's *Victorious Love* (1698), a tragedy based on Southerne's play, which had a comic underplot, omitted by Walker.
[2] Unless it was derived from the name of the river Orinoco, which Defoe in *Robinson Crusoe* calls the Oroonoque.

touching scene, and are suffered to be reunited. Oroonoko distinguishes himself by his good conduct and his fearlessness of danger. But he quickly finds that his tyrants promise freedom to himself and Imoinda merely to delude them into submissive behaviour. He flees into the wilderness at the head of a body of slaves. The planters follow ; the blacks fling down their arms, and Oroonoko surrenders on the assurance that they shall not be chastised. But the white governor is a scoundrel. The magnanimous Negro is put in irons and ruthlessly tortured. Imoinda is set apart for a worse fate. But she dies by the hand of the loved Oroonoko, rather than bear dishonour. The royal slave, with Roman fortitude, kills his wife, and with the stoicism of an Indian brave smokes a pipe of tobacco while his captors execute him piecemeal.

The story would fit happily into the scheme of a romantic play, the earlier acts being separated from the later by an interval like that in *A Winter's Tale*. The love-making and intrigue in the first part are managed with the deftness of an experienced playwright ; the final scenes are notably impressive. Southerne thought it necessary, in dramatizing *Oroonoko*, to conciliate prejudice by making Imoinda the child of a European who had adopted a savage life ; he also introduced a comic element and much superfluous coarseness. Perhaps Mrs Behn would have done much the same had she turned the story into a play ; her stage record is pretty bad. Anyhow, as it stands, *The History of the Royal Slave*, in spite of considerable crudeness, is as good a piece of dramatic story-telling as had yet been produced.

But the story has made a further mark on literary history by virtue of the humanitarian feeling that pervades it. *Oroonoko* has been described as the first emancipation novel, the first protest against the brutal exploitation of the weaker races in the name of progress. Mrs Behn was a woman of ardent sensibility, prone to be carried away by the dominant sentiment of any story in which she was thoroughly interested. In *The Fair Jilt*, her enthusiastic acceptance of the romantic doctrine of the sovereignty of love makes her blind to the flagitiousness of her hero and heroine. No doubt some such allowance must also be

Humanitarian feeling in " Oroonoko "

made for the indecency of her plays. In *The Unfortunate Happy Lady*, on the other hand, she is a warm champion of virtue and constancy ; and in *Agnes de Castro*, again, loyalty wages a sore struggle with passion, and wins the day. In *Oroonoko*, the contrast between the noble slave and the sordid, vicious, and unscrupulous planters who did him to death, inspired her, for the moment, with the idea of man's innate goodness before he is corrupted by the arts of civilization. Her noble savage foreshadows Rousseau's conception of man in a state of nature. In describing the natives of Surinam, as she alleges that she saw them, she says :—

These people represented to me an absolute idea of the first state of innocence, before man knew how to sin : And 'tis most evident and plain, that simple Nature is the most harmless, inoffensive and virtuous mistress. It is she alone, if she were permitted, that better instructs the world than all the inventions of man : religion would here but destroy that tranquillity they possess by ignorance ; and laws would but teach them to know offences of which now they have no notion. They once made mourning and fasting for the death of the English governor, who had given his hand to come on such a day to them, and neither came nor sent ; believing when a man's word was past, nothing but death could or should prevent his keeping it : and when they saw he was not dead, they asked him what name they had for a man who promised a thing he did not do ? The governor told them such a man was a liar, which was a word of infamy to a gentleman. Then one of them replied, " Governor, you are a liar, and guilty of that infamy." [1]

A little further on she says : " Such ill morals are only practis'd in Christian countries, where they prefer the bare name of religion ; and, without virtue and morality, think that sufficient." What more scathing contrast could there be than that between the lofty Oroonoko and the perjured captain who feasts him on board his vessel only to kidnap him and his followers and sell them to the planters ! When the captain hesitates to accept the parole of a savage, Oroonoko replies, that " He was sorry to hear that the captain pretended to the

[1] *Novels*, ed. E. A. Baker, 4-5.

knowledge and worship of any gods, who had taught him no
better principles than not to credit as he would be credited."
And when he quits the ship for the slave-mart he takes leave
with the biting words, " Farewell, sir, 'tis worth my sufferings
to gain so true a knowledge, both of you and of your gods, by
whom you swear." And desiring those that held him to forbear
their pains, assuring them he would make no resistance, he cried,
" Come, my fellow-slaves, let us descend, and see if we can meet
with more honour and honesty in the next world we shall touch
upon."

Mrs Behn even anticipates Swift in the vehemence of her
satire on the vile miscreants who were sent by the deputy-
governor to bring back Cæsar—Oroonoko's slave-name—who
had led the revolted Negroes into the woods :—

Cæsar told him there was no faith in the white men, or the
gods they adored ; who instructed them in principles so false,
that honest men could not live amongst them ; though no
people professed so much, none performed so little : that he
knew what he had to do when he dealt with men of honour ;
but with them a man ought to be eternally on his guard, and
never to eat and drink with Christians, without his weapon of
defence in his hand ; and, for his own security, never to credit
one word they spoke. As for the rashness and inconsiderateness
of his action, he would confess the governor is in the right ;
and that he was ashamed of what he had done, in endeavouring
to make those free who were by nature slaves, poor wretched
rogues, fit to be used as Christians' tools ; dogs, treacherous
and cowardly, fit for such masters ; and they wanted only
but to be whipped into the knowledge of the Christian gods,
to be the vilest of all creeping things ; to learn to worship such
deities as had not power to make them just, brave, or honest.[1]

In the third novel contained in the same volume as *Oroonoko*,
Mrs Behn gave her version of a tragical episode of Portuguese
history much celebrated by Peninsular and French and English
poets, dramatists, and romancers.[2] *Agnes de Castro, or The Force*

"*Agnes
de
Castro*"

---

[1] *Novels*, ed. E. A. Baker, 68-69.
[2] It is curious that a translation by P. B. G. (Peter Ballon, Gent.) of the
novel on which Astrea's was based, viz., Mlle S. B. de Brillac's *Agnès de
Castro, nouvelle portugaise* (1688), came out this same year in *Two New Novels :*

of Generous Blood, is the tale of Ines de Castro, daughter of a great Spanish noble and maid-of-honour to Donna Constantia, wife of the Infante Don Perdo. She has the misfortune to be loved by the husband of her mistress, to whom she is tenderly attached. There is no foul intrigue in the story. Don Pedro struggles honourably against his passion : " his fault was not voluntary . . . a commanding power, a fatal star, had forc'd him to love in spite of himself." The princess herself admits his innocence, and harbours no resentment against her spotless friend. She tells her husband, " I have no reproaches to make against you, knowing that 'tis inclination that disposes hearts, not reason." In spite of irrepressible regret she loves her husband so unselfishly that she conjures Agnes not to deprive him of her society, since it is necessary to his happiness. But the truce is brought to a fatal ending by the malice of an envious woman, who persuades Constantia that the lovers are guilty, and so breaks her heart.

" The Lucky Mistake "

Probably Mrs Behn's next novel was *The Lucky Mistake* (1689), which, she says, in the dedication to George Greenviel, " has more of realty than fiction," and, she continues, " if I have not made it fuller of intrigue, 'twas because I had a mind to keep it close to the truth." It is a Romeo and Juliet story of the son and daughter of two counts living in adjoining houses in Orleans. The fathers are not at feud, but only of different fortunes. Hence Rinaldo's sire warns him not to fall in love with Atlante. But he does fall in love, and carries on a secret correspondence with the young lady through her pert and enterprising sister. On discovering this manœuvre, Atlante's father packs Charlot off to a nunnery. But the lovers still carry on their affair, the time-honoured balcony of romance aiding their purpose. The lady's father presently tries to marry her to an elderly friend ; this brings matters to a head, and she refuses ; so she too is packed off to a nunnery. Now comes the lucky mistake, which is not the most ingenious stroke one could have wished for to solve the dilemma. Rinaldo determines to carry

I. *The Art of Making Love.* II. *The Fatal Beauty of Agnes de Castro : Taken out of the History of Portugal* (1688). See Esdaile, 160, where the volume is catalogued under Mrs Behn.

off his mistress, and employs her sister as his envoy. This young minx has now a mind to be married herself, and knows that the respective fathers would smile on such an alternative to the other match. So she slips out instead of her sister at the time appointed. But at that moment her sister's elderly suitor arrives on the spot with a band of armed servants, and whilst Rinaldo is fighting them he carries off the supposed Atlante. When he realizes his error, he decides to make the best of a bad business, and offers to marry Charlot. She is nothing loth. Rinaldo comes home to find a wedding going on next door ; he swoons and is like to die. But he comes round when it proves to be not Atlante after all. The reader is kept in the titillations of suspense to the last page, when his natural desires are gratified.

Two of Mrs Behn's novels bear the title of *The Nun*,[1] much to the embarrassment of bibliographers. The title was much overworked after the Portuguese letters had given a fillip to tales of love in a nunnery. *The Nun ; or, the Perjured Beauty* is the story of Ardelia, another Fair Jilt. Astrea frankly accepted, save when a different fancy inspired her, Charles the Second's wellknown adage on the frailty of woman. "Virtue," she makes one of her characters say, "is but a name kept from scandal, which the most base of women best preserve." But Ardelia does not even trouble about appearances. She is one of those passionate, insatiable, capricious women who play a leading rôle in every one of Astrea's comedies, and are always drawn with energy and truth because their author's heart was in them. The plot is worked out with ingenuity, but the story, with its holocaust of lovers, is but a debased *novella*. The author described it as " a true novel."

The History of the Nun, or The Fair Vow-Breaker (1689), which also claims to be true, " as it is on the records of the town," videlicet, the town of Ypres, is a very grim variant of the oft-told story of a husband coming home after long absence and finding his wife married to another, the story best known to modern readers from Tennyson's *Enoch Arden*. In Mrs Behn's novel the second husband was Isabella's first lover : this makes

Marginal notes:
" *The Nun, or the Perjured Beauty* "

" *The Nun, or the Fair Vow-Breaker* "

[1] Now to be found in the Rev. Montague Summers's edition of the *Works*, v.

it a rather complicated story. The young lady is as beautiful and courted as the previous heroines, and all her friends are deeply afflicted when she rejects the admirable Villenoys and resolves to bury herself in a convent. The lover departs to fight against the Turks. Isabella takes the final vows. But one of the sisters has an irresistible brother; Henault and Isabella fall headlong in love. The nun's vacillations between duty and passion are analysed with mature knowledge of the amorous heart of a girl, a subject thoroughly congenial to Astrea : the inner drama in the two breasts, and the comedy of shifts and deceptions by which they hoodwink the argus eyes about them, are prettily treated. Isabella escapes from the cloister, the pair are married. But Henault's father disinherits him, and when they are reduced to poverty the young man consents to enlist in the expedition for the relief of Candia in order to earn his pardon. Isabella receives absolution for her broken vows. Then comes the news that her husband has fallen in battle ; his dying message is brought by Villenoys, who had become his most intimate comrade. Time elapses, and at length Isabella accepts the lover whom she had long before rejected, and they become the happiest and most envied of wedded pairs. But one night a bearded and ragged stranger comes to the house, whilst Villenoys is away. It is Henault, who had not been killed, but after grievous sufferings has come home to his wife.

Isabella is in consternation ; a thousand thoughts rush through her mind, as the poor husband stares at her in bewilderment. Had she known him to be alive, " she had lov'd to the last moment of their lives ; but, alas ! the dead are soon forgotten, and she now lov'd only Villenoys." She comes to a fearful decision. Keeping her servants out of the way, she lodges him in a rich chamber, which rouses some jealous suspicions in his mind, but he is too worn out to ask any questions. Then, so convulsed with horror that she is on the point of killing herself, she smothers the sleeping man. Hardly the deed is done when Villenoys returns unexpectedly, and finding his wife delirious with remorse and fear, exacts from her the confession that Henault has returned. But she says that he had died of the shock of hearing that she was remarried. To avert suspicion, he proposes to put the body in a sack and throw it into the river. Then comes a touch beyond the melodramatic level of the foregoing. "Isabella all this while said but little, but, fill'd with thoughts all black and hellish, she ponder'd within, while the fond and passionate Villenoys was endeavouring to hide her shame, and to make this an absolute secret : she imagin'd, that could she live after a deed so black, Villenoys would be eternal reproaching her, if not with his tongue, at least with his heart, and embolden'd by one wickedness, she was the readier for another, and another of such a nature as has, in my opinion, far less excuse than the first; but when fate begins to afflict, she goes through stitch with her black work." Villenoys performs his ghastly office, and ties up the body. "When he had the sack on his back, she cried, 'Stay, my dear, some of his clothes hang out, which I will put in '; and with that, taking the pack-needle with the thread, sew'd the sack, with several strong stitches, to the collar of Villenoy's coat, without his perceiving it, and bid him go now ; ' and when you come to the bridge,' said she, ' and that you are throwing him over the rail, which is not above breast high, be sure you give him a good swing, lest the sack should hang on anything at the side of the bridge, and not fall into the stream.' ' I'll warrant you,' said Villenoys, ' I know how to secure his falling.' " He swung the body over, the weight pulled him with it, and the live and the dead man were carried down. Isabella would have escaped punishment, except from her unhappy conscience, but that an accident brought her under suspicion, and she was executed.

Mrs Behn was no realist, but one brought up in the school of romance and unable to take any but a romantic view of life, who felt the need, however, of breaking away from the unreality of the romances. She imagined this was to be done merely by seasoning her narratives with facts, real or spurious, with familiar names and places, and the like. But realism can dispense with all that, as Bunyan had recently shown. Though she understood the need for verisimilitude, she never found out how to secure it, never evoked for an instant the illusion of real life. She could interest us in her characters, or rather in the doings and volitions of her characters ; but even Oroonoko and Imoinda are only fine

Mrs Behn's contribution to the novel

conceptions whose pretence at being human realities would not impose upon any but the most uncritical imagination. Her theatrical expertness and her cultivation of the *novella* helped her to make effective play with the reader's sense of curiosity, surprise, wonder, suspense, dread, pity, or indignation ; she often showed ingenuity, and sometimes attained the neatness at which she always aimed. Her prose style was still too emotional and inflated, and her dialogue lacked the colloquial accent ; but it is to her credit that she tried not to write " loftily " nor yet in the " low stile that is yet something worse." [1] She kept the tastes and infirmities of the contemporary reader in her mind's eye, as is well manifested by such a work as her rendering of Fontenelle's *Theory or System of Several New Inhabited Worlds* into a familiar conversation making a recondite subject intelligible to untrained intellects. " I would treat of philosophy in a manner altogether unphilosophical," she says in the essay " On Translated Prose." [2] And, in the same way, she brought romance down from its spavined and limping Pegasus to walk the pavement with the crowd of ordinary cits.

Anti-romance —" Zelinda "

This was almost to meet the anti-romance half-way, but she got no farther even when she attempted a comic tale of everyday London people. Only two scions of that foreign stock are worth recognizing among English novels of the period, the romance *Zelinda*, the plot of which is borrowed from Voiture, and Congreve's youthful novel *Incognita*. [3] *Zelinda : An Excellent New Romance* (1676) was announced on the title-page as " Translated from the French of Monsieur de Scudéry. By T. D. Gent." It pokes fun at Scudéry romances and their imitators, but whatever larceny there was committed was upon Vincent de Voiture, the plot of whose unfinished *Histoire*

---

[1] Preface to her translation of the *History of Oracles*.
[2] See above, p. 83.
[3] Such ephemeral skits as *The Essex Champion : or, The Famous History of Sir Billy of Billerecay and his Squire Ricardo* (c. 1685), a burlesque of the same stamp as *Don Juan Lamberto* (see above, p. 39 n.), and Samuel Holland's *Don Zara del Fogo : A Mock-Romance. Written originally in the British Tongue, and made English by a person of much honor, Basilius Musophilus* (1656), are tomfooleries that merely illustrate our bareness in this particular genre. The last-named was thrice reissued and thrice rechristened, as *Wit and Fancy in a Maze* (1656), *Romancio-Mastix, or a Romance on Romances* (1660), and *The Spaniard : or, Don Zara del Fogo* (1719).

d'Alcidalis et Zélide (1678) [1] it purloins and turns topsy-turvy. In an amusing preface, T. D. smiles at his publisher's flattering impeachment that this is an excellent romance, and as to its being a translation, " 'tis no more so than the mother that bore me."

I write not for glory, nor self-interest, nor to gratify kindness nor revenge. Now the impertinent critical reader will be ready to ask, for what then ? For that and all other questions to my prejudice, I will borrow Mr Bays's answer and say, Because—I gad, sir, I will not tell you—I desire to please but one person in the world, and, as one dedicates his labours and heroes to Calista, another to Urania, etc., at the feet of her, my adored Celia, I lay all my giants and monsters.

The giants and monsters are only figurative ; but after this admonition any extravagance can be accepted in the proper spirit. The exalted passions, furious jealousies, hopeless separations, and miraculous reunions of ancient and modern romance are all introduced, but only in mockery. A king and queen of Aragon had children by their previous consorts, and the ambitious queen intrigues to marry the young prince Alcidalis to her daughter. But she unfortunately takes under her care the orphan child of an Italian nobleman, and brings her up with the young princess. The result can be foreseen : Alcidalis and the stranger fall in love. As they grow up, their passion for each other excites every one's notice, and the queen is at her wit's end to get over this obstacle to her scheme. Finally, she takes Zelinda aboard a ship, informs her that she is to marry the Duke of Tarentum, and leaves her in the captain's charge. Determined to escape the hateful match, Zelinda persuades the captain to dress up a young lady to impersonate her, and willingly endows this deputy with all her portable wealth and with the fee simple of her lands and title. The impostor having been easily palmed off on the elderly duke, Zelinda sails away ; but the ship falls into the hands of pirates. Reversing the rôle of Sidney's Zelmane, Zelinda dons male attire, distinguishes herself by her valour and charms every one with her debonair

[1] A translation of this, *Alcidalis and Zelinda*, appears in *The Works of Mr de Voiture. Translated by Mr Ozell* (1726).

person. Meanwhile, the distracted Alcidalis is in pursuit, and knowing nothing of Zelinda's stratagem makes his way to the palace of the duke, now, he believes, in possession of his mistress. Disguised as a slave, he penetrates to the private apartments, sends a *billet-doux* making himself known to the duchess ; and the sham Zelinda, disenamoured of her elderly husband, is only too delighted to give him a warm reception. But they are interrupted by the unseasonable return of the duke. The lady, however, is clever enough to be the one to take offence, and heaps reproaches on the down-trodden husband's head until he meekly sues for pardon.

The true Zelinda, under the masculine anagram of Zelidan, is now back in Spain,[1] where she finds the king dead, the populace in revolt, and the queen and her daughter's lives in danger. Hardly has she quelled the outbreak, when a fresh attack is made on the palace. This time it is Alcidalis returning to vindicate his rights. In the confused fighting Zelidan is struck down by her lover, and her would-be rival, the young princess, is killed. All this is a caricature of scenes in the *Arcadia*, like an antecedent episode, in which Zelidan, the woman disguised as a man, has been the embarrassed object of the passions of both mother and daughter. Of course, the end turns out all that could be wished. The style is sprightly and the digressions are droll ; but *Zelinda* is not quite such a masterpiece as to sustain the author's concluding challenge—" Gentle Reader, I may safely call you so now, for I am sure you are tired as well as I."

The year that *Zelinda* was published, Orrery, the author of *Parthenissa*, published a novel, *English Adventures* (1676), " by a Person of Honour," in which romance underwent further deterioration. It is an indigestible mixture of the pastoral and the picaresque, erotic romance and the novel of intrigue, and an early example of numerous chronicles of scandal cloaked in an historical setting. The amours of the young Henry VIII. with a certain Isabella, betrothed and then married to a poltroon, and the rivalry and intrigues of Brandon and Howard, are related with the debauched cynicism of a romancer corrupted by a long life at the Restoration court, who announces,

----

[1] Syracuse = Saragossa.

" Love which terminates in marriage is not of the essentials of my history." Brandon tells a story for the general entertainment which furnished the plot for Otway's *Orphan*.

Much more able than this meretricious performance is a direct imitation of French anti-romance entitled, *The Adventures of Covent Garden, in Imitation of Scarron's City Romance* (1699), which is actually an attempt after Furetière's *Roman Bourgeois*. The experiences of the young man about town, at the theatre, at Wills's coffee-house and the Rose, at Bartholomew's Fair and other resorts, read as if the author were reporting his own impressions, and so do the love episodes with Selinda and the demirep Emilia. There is alternate interest between the realistic descriptions of middle-class life and the analysis of a hesitating lover's sensations, and between this and some gossiping discussions of the drama.[1] The realism of another story that came out this year has led some critics to ascribe it to Defoe. *The Compleat Mendicant : or, Unhappy Beggar. Being the Life of an Unfortunate Gentleman* (1699) is that queer thing, a picaresque story with a virtuous hero. He leaves Oxford on foot, and after being fleeced by various rogues becomes usher in a school. He takes Holy Orders, but ill-luck still pursuing him he turns shepherd, but again is compelled to follow the footpath way. With an excess of moralization, the first part comes to an end, and nothing is known of the promised sequel.

Congreve's *Incognita : or, Love and Duty Reconcil'd* (1692) is not perhaps an anti-romance after the manner of Sorel, Furetière, or Scarron, but it probably owes something to them, and is certainly mock-romantic. In the oft-quoted preface he lays it down :

> Romances are generally composed of the constant loves and invincible courages of heroes, heroines, kings and queens, mortals of the first rank, and so forth ; where lofty language, miraculous contingencies and impossible performances, elevate and surprise the reader into a giddy delight, which leaves him flat upon the ground whenever he gives off, and vexes him to think how he has suffered himself to be pleased and transported,

Marginal notes: "The Adventures of Covent Garden"; *Congreve's "Incognita"*

---

[1] Quoted by Jusserand, pp. 404-406. A clumsier but earnest attempt at the analysis of thoughts and feelings in a drama of thwarted love was *The Player's Tragedy : or, Fatal Love, a New Novel* (1693).

concerned and afflicted at the several passages which he has read
. . . when he is forced to be very well convinced that 'tis all a
lie. Novels are of a more familiar nature ; come near us, and
represent intrigues in practice, delight us with accidents and
odd events, but not such as are wholly unusual or unprecedented, such which not being so distinct from our belief brings
also the pleasure nearer us. Romances give more of wonder,
novels more delight.

In such admirable criticism and in the bantering digressions
in which Congreve, as it were, picks up the story from time to
time and asks us to see how nicely he is getting on, there is a
foretaste of Fielding.

Most writers of fiction, from Mrs Behn to Fielding, were
also writers of plays, and the effect of this upon their story-
telling cannot easily be overlooked. Congreve, however, had
not noticed the circumstance, being most familiar with the
tedious epical procedure of the romancers. He proposed, he
said, to add another beauty, " to imitate dramatic writing,
namely, in the design, contexture and result of the plot." And
he remarks, " I have not observed it before in a novel." He had
not yet written any plays himself, unless he was at work at this
date on *The Old Bachelor* ; but *Incognita* is, obviously, planned
and executed by one with an unerring eye for stage effects.
The plot is a clever piece of ingenuity, hingeing on the simple
device of an exchange of names between two young men of
fashion going for a revel to Florence and there incontinently
falling in love.[1] This is combined with the ironical misunder-
standing that produces so much diversion in *The Rivals* and in
Nightmare Abbey, a lover obstinately resisting his father's choice
which turns out to be the young lady whom he has been madly
in love with all the time. But here there are two lovers and
two young ladies and a double complication of mistaken
identities. The comedy of errors is crowded with sardonic
situations and dramatic surprises. Don Fabio and the Marquess

---

[1] It does not detract a whit from its ingenuity if the plot is based on an
actual experience, as Congreve himself avers (" the Copy which I imitate ") in
his preface. His biographer of 1730, the *Biographia Britannica*, and Mr Brett-
Smith himself, the recent editor of *Incognita*, make unnecessary fuss about this
point (see *Incognita*, ed. H. F. B. Brett-Smith, introd., viii-ix).

of Viterbo, the Montagu and Capulet of the story, are looking
anxiously for the young people whose union is to end their
ancient feud ; the pair of cavaliers are playing hide and seek,
in momentary dread of being summoned to a hated betrothal ;
the young ladies are in a like state of ignorance that their hands
are promised where their hearts have already been bestowed.
Such a posture of circumstance is fertile in comic issues. It was
a loss to the stage when Congreve contented himself with
making a novelette of *Incognita*.

Merely as romance, the story is better than the romances.
Love is a kind of madness, and every lover is a mad romanticist.
Thus the thrills and ecstasies are so perfectly in character that
we can freely take part in them and yet enjoy the irony that
shows up the madness.

At that (as Aurelian tells the story) a sigh diffused a mournful
sweetness through the air, and liquid grief fell gently from her
eyes, triumphant sadness sat upon her brow, and even sorrow
seem'd delighted with the conquest he had made. See what a
change Aurelian felt ! His heart bled tears, and trembled in
his breast ; sighs struggling for a vent had choked each other's
passage up ; his floods of joy were all suppressed ; cold doubts
and fears had chill'd 'em with a sudden frost, and he was troubled
to excess ; yet knew not why. Well, the learned say it was
sympathy ; and I am always of the opinion with the learned,
if they speak first.[1]

Elsewhere, Congreve is frankly mock-heroic, as when a passage
of magniloquent description ends with this postscript :

You must know, that about the fall of the evening, and at
that time when the *æquilibrium* of day and night, for some
time, holds the air in a gloomy suspense between an unwilling-
ness to leave the light and a natural impulse into the dominion
of darkness, about this time our heroes, shall I say, sallied or
slunk out of their lodgings, and steered towards the great
palace, whither, before they were arrived, such a prodigious
number of torches were on fire, that the day, by help of these
auxiliary forces, seem'd to continue its dominion ; the owls
and bats apprehending their mistake, in counting the hours,
retir'd again to a convenient darkness ; for Madam Night was

[1] *Incognita*, ed. H. F. B. Brett-Smith, 1922, p. 55.

no more to be seen than she was to be heard ; and the chymists were of opinion that her fuliginous damps, rarefied by the abundance of flame, were evaporated.[1]

The intrinsic merits of the little story—it is only a miniature, " the time from first to last is but three days " [2]—its ingenuity and finish are not of more importance historically than the careless ease and the assurance of perfect mastery with which it is handled. This was essential if the raillery was to be effective. T. D. in *Zelinda* had tried to assume the same air of superiority ; Congreve wore it without effort. The novel must have been finished by the time he was twenty-one ; there is an unconfirmed tradition that he wrote it at seventeen. That sounds precocious. But perhaps the self-confident air and the assumption of ripe worldly wisdom are really less to be wondered at if it is the work of a young fellow first asserting his manhood. At all events, in this " trifle " as he called it,[3] style, in a fuller sense than in Lyly or Sidney, takes a place in fiction that otherwise it would not have come into before Fielding, and fiction is so much the nearer to becoming a fine art.

[1] *Incognita*, ed. H. F. B. Brett-Smith, 1922, pp. 13-14.
[2] Congreve's Preface.
[3] The *D.N.B.* calls it " a feeble novel " (*Epitome*, 269).

CHAPTER V

THE FOLLOWERS OF MRS BEHN

MRS BEHN started a regular school. Her pen was taken up by *Mrs* Mrs Manley and then by Mrs Haywood, Grub Street writers *Behn's* who neglected no branch of their predecessor's trade, and *followers* though they failed of her success in drama, were very enterprising in following up the lines of sentimental, pseudo-historical, and domestic fiction which she had initiated. They were more under the sway of foreign fashions, however, than she was ; they revelled in the scandal-mongering chronicle now enormously popular in France, and they imbibed the cynicism and levity of the anti-romances without the wit and humour. Hence a peculiar nastiness in Haywood's sneers at romantic constancy in the midst of luscious eroticism. There were other women writers of more limited range belonging to the school, such as Mrs Barker, Mrs Mary Davys, Mrs Aubin, and the moral Mrs Rowe. The service they rendered was to have kept up a supply of novels and stories, which habituated a larger and larger public to find their amusement in the reading of fiction, and which, poor in quality as they were, provided the original form for the eighteenth-century novel of manners. Defoe, for the most part, took a line of his own ; yet he was not entirely out of their debt. Richardson and Fielding were less innovators · than is usually supposed ; in turning to novel-writing, they entered upon an established and thriving business, and they adopted many tricks of the trade from these humble precursors.[1]

Mary de la Rivière Manley (1672-1724) was the daughter *Mrs* of Sir Roger Manley, who fought for Charles I., was made *Manley* lieutenant-governor of the forces in Jersey under his son, and wrote a couple of historical works. In temperament and in

[1] Fielding spoke contemptuously of Mrs Haywood and put her into *The Author's Farce*. Perhaps the geniuses who create genuine film-plays, in the times yet to be, will so regard the contemptible productions of the present age.

career she was not unlike her elder, Astrea. Left an orphan, she had the misfortune as a girl of sixteen to be enticed into a bigamous marriage by her cousin, John Manley. When he left her, she was taken up by the Duchess of Cleveland, and lived for a time in her household. Then she found she could produce marketable plays and other works. *The Lost Lover ; or, the Jealous Husband*, a comedy in verse, was successful at Drury Lane (1696) ; Betterton brought out her verse tragedy, *The Royal Mischief*, at Lincoln's Inn Fields the same year. *Almyra ; or, the Arabian Vow*, a fantastic play based on the *Arabian Nights*, was presented at the Haymarket (1706). The first of her productions that can be called fiction was a series of eight *Letters Written by Mrs Manley. To which is added A Letter from a supposed Nun in Portugal, to a Gentleman in France, in Imitation of the Nun's Five Letters in Print, by Colonel Park* (1696). This was republished in 1725, the year after her death, as *A Stage-Coach Journey to Exeter. Describing the Humours of the Road, with the Characters and Adventures of the Company*.[1] It is her best work, but less notorious than a series of so-called secret histories, or chronicles of scandal of an unsavoury and libellous nature, which began with *The Secret History of Queen Zarah and the Zarasians* (1705), a miscellany of anecdote and scurrilous imputation aimed chiefly at the Duchess of Marlborough.[2] This was in two volumes. It was followed by three more parts, the second in two volumes, all together forming a series with the general title, *The New Atalantis*. First of these sequels was *Secret Memoirs and Manners of several Persons of Quality, of both Sexes. . . . From the New Atalantis, an Island in the Mediterranean* (1709). Next came a second edition comprising a second part, which also appeared separately as *Memoirs of Europe*,

Her secret histories

---

[1] *The Nun's Letter*, by Richardson Park, is reprinted here as *The Force of Love : or, The Nun's Complaint*. It is one of many feeble attempts in the manner of the famous Portuguese letters.

[2] It is described on the title-page as "Faithfully Translated from the Italian Copy now lodg'd in the Vatican at Rome, and never before Printed in any language." Reprinted in 1711, with the addition, "Containing the True Reasons of the Necessity of the Revolution that lately happen'd in the Kingdom of Albigion. By Way of Appendix to the New Atalantis." One of the French editions bears candidly the title, *Histoire secrète de la reine Zarah ou la Duchesse de Marlborough démasquée . . . traduite de l'original Anglais* (1711).

Towards the close of the Eighth Century. Written by Eginardus, Secretary and Favorite to Charlemagne (1710), and then *Court Intrigues, in a Collection of Original Letters, from the Island of the New Atalantis* (1711). For her libels on the Whigs, in which she is said to have been aided and abetted by Swift, the author, printers, and publishers of *The New Atalantis* were arrested on a warrant from the Earl of Sunderland (1709). She escaped punishment, but was not discharged till next year.

Swift was caustic at the expense of Mrs Manley in the *Tatler* (1709) ;[1] but in the stress of political warfare he made friends with her, and gave her hints for various pamphlets supporting the Harley administration.[2] When he gave up the editorship of *The Examiner* (June 1711), she took his place, and he spoke warmly of her efficiency.[3] Mrs Manley was not in flourishing circumstances at this period. Swift supported a memorial to get her a pension, shortly before she took over *The Examiner*. A little later he reported to Stella that " poor Mrs Manley, the author, is very ill of a dropsy and sore leg : the printer tells me he is afraid she cannot live long. I am heartily sorry : she has very generous principles for one of her sort and a great deal of good sense and invention : she is about forty, very homely, and very fat." [4] In *The Adventures of Rivella ; or the History of the*

---

[1] " Epicene, the writer of *Memoirs from the Mediterranean,* who, by the help of some artificial poisons conveyed by smells, has within these few weeks brought many persons of both sexes to an untimely fate ; and, what is more surprising, has, contrary to her profession, with the same odours revived others who had long since been drowned in the whirlpools of Lethe " (*Tatler,* 63). Mrs Manley thought Steele had written this, and retaliated in *The New Atalantis,* but accepted and printed his denial in the *Memoirs of Europe.* She made it up with Steele by dedicating to him her *Lucius,* presented at Drury Lane (1717).

[2] *Journal to Stella,* 16th April 1711 : " I sent my hints to the author of the *Atalantis,* and she cooked it into a sixpenny pamphlet, in her own style ; only the first page is left as I was beginning it."

[3] *Ibid.,* 3rd November 1711 : " The last six were written by a woman. Then there is an account of Guiscard by the same woman, but the facts sent by Presto. Then an answer to the letter to the Lords about Gregg by Presto ; Prior's *Journey* by Presto ; *Vindication of the Duke of Marlborough,* entirely by the same woman ; *Comment on Hare's Sermon* by the same woman, only hints sent to the printer from Presto to give her.'" He had previously singled out the *Vindication* as the best of five pamphlets which he had either written or contributed to, all except this one. Apparently, she had done the " donkey-work " on the whole lot. The printer alluded to was John Barber, afterwards Lord Mayor. Mrs Manley was his mistress.

[4] *Ibid.,* 28th January 1712.

Author of the Atalantis. With Secret Memoirs and Characters of several considerable Persons her Contemporaries (1714), which she pretended was " done into English from the French," she gave the world a romanticized account of her own life. It was re-issued frankly as *Memoirs of the Life of Mrs Manley* (1717), with " A Compleat Key." Her last work was *The Power of Love : in Seven Novels* (1720), described as " Never before Published," but partly if not entirely derived from Bandello through Painter's *Palace of Pleasure.*

Mrs Manley was not the original begetter of the scandalous chronicle disguised as fiction. Instances have already come to light of oblique references to actual people, in the personages of romance or anti-romance. With the decline of romance, there was a strong temptation to utilize the device to hit at one's enemies; and the practice had come into high favour, in spite of its serious risks, in France, where Bussy-Rabutin had produced something like a classic in his *Histoire amoureuse des Gaules* (1660).[1] The *romans à clef*, secret histories, or spurious memoirs, were generally based on the principle *cherchez la femme*, and the authors were as keen as Freudian psycho-analysts at discovering sexual motives at the bottom of every political affair, from the days of the Merovingians to their own time. The strange thing is that Mrs Manley, in the preface to *Queen Zarah and the Zarazians*, assumes a moral pose : she intends " to instruct, and to inspire into men the love of virtue and abhorrence of vice, by the examples proposed to them." She condemns the reading of romances as " a vice," but notes with relief that the " fury is very much abated." Hence she is inspired with confidence in bringing forward—

these little pieces which have banished romances [and which] are much more agreeable to the brisk and impetuous humour of the English, who have naturally no taste for long-winded performances, for they have no sooner begun a book but they desire to see the end of it.[2]

[1] For a summary of the history of the *chronique scandaleuse*, see Tieje, 54-57.
[2] A recent version of Heliodorus, advertised on the fly-leaves of Mrs Manley's *Stage-Coach Journey*, aptly illustrates this remark. The long-winded romance is cut up into novels of moderate length, each with a " snappy " modern title, the whole book, instead of *Theagenes and Chariclea,*

And she intends to depict the world of the present day :

> For the reader's better understanding we ought not to choose too ancient accidents, nor unknown heroes, which are sought for in a barbarous time, for we care little for what was done a thousand years ago among the Tartars or Abyssinians.[1]

Fiction, fact, and scandalous gossip are mingled in *The New Atalantis*. The appeal to the prurient was in the half-disguised versions of intrigues and adulteries committed by persons of rank, some of them now dead, many still in the public eye. Everybody recognized the personages implicated : Sigismund II. was Charles II. ; the Prince of Tameran, James II. ; the Marquess of Caria, the Duke of Marlborough, and so on. Mrs Manley did not waste her time in devising any artistic form for her pretended revelations ; she scribbled at high speed for readers eagerly awaiting the next number, and demanding edition after edition. The machinery is of the clumsiest. Thus we have a dialogue between Astrea and Virtue, who are subsequently joined by Intelligence, about what is going on in the Metropolis of France or Great Britain, " places renowned in the Court of Jupiter for hypocrisy, politics, politeness and vanity." Intelligence relates incidents of the most profligate nature, in voluptuous and seducing language, and dwells on every detail with sentimental gusto. Earthly characters appear on the stage, and the celestial emissaries eavesdrop. This is her ordinary method.[2] But the influence of Elizabethan translations of

" The New Ata-lantis "

---

being called, *The Reward of Chastity, illustrated in the adventures of Theagenes and Chariclia, a Romance : being the Rise, Progress, Tryals, and happy Success of the Heroic Loves of those two illustrious persons ; wherein the following Histories are intermixed. 1. The Treacherous Slave : or, The Cruel Stepmother. 2. The Wandering Prelate. 3. The Fighting Priest. 4. The Royal Adultress : with several other curious Events : Written originally in Greek by Heliodorus, Bishop of Tricca, in the fourth century of Christianity ; who chose to be deprived of his Bishoprick rather than destroy this Book, design'd by him for the Promotion of Virtuous Love : Made English from the Greek Original : with a Character of the Author and this Work, by Sir Richard Blackmore.* In fact, the long romance is passed off on the bookseller's customers as a collection of short stories. The description of the easy-going bishop as a martyr for conscience' sake is particularly amusing.

[1] Preface to *Queen Zarah.*

[2] There is a slight resemblance here to the device of the foreign observer used in the *Turkish Spy*, etc., and a closer one to the supernatural object, in the *Adventures of a Guinea*, etc.

novelle is patent in the melodramatic roundness given to many of the histories, as well as in the general picture of society, like that of Bandello's Italy, permeated with intrigue, lust, jealousy, and crime. Take, for example, the story of Mr W—— in *Court Intrigues*. A wealthy lady receives this gentleman in her chamber night after night, but under the strict condition that he must never see her face. It is a variant of the tale of Psyche. When he grows dissatisfied with this blind man's holiday, and she apprehends that he may betray her profligacy, she suborns a bravo to kill him in a duel.

In her cross-examination by Sunderland, Mrs Manley steadily declined to reveal the sources of her information. She protested that her work was entirely imaginative, and that if there was any truth in it this must have come from inspiration. When the prosecutor objected that such an immoral work could not have been inspired from above, she reminded him that there were evil angels as well as good. *The New Atalantis* was the immediate pattern for Mrs Haywood's secret histories, and the starting-point for a number of key-romances and calumnious satires during the eighteenth century. It has the higher distinction, in spite of all its crudeness, of having suggested the plan of *Gulliver's Travels*.

"*The Adventures of Rivella*" Mrs Manley's autobiographical novel, *The Adventures of Rivella*, which is stated to be " Deliver'd in a Conversation to the young Chevalier D'Aumont in Somerset-House Garden, by Sir Charles Lovemore," and " Done into English from the French," is a sort of appendix to *The New Atalantis*. Lovemore was Lieut.-General John Tidcomb. Rivella is, of course, Mrs Manley herself, who had figured in *The New Atalantis* as Delia. Count Fortunatus is Marlborough ; and Lysander, the handsome ensign with whom Rivella becomes infatuated, may be the third Earl of Carlisle.[1] Lord Crafty is the Duke of Montagu. The youthful Rivella has an unhappy passion for a young officer who makes no return, and is ordered on foreign service. The four years, of her own misfortunes, that ensue have been recounted by Mrs Manley in the story of Delia. Lovemore, who

---

[1] She says, "The námes of persons ought to have a sweetness in them, for a barbarous name disturbs the imagination."

adores Rivella, hears of her ruin, and finds her in Paris, living with Hilaria, mistress of a former king : Hilaria is the Duchess of Cleveland. Hilaria ere long abandons her. The portraits are done in the established romantic style. A pathetic turn is given to Rivella's story by an episode of self-renunciation. She might have married her lover Cleander on the death of his wife, but magnanimously persuades him to accept the hand of a rich widow, " rather than to see him poor and miserable, an object of perpetual reproach to her heart and eyes, for having preferred the reparation of her own honour to the preservation of his."

In *A Stage-Coach Journey*, Mrs Manley sketches the travellers and describes the humours of the road in a fairly amusing manner, the epistolary form lending itself aptly enough to a purpose akin to that of the character. The impertinent beau, the jovial sea-captain, the prude, the over-familiar and talkative mayoress of Totnes, and the originals met with at the various inns, are all depicted in a lively style. Needless to say, they have their love-stories to tell ; those of the beau and captain being as free as might be expected, those of the ladies plaintively sentimental. No doubt, this sketch gave Mrs Haywood the cue for her *Bath-Intrigues*, also in letters.

Most—perhaps all—of the seven stories in *The Power of Love* (1720) were adapted from Painter's *Palace of Pleasure*, and come ultimately from Bandello ; Mrs Manley does not acknowledge the loan, though she did not take the precaution to change the characters' names. *The Fair Hypocrite* is Painter's *Duchess of Savoy*,[1] retold with a new attention to character. The duchess is an innocent girl married to the aged duke, and she lives happily and virtuously until a Spanish lady breeds such a longing in her heart with talk about her accomplished brother, Don Carlos, that the susceptible duchess prevails upon her husband to let her go on pilgrimage to Spain. Thus she begins to slide on the downward path, till, through her liaison with Don Carlos, she is verily the fair hypocrite. The next, *The Physician's Stratagem*, is a pathetic story on the Italian pattern. *The Wife's Resentment*, also tragic, is from Painter's *Didaco and Violenta*.[2]

" A Stage-Coach Journey"

Imitations of Bandello

[1] 45th novel.   [2] 42nd novel.

The Husband's Resentment is concerned with two instances of faithlessness : the one from Painter's *Of a Lady of Thurin*,[1] the poor maid of Turin who marries a marquess and then is discovered to be no better than she should be ; the other from his *President of Grenoble*,[2] in which the lady is shown up by one of the president's men. Mrs Manley alters the story, and makes a jealous old housekeeper expose her unfaithful mistress in the hope of regaining her master's favour. *The Happy Fugitives* is from Painter's *Alerane and Adelasia*[3] ; *The Perjur'd Beauty* from the St Gregory legend, basis of Walpole's play, *The Mysterious Mother*. The story is well and movingly told : all that is within Mrs Manley's reach. But it is not enough to show men or women feeling thus and thus or doing this or that : not so does a clear portrait of character emerge. There, however, is her limit. We know what her characters want and what they do ; but we know them as interests, not as interesting personalities.

Mrs Haywood   Nor can anything better be said of the more prolific Mrs Eliza Haywood (1693 ?-1756), except perhaps of two novels written after Defoe and Richardson had given her a lesson in the art of drawing from life.[4] She left her husband (1721), and began writing for the stage, on which she had appeared some years before in Shadwell's adaptation of Timon of Athens. Rich commissioned her to rewrite *The Fair Captive*, and her comedy, *A Wife to be Lett* (1723), was acted at Drury Lane. She had to be contented with publishing a tragedy, *Frederick, Duke of Brunswick-Lunenburgh* (1729). But long before this her novels had made a sensation ; and it was to fiction chiefly, with some translations, letters, and writings in two periodicals—*The Female Spectator* (1744-1746) and *The Parrot* (1746)—that she applied herself strenuously for the next thirty years. Her novels fall roughly into three groups : the first, " the finest love-sick passionate stories," approved ironically by Mrs Lennox, are after the model set by Mrs Behn ; then come a series of secret histories in the style of Mrs Manley ; and lastly her *Betsy*

---

[1] 43rd novel.   [2] 58th novel.   [3] 44th novel.
[4] There is a monograph on her by G. F. Whicher : *The Life and Romances of Mrs Haywood* (Columbia University Press, 1915).

Thoughtless and *Jemmy and Jenny Jessamy*, which are among the better novels of sensibility.

The first of some twenty or more novels was *Love in Excess : or, the Fatal Enquiry* (1719-1720), which was in a sixth edition when it went into her collected *Secret Histories, Novels, and Poems* (4 vols., 1725). The languishing and lachrymose novel, *The British Recluse : Or, Secret History of Cleomira, Suppos'd Dead* (1722), was not quite so well received. Neither is so fair an example of her work as *Idalia : Or, The Unfortunate Mistress* (1723). In this she vies with the creator of the nun Isabella in the analysis of a tortured heart ; but she is still more melodramatic, rhetorical, and high-flown. Idalia, the daughter of a Venetian grandee, being mildly in love with the rakish but personable Florez, is entrapped by this wretch into an assignation which the powerful Lord Ferdinand, nephew of the Doge, has suborned him to contrive. Ferdinand ravishes Idalia. To escape the hue and cry, he commits her to his friend Don Henriques, who carries her away but falls in love with her himself. There is a duel, in which both the ravisher and Henriques are killed. Myrtano, the brother of Henriques, now tries to seduce the unfortunate lady under a promise of marriage, and to escape him she flees to Verona. Here the tale breaks off ; but in the ultra-romantic second part she is carried away by pirates, and suffers a train of misfortunes, being at length shipwrecked and cast ashore, to be sheltered by a lady and her husband. The latter is Myrtano, and the result is a triple drama of jealousy, in which the wife tries to poison the fair interloper and is generously forgiven. *Lasselia : Or, The Self-Abandon'd* (1723), a tale of court intrigue in which Louis XIV. appears, came next. The inevitable essay in the Portuguese style, *Letters of a Lady of Quality to a Chevalier* (1721), had been a free paraphrase of a set by Edme Boursault (1699). Mrs Haywood was fond of the epistle. Later she published a volume of *Love-Letters on all Occasions lately passed between Persons of Distinction* (1730) and another of *Epistles for the Ladies* (1749-1750). They express the doubts and fears and jealousies in the mind of a woman, but do not tell a story. In her novels, also, the most intense passions and sensations are put into the letters between the characters,

Her novels, secret histories, and love-letters

and these are vehement and fairly natural in expression ; but Mrs Haywood never acquired the art of making the letter an integral part of the action. Her *Letters from the Palace of Fame. Written by the First Minister in the Regions of Air, to an Inhabitant of this World* (1727), is an effort in the style of *The Turkish Spy*,[1] and may have owed something to Montesquieu's *Lettres Persanes* (1721). She describes it as " Translated from an Arabian Manuscript."[2]

Novels written under French influence

The Fatal Secret : Or, Constancy in Distress (1724), and possibly some of the stories already mentioned, were influenced by Madame de Gomez and other French writers who were producing short romantic tales of contemporary life and making an earnest attempt to bring fiction of the Scudéry type into some approximation to nature. *La Belle Assemblée : Or, The Adventures of Six Days,* a series of conversations on love, despair, conduct and etiquette, learning and wit, was translated from that lady this same year, partly at any rate by Mrs Haywood, who was wholly responsible for the Englishing of its sequel, *L'Entretien des Beaux Esprits* (1734). *The Fatal Secret* depicts a young girl distracted between duty and love, when her father has chosen her a husband and she is smitten with passion for another.

Her once calm and peaceful bosom was now all hurry and confusion : the esteem which she had been long labouring to feel for the Chevalier was now turned to aversion and disdain ; and the indifference she had for all mankind was now converted into the most violent passion for one.

This expatiation on Amadea's feelings is carried on for pages ; it is the sort of thing that Mrs Haywood and her fellow-novelists fondly imagined to be enthralling drama. But the beings who experience these emotional tempests are too thin and lifeless for the reader's heart to throb in sympathy. They are not persons, but merely bundles of impersonal feelings. Mrs Haywood could make some show of the working of motive,

---

[1] See below, p. 143.
[2] *A Letter from H—— G——* (1750) is sometimes attributed to Mrs Haywood. It makes a journalistic pretence of confidential information about the Pretender. H. G. stands for Henry Goring, and the work is of the nature of a key-novel.

THE FOLLOWERS OF MRS BEHN 117

especially under the influence of febrile sentiment; she lacked the power of giving individuality to the figures swayed by these gusty emotions.

There is plenty of the same sort of thing in *The Life of Madam de Villesache* (1727). In *The Mercenary Lover : Or, The Unfortunate Heiresses. Being a True Secret History of a City Amour* (1726), interest, however, centres first in the undermining of a girl's morals by her brother-in-law, who corrupts her so that he may get hold of her fortune as well as her sister's, and secondly in her death and the detection of his guilt. In *The Padlock : or, No Guard without Virtue*, printed with the third edition of this (1728), an ill-used wife is rescued by her lover, and, living virtuously until she has been divorced, receives her reward in a devoted husband. *Philidore and Placentia : Or, L'Amour trop Delicat* (1727) has been aptly called " a mosaic of romantic adventures." [1] In this and other short stories Mrs Haywood found plots and motives from the French writers who were converting romance *à la Scudéry* into little histories with as much realism and modernity as was within their limited grasp. Like Mrs Behn and Mrs Manley, she localized her scenes in a perfunctory way, described her heroines and her heroes in minute detail, and made them express their feelings in vigorous language; but she does not succeed any better than they, if as much, in making any of her creations live.

Her *Bath-Intrigues : in four Letters to a Friend in London* (1725) is like Mrs Manley's *Stage-Coach Journey* in its incisive sketches of local characters and manners, and like her *Court Intrigues* in its scandal-mongering. It can be grouped with her two more celebrated secret histories, the *Memoirs of a Certain Island Adjacent to the Kingdom of Utopia. Written by a Celebrated Author of that Country. Now Translated into English* (2 vols., 1725-1726), and *The Secret History of the Present Intrigues of the Court of Caramania* (1727).[2] It is *The New Atalantis* all over

Novels and secret histories after Mrs Manley

[1] Whicher, p. 63. Dottin (*Daniel de Foe et ses romans*, p. 643) is of opinion that Mrs Haywood borrowed the idea of her hero and heroine stranded on a desert island from *Captain Singleton*.
[2] The year before had appeared *The Masqueraders ; or Fatal Curiosity: Being the Secret History of a Late Amour* (1724), and this year (1725) a spurious history entitled *Mary Stuart, Queen of Scots : Being the Secret History of her*

again ; not even all the personages are changed, for the Duchess of Marlborough, now a dowager, was still alive and the subject of a vicious portrait. The affair of Lady Macclesfield, formerly Anne Mason, and Lord Rivers, putative father of the poet Savage, is given a lurid form in the episode of Masonia and Riverius. Prince Theodore, in the *Court of Caramania,* was easily recognized as the Prince of Wales. Showèrs of abuse descended on Mrs Haywood's head ; but the coarse invective of Pope in the *Dunciad* merely served to excite feeling in her favour.

Her last novels— "Betsy Thought-less" and "Jemmy and Jenny Jessamy"

By the date of Mrs Haywood's last novels, for she was active for another thirty years, a famous revolution had taken place in the world of letters, and prose fiction, instead of being the Cinderella of the literary arts, was now on the way to becoming the most highly favoured. Defoe and Richardson had written, and also Fielding, though the latter's greatness was as yet recognized by few of his peers. *Betsy Thoughtless* (1751) and *Jemmy and Jenny Jessamy* (1753), as we might expect, reveal that Mrs Haywood had learned something from *Moll Flanders,* and more from *Clarissa Harlowe.*[1] She always had a receptive mind, though by now she was too old to change very deeply. Yet *The History of Miss Betsy Thoughtless* is a totally different kind of novel from *Idalia* : the figures appearing in it are not devoid of individual traits ; the incidents do not occur in empty space, but some vestiges at least of an outside world are brought into the sphere of vision. The main situation, that of an inexperienced girl entering upon the trials and deceptions of

Life, and the Real Causes of all Her Misfortunes. Containing a Relation of many particular Transactions in her Reign. . . . Translated from the French. It competed with another work of the same year, entitled *The History of the Life and Reign of Mary Stuart.* Several other of her novels, as indeed is indicated in the title of the collected editions, comprise secret histories, and won extra popularity on that account. " Secret history " was a phrase to conjure with, like the modern " indiscretions," " uncensored recollections," etc.

[1] *Pamela* also had not failed to give her hints. *A Present for a Servant-Maid : or, the Sure Means of gaining Love and Esteem* (with the additions in the second issue) *containing Rules for her Moral Conduct, both with respect to herself and her Superiors : the Whole Art of Cookery, Pickling, and Preserving. . . . With Marketing Tables,* etc., shows the Richardsonian influence in its " kitchen morality," and so likewise does her contribution to the Foundling literature common at the time of Captain Coram's charitable foundation in Bloomsbury, *The Fortunate Foundlings* (1748), the " Genuine History " of a pair of twins of that ilk.

life, probably deserves the credit of suggesting to Fanny Burney
the scheme of *Evelina*.

Betsy Thoughtless is a spirited and coquettish but not a
giddy person, whose troubles are partly the result of the skittish-
ness or worse of her schoolfellow Miss Forward, and partly due
to the coarse and dissolute Lady Mellasin, wife of her guardian,
and the jealousy of Flora Mellasin, the daughter. The Forward
girl promptly falls a victim to the temptations that Betsy resists.
Betsy has three admirers, Staple, Hysom, and Trueworth.
Captain Hysom, who may have suggested Fanny Burney's
Captain Mirvan, is a bluff and hearty seaman. Trueworth is the
Orville of the story, a paragon of worth and delicacy who wins
Betsy in the end, but, alas! is a prig.[1] The end is too long
deferred. Betsy first plays off her lovers against each other for
the mere fun of the game. She treats Captain Hysom, who is
uncouth but good-natured, with unpardonable levity. Meanwhile, trouble is brewing in the misdoings of Lady Mellasin,
who is extravagant, and carries on an illicit amour. She is black-
mailed, and barely escapes a spunging-house. Last of all, when
her husband is dying, she forges a will. Betsy is beset by the
plots of illegitimate lovers as well as the addresses of the honest
three. A vicious peer makes a show of rescuing her from a band
of rakes, in Westminster Cloisters, and this leads to a duel,
which the crafty viscount contrives to have interrupted. Her
friend and confidant Flora Mellasin slanders her to Trueworth,
whose misdoubts are deepened by the discovery of her friendship for the abandoned Forward. We have intrigues, false
accusations, anonymous letters, and numerous complications,
but not an orderly plot.

In one episode, of picaresque origin, Betsy is prevailed upon
to visit a dying baronet, who implores her to marry him in his
last moments so that he may have the consolation of leaving her
his fortune. When the ceremony—a bogus ceremony—is over,
he jumps out of bed and tries to consummate the marriage. She
is rescued in the nick of time, to find that the supposed baronet

*" Betsy
Thought-
less "*

---

[1] Dunlop's elaborate comparison of *Evelina* and *Betsy Thoughtless* is examined
by Dr. G. F. Whicher (*Life and Romances of Mrs Haywood*, p. 161), who observes
that there is no evidence that Fanny Burney had read the previous work.

is a hardened criminal. At length, Betsy is drawn into a marriage with a Mr Munden, who deceives her and compels her to seek a refuge with her brother, but opportunely dies. Then the widow, chastened by experience, marries the much-enduring Trueworth.

Compared with Richardson's, the character-drawing is almost null. Mrs Haywood, although she must have read *Pamela* and *Clarissa*, has not learned to touch in the little mannerisms that accentuate individuality ; she sets down what her characters do and say, but not how they act and speak. The letters are given at full length, with all the formalities, and are a contrast to the pith and dramatic force of Richardson's. She comes nearer to, though still a long way behind, the simpler narrative method of Defoe in *Moll Flanders* and *Roxana*. And she lacks the art of economy, of concentration : *Betsy Thoughtless* and *Jemmy and Jenny Jessamy* both contain the rough material of many stories, flung together without any sense of selection.

" *Jemmy and Jenny Jessamy* "

Jemmy and Jenny Jessamy (1753) has a capital opening. Sophia's brother brings his mistress home, and prepares to marry her next day, whereupon the lady refuses, and presently lets out that she is married already. Jemmy and Jenny are cousins and lovers from infancy, meant by their parents to marry when they come of age ; and, contrary to usage, they do not rebel against this understanding. Fond of each other, but both desirous of seeing the world and gaining experience before tying themselves up, they go forth to collect and compare observations. Some of the types they meet with are amusing, some already hackneyed; for instance, the lady who lets her men pay her gambling debts—for love—and withholds the expected recompense. Jenny goes to Bath, and Jemmy is prevented from joining her there by various accidents, which are by way of a trial of her constancy. This is severely tested by the addresses of a gentleman of worth, and by the report that Jemmy has been unfaithful. There is the usual attempt at rape by a profligate—a regular feature in Mrs Haywood's stories. Beset with other perplexities and misunderstandings, she has to return to London, just before Jemmy at length follows her to Bath. The trite incident of two love-letters put in the wrong envelopes is used, but not very effectively. Jemmy sends one to an old flame of his undergraduate days, Celia of the Woods ; the other to his sweetheart. Celia, whom Jemmy has met accidentally in town, proves to be now the wife of a baronet, to whom Jemmy's false friend Bellpine is heir presumptive. Bellpine tries to ruin Jemmy by involving him with a third lady and betraying the affair to Jenny. But she forgives even this infidelity, which she does not think serious. When Bellpine's villainy comes to light he and Jemmy fight a duel, and Bellpine is given out for dead. Jemmy escapes to the Continent, but later Bellpine recovers, and there is a general clearing up of things and final reconciliation, the well-tried lovers entering on the long-deferred estate of matrimony.

The main story is encumbered with various inset stories, in spite of which the plot-work is not unskilful, and this, in spite again, of the clumsy use of full-length letters. The realism is as thin as in *Betsy Thoughtless*. In both works the moral intention is obvious ; but in these two novels Mrs Haywood laid herself less open to the objection that, while the formal lesson was unimpeachable, the mode of inculcating it led the reader into the perilous seductions that he was charged to avoid. She had had the face to declare in the preface to *Queen Zarah* that the object was " to instruct, and to inspire into men the love of virtue and abhorrence of vice, by the examples proposed to them." And when her sincerity was impugned, and some of her own sex had been unkind enough to insinuate that " I seem to endeavour to divert more than to improve the minds of my readers," she rejoined, in her preface to *Lasselia* :

How far I have been able to succeed in my desires of infusing these cautions, too necessary to a number, I will not pretend to determine ; but where I have had the misfortune to fail, must impute it either to the obstinacy of those I would persuade, or to my own deficiency in that very thing which they are pleased to say I too much abound in—a true description of Nature.

The women writers who followed in her and Mrs Manley's wake were still more earnest. The word " instructive " is not less prominent than the word " entertaining " in the titles of

Followers of Mrs Manley and Mrs Haywood

Mrs Barker's novels. Mary Davys announced that she wrote *The Reform'd Coquet* to serve the public by showing :

> How amiable a lady is without the blots of vanity and levity, which stain the mind and stamp deformity where the greatest beauties would shine, were they banished.

Penelope Aubin wrote *The Life of Madam de Beaumont* for the purpose of " pleasing, and at the same time encouraging virtue " in her readers, and says at the end :

> Such histories as these ought to be published in this age above all others, and if we would be like the worthy persons whose story we have here read, happy and blessed with all human felicity, let us imitate their virtues, since that is the only way to make us dear to God and man, and the most certain and noble method to perpetuate our names, and render our memories immortal and our souls eternally happy.

She was much distressed by the frivolity of her time. In the preface to *The Count de Vinevil* she observes :

> Since serious things are in a manner altogether neglected, by what we call the gay and fashionable part of mankind, and religious treatises grow mouldy on the booksellers' shelves in the back shops ; when ingenuity is, for want of encouragement, starved into silence, and Toland's abominable writings sell ten times better than the inimitable Mr Pope's " Homer " ; when Dacier's works are attempted to be translated by a hackney-writer, and Horace's odes turned into prose and nonsense ; the few that honour virtue, and wish well to the nation, ought to study to reclaim our giddy youth ; and since reprehensions fail, try to win them to virtue by methods where delight and instruction may go together. With this design I present this book to the public, in which you will find a story, where Divine Providence manifests itself in every action, where virtue is tried with misfortunes, and rewarded with blessings. In fine, where men behave themselves like Christians, and women are really virtuous, and such as we ought to imitate.

Mrs Eliza-beth Rowe Elizabeth Rowe, the venerated author of *Friendship in Death* and *Letters Moral and Entertaining*, the friend of the hymn-writer Dr Watts, the eulogized of Klopstock, Wieland, and Dr Johnson, was equally serious, and was

THE FOLLOWERS OF MRS BEHN 123

taken more seriously still by her readers. Her *Friendship in Death, in twenty Letters from the Dead to the Living* (1728) aimed " to impress the notion of the soul's immortality ; without which, all virtue and religion, with their temporal and eternal consequences, must fall to the ground " ; and she hoped " endeavouring to make the mind function with the thoughts of our future existence, and contract, as it were unawares, an habitual persuasion of it, by writings built on that foundation, and addressed to the affections and imagination, will not be thought improper, either as a doctrine, or amusement." [1] Here are the superscriptions of the more striking epistles : " To the Earl of R——r from Clerimont, who had promised to appear to him after his death " ; " To the Countess of —— from Narcissus, her only son and heir, who died when he was but two years old " ; " To —— from Junius, giving his friend a description of the planetary worlds " ; " To Emilia from Delia, giving her a beautiful description of the invisible regions " ; " To Sylvia from Alexis, acquainting her, that she is the natural daughter of a person of quality, and not the real issue of her supposed parents." The didactic and pietistic nature of the letters is fairly indicated. They were very popular, much more so than the *Letters Moral and Entertaining* (1729-1733) which followed, although these were not so crude, and comprised little stories and bits of dialogue inserted, not unskilfully, as they might be in a modern religious tract. In some the art of the *novella* is employed for purposes of edification. Others are pleasant tales of rural life, almost pastorals, with idyllic painting of scenery, in a manner afterwards followed by the author of *John Buncle*. The letters are supposed to be written between intimate friends, who are given a true account of events about which they had been in the dark. Such is the letter " To Belinda from Sylvia, ingenuously confessing, that a guilty passion was the real cause of her sudden retirement into the country," [2] supplemented in the second part by one " To Belinda from Sylvia, giving her the sequel of her story." [3] The three letters beginning the second part, " To Lady Sophia, from Rosalinda, relating the true occasion of her flying from France, and leaving her father's

[1] Preface.   [2] Part I., letter 3.   [3] Part II., letter 5.

house in the disguise of a country girl," have the sequel expounded in the three at the beginning of the following part. Mrs Rowe had no gift for character-drawing, and her treatment of motive is the shallowest sentimentalism. She fails to attain any loftier moral standpoint than the axiom that rectitude will have its reward. Her heroines are models of sensibility, but their pious sentiments are no more elevated than the ethics of *Pamela*. Both as moralist and as novelist, Mrs Rowe stands on a lower plane than her literary descendant Hannah More.

Mrs
Barker

Jane Barker (*c.* 1675-1743) is said to have been a young associate of the Orinda circle, and to have belonged to a similar coterie of literary aspirants at Cambridge. She contributed to a series of *Poetical Recreations* (1688), which also contains some tributes from other versifiers to her genius. But she was of riper age when she published a feeble didactic work, *Exilius : Or, The Banish'd Roman . . . A New Romance. Written After the Manner of Telemachus, For the Instruction of Some Young Ladies of Quality* (1715). As fiction this is naught, the stories told are ultra-romantic ; but the counsels vouchsafed on manners and the practical affairs of life are sensible, and prepare the way for Richardson. A later novel has a suggestive title, but the promise of something unprecedented is hardly made good. *A Patch-Work Screen for the Ladies ; or, Love and Virtue Recommended, in a Collection of Instructive Novels. Related After a Manner Intirely New, and interspersed with Rural Poems, describing the Innocence of a Country Life* (1723), and *The Lining of the Patch-Work Screen ; Design'd for the Farther Entertainment of the Ladies* (1726), are but two more sets of improving tales, the moral of which is of the worldly-wise rather than the ethical order. Mrs Barker's stories were at any rate popular. There was a collective edition, *The Entertaining Novels of Mrs Barker,* which reached a third edition by 1736.

Mrs
Aubin

Penelope Aubin came under the spell of *Robinson Crusoe,* and in several of her novels produced a curious mixture of romantic adventure and love matters in which faith and virtue were tried by many afflictions and rewarded according to merit, the vicious being shown " unfortunate in the end," and their death " accompanied with terrors." She was a religious as well as a moral teacher, and assured the reader that " the virtuous shall look dangers in the face unmoved, and putting their whole trust in the Divine Providence, shall be delivered, even by miraculous means ; or dying with comfort be freed from the miseries of this life, and go to taste an eternal repose." [1]

To encourage virtue and induce her readers to confide in Providence and look on death with indifference is her whole aim in *The Life of Madam de Beaumont* (1721), which is the history of a French lady " who lived in a cave in Wales about fourteen years undiscovered, being forced to fly France for her religion, and of the cruel usage she had there. Also her Lord's Adventures in Muscovy where he was prisoner some years, with an Account of his returning to France, and her being discovered by a Welsh Gentleman, who fetched her Lord to Wales ; and of many strange accidents which befell them and their daughter Belinda, who was stolen away from them, and of their Return to France in the year 1718." This was exceeded in improbability by *The Strange Adventures of the Count de Vinevil and his Family. Being an Account of what happen'd to them whilst they resided at Constantinople. And of Mlle Ardelisia his daughter's being shipwrecked on the Uninhabited Island Delos in the Return to France, with Violetta, a Venetian Lady, the Captain of the Ship, a Priest, and five Sailors. The manner of their living there, and strange Deliverance by the arrival of a Ship commanded by Violetta's father. Ardelisia's Entertainment at Venice and safe return to France* (1721). It is unnecessary to quote more than the titles, which give the whole bill of fare ; there is a sameness and a staleness about the viands offered. Mrs Aubin's next was *The Noble Slaves : Or, The Lives and Adventures of Two Lords and Two Ladies, who were shipwrecked and cast upon a desolate Island* (1722). Then, after translating a work quite as marvellous which professed to be historical, Petis de la Croix' *History of Genghizcan the Great, First Emperor of the Antient Moguls*

[1] Preface to *Adventures of the Lady Lucy*, in " A Collection of Entertaining Histories and Novels designed to promote the cause of Virtue and Honour, Principally founded on facts and instructive incidents " (3 vols., 1739); contains *The Noble Slaves, Life and Amorous Adventures of Lucinda, Strange Adventures of Count de Vinevil, Life and Adventures of the Lady Lucy, Life and Adventures of Count Albertus, Life of Charlotte Du Pont, Life of Madam de Beaumont.*

and Tartars (1726), she returned to her own vein in *The Life and Adventures of the Lady Lucy* (1726), which incidentally brings in what almost look like first-hand experiences of the Irish wars after the Revolution. Mrs Aubin undertook two other congenial pieces of translation : *The Illustrious French Lovers ; Being the True Histories of the Amours of Several French Persons of Quality* (1727), and *The Life of the Countess de Gondez. Written by her own Hand* (1729). Her last original work was a picaresque novel, *The Life and Adventures of the Young Count Albertus, The Son of Count Lewis Augustus, by the Lady Lucy* (1728), the hero of which, hard hit by the death of his wife, seeks forgetfulness in foreign travel. In the first part of the story, he meets various persons who relate their tragic lives, the best of these insets being a grimly dramatic account of the abduction of both daughter and treasure of an old miser in Madrid. The upshot of his reflections on these gloomy occurrences is that Albertus becomes a Benedictine, and sails with three Jesuits to China as a missionary, ending his life a martyr to the Christian faith. In the narrative of the oriental adventures, Mrs Aubin evidently utilized the accounts of travel in the Near and the Far East which were growing plentiful at this period.

Mrs Davys

Mary Davys was the widow of a schoolmaster at York, and an acquaintance of Swift. " Left to her own endeavours for twenty-seven years together," she wrote plays, novels, poems, and familiar letters, " for that bread which they that condemn her would very probably deny to give her." It was thus that she defended herself against uncharitable opinions on the profession she had adopted, in the preface to her collective works (1725). She had definite views on the right structure for a novel, and on the need for making the extraordinary seem probable.

I have in every novel proposed one entire scheme or plot, and the other adventures are only incident or collateral to it ; which is the great rule prescribed by the critics, not only in tragedy, and other heroic poems, but in comedy too. The adventures, as far as I could order them, are wonderful and probable.

One of her tales, *The Merry Wanderer*, describes incidents of travel, the odd characters met with at an inn, and the niggardly treatment received at a friend's house, just as Mrs Manley and Mrs Haywood had recounted similar experiences, but with a stronger flavour of the picaresque. All this is but the prologue, however, to a comic tale of amorous intrigue. Her comedy, *The Northern Heiress ; or, the Humours of York* (1716), offered similar entertainment. In her best novel, *The Reform'd Coquet, or Memoirs of Amoranda* (1724), she describes how the giddy young heroine is rescued from the compromising or mercenary gallantries of a crowd of admirers by a perfect young nobleman, who at length exchanges the part of mentor for that of wooer, and becomes the perfect husband. And it is all written for the purpose of warning the ladies :

When you grow weary of flattery, and begin to listen to matrimonial addresses, choose a man of fine sense, as well as a fine wig, and let him have some merit, as well as much embroidery ; this will make coxcombs give ground, and men of sense will equally admire your conduct with your beauty.

Mrs Davys-did not escape the Portuguese fashion : she too has her set of *Familiar Letters betwixt a Gentleman and a Lady* included in the *Works* (2 vols., 1725). *The Cousins* is a regular *novella* in a Spanish setting.

It is interesting to find one of these women writers, Mrs Arabella Plantin, deliberately opposing middle-class fiction to those modish stories that dazzle the reader with pompous titles and the life of shining courts, in a word, adopting the anti-romantic attitude. In *Love Led Astray ; or, The Mutual Inconstancy* (1727) [1] she writes thus :

It is not among the most exalted characters, nor in the highest rank of life, that the strange effects of Love most frequently appear ; this little deity extends his empire to the most obscure retreats, as well as to the most shining courts. I know that the name of a prince embellishes a story, and seems to interest a reader in it, tho' that pompous title is not always attended with all the gallantry which is often found in a private person ; therefore I leave the Historians the choice of their illustrious name. I intend to confine myself to the passion of love, and as

[1] Two novels—I. *The Ingrateful : Or, The Just Revenge.* II. *Love led Astray : Or, The Mutual Inconstancy* (in *Whartoniana*, 1727).

I am persuaded that a shepherd may in this point exceed the greatest king, I shall not go beyond the bounds of a forest to convince my readers of this truth.

Nevertheless, after all this talk about the probabilities, we are fobbed off with a pastoral, in truth two pastorals, miniature *Arcadias*, with the Sidneian characters merely reduced a peg or two in rank.

Mrs Boyd

The ingenious Mrs Elizabeth Boyd resuscitated Behnesque fiction in *The Female Page: A Genuine and Entertaining History, Relating to Some Persons of Distinction. Intermix'd with A great Variety of affecting Intrigues in Love and Gallantry. Also the remarkable Letters that passed between the several Persons concerned* (1737). In the preface, she seems to deprecate the supposition, yet slyly hints, that the actual goings on of certain people of note are recorded in the story, though she refuses indignantly to adopt the practice of a key. It is a tale of roving loves and confused intrigues, with many scenes of unrestrained voluptuousness and dithyrambic emotion. Here is a sample of Mrs Boyd's semi-metrical fustian, printed as it ought to have been printed, in the form of verse:

> Unhappy Sex! forbid by prudent Thought
> to breathe a Sigh, or dart a meaning Look,
> lest a censorious World name it a Crime;
> and when the sad Relief of Words would ease,
> nay calm, and cessate Wars, dread to unfold them,
> and have we ought of Conduct, must deceive,
> Lye to the Friend we hug, yet call them dear:
> Such are the base Reserves of modern Friendships.
> Oh, Jupiter, forbid the foul Injustice!
> Defraud of Thought, and Perjury of Souls!
> yet, so much she who hath a fame to lose,
> or any spark of modest thinking act,
> or be the Laugh of Crouds, the Fop's remark.[1]

The scene is Cyprus, whither apparently a dissolute Restoration or Regency court has been transplanted. Of course, the Female Page is a woman in love with the principal character, Duke Bellfont, and her sex is disclosed in the most provocative

---

[1] *The Female Page* (1737), p. 102.

circumstances. The duchess falls in love with the handsome page; the duke's brother tries to ravish her. After all that happens, it seems a superfluous concession to formal morality to conclude with the marriage of the lovers through the death of the duchess.

Between Mrs Behn and Mrs Boyd fiction had on the whole, however, begun to settle down to its own proper sphere. *Summary* Novelists were growing more clearly aware that their business was with life as it is. Romance was getting old-fashioned and ridiculous. The *novella* offered inadequate resources, though it taught the importance of unity, of the strict connexion of action and motive, and of liveliness of manner and style. The object of both romance and *novella* was to tell a touching or exciting story. The novel, as it was gradually evolving, has a further duty to perform, to exhibit life actually going on. This the professional writers were beginning dimly to understand. They acknowledged the need for verisimilitude. But the kind of verisimilitude they observed was, after all, only a negative virtue, the avoidance of improbability. To insist that a story must be plausible in its circumstances and incidents is but a small advance on the road to realism; it is to eschew an ancient weakness, but not to attain a new strength. When the novelist had acquired the art of conveying the illusion of life, he would be able to present the improbable and even the impossible without infringing verisimilitude. Defoe and Swift were now demonstrating this, and making such a contribution to the technique of realism as marks a great epoch in the history of the novel.

CHAPTER VI

THE ESTABLISHMENT OF REALISM—
DEFOE AND *ROBINSON CRUSOE*

*A new
beginning
with
Defoe*

THE turning-point in the history of the English novel has now been reached. With Defoe fiction seems to make a new start, and to recapitulate in the course of one man's miscellaneous output the whole process by which, at various dates, historical writing, lives of celebrities, narratives of travel in unknown regions, and other accounts of real or alleged facts, gave rise to arbitrary invention. Not that Defoe ignored all that had been accomplished by others. On the contrary, he was not only a man of exceptionally wide reading who ignored nothing that could be of the slightest interest to him, but he was also one who would without scruple make free with any building material or literary device that came in useful from any source whatever. But it so happened that other writers served his purposes better, and he accordingly borrowed as little as Bunyan had done from novelists of the past or the present. *Robinson Crusoe* and *Captain Singleton*, *Moll Flanders* and *Roxana*, have a better right than anything previously written in English to be classed as novels ; yet not one of them was candidly given to the world as a work of fiction. The public for whom Defoe catered was more insistent even than the readers who believed in Mrs Behn's and Mrs Manley's reliability on being supplied with genuine information. Fiction was a thing they despised ; they left it to the childish people who liked fairy-tales. Defoe's predecessors flattered this superiority by seasoning their fiction with fact or the pretence of fact : Defoe dished up facts themselves to make fiction. In order to convince readers that what he was telling them, however incredible it sounded, was indubitably true, Defoe invented a special technique, the circumstantial method, a technique that has been used since only when writers have had to secure suspension of disbelief in the absolutely impossible ; and the result was that he set an example of such realism as skirts the limits, if it does not trespass beyond them, of legitimate art.

Daniel Defoe (1659 ?-1731) [1] was nearly sixty when he published the first of his great works of fiction, *Robinson Crusoe*. He had begun writing as a pamphleteer, newsmonger, and publicist at the age of thirty-seven, and already had an enormous list of works to his credit—and some to his discredit. By birth and upbringing a Nonconformist, he had been first intended for the ministry, but instead he went into business, though he never resigned his active interest in the religious questions that agitated the time or in the political controversies hinging upon them. He was out with Monmouth in 1685, but did not make himself conspicuous, and found his way back to London unmolested. When William of Orange landed at Torbay, he once more volunteered against James II., and joined the invading army at Henley only in time to learn that the king had secretly left London, and had been intercepted at Sheerness and taken to Faversham. To glean what facts he might, Defoe rode to Faversham, and afterwards witnessed the triumphal entry of William and Mary into the capital, and was present at the subsequent meetings of the two Houses of Parliament.

Defoe's life and works

He had set up as a hosier or hose-factor, and implicated himself in various speculative transactions. Instead of making a fortune, he went bankrupt (1692), but came to an amicable arrangement with his creditors. His next trading venture was more prosperous. He ran an extensive brick-factory at Tilbury for some ten years (1694-1705), and was able to reduce his debts from £17,000 to £5000, and ultimately to pay them off entirely. When a tax on glass was voted (1695), Defoe was appointed accountant to the commissioners, and held the post for four years, when the tax was withdrawn. He was consulted by the Government on such matters as the proposal to establish lotteries for the benefit of the Exchequer, and twice held office as one of the controllers of a royal lottery. His wide and accurate knowledge of the body politic and economic, his speculative boldness, and his instinctive bent for thinking out

[1] Professor W. P. Trent on " Defoe " (*Camb. Hist. of Eng. Lit.*, ix. 6).

how things should be done, are strikingly shown in his *Essay on Projects* (1698), which propounds a number of schemes for commercial, fiscal, educational, and military reforms, most of them sound and far-seeing, others wildly Utopian.

*Polem-
ical
writings*
Defoe's many-sided abilities and his devotion to the Protestant cause marked him out for employment as a controversialist in matters of more immediacy. He championed the war policy of the king in pamphlets exposing the danger of letting Louis XIV. have his way over the Spanish succession. He made game of those who disparaged William III. as a foreigner by publishing a ballad, *The True-born Englishman*, reminding the nation, in trenchant doggerel terms, that they were as mongrel a breed as ever peopled the earth. Far from exciting indignation, the satire sold in tens of thousands, and made Defoe the most popular man in England. But his strong-mindedness and independence were less happy when he dealt with the troubles of his co-religionists. He failed to please the Dissenters with his tracts on the practice of occasional conformity, and his sarcastic adoption, in *The Shortest Way with the Dissenters* (1702), of the most violent and extreme sentiments of a High Churchman, ready to put down Nonconformity by the method of hanging the preachers and banishing their congregations, embroiled him with both parties at once. Many of the high-flying Tories were foolish enough to take the advice in earnest ; their opponents were alarmed. Hearing that proceedings were in train against him, Defoe went into hiding, and issued a defence of his conduct. Eventually, however, he stood his trial, and was sentenced to a fine, to stand three times in the pillory, and to be imprisoned during the queen's pleasure. His three days in the pillory were a triumph for Defoe. He was encircled by a bodyguard of admirers, while the populace drank his health and shouted lines from the *Hymn to the Pillory*, in which he boldly declared that he had been punished for telling " those truths that should not have been told."

> " And thus he's an example made
> To make men of their honesty afraid."

Released from gaol in November 1703, Defoe, whose works at Tilbury had been dismantled, leaving him with no support

for his wife and family except his pen, went on with his pam- *" The*
phleteering: started the *Weekly Review of the Affairs of France* *Jour-*
(1704-1713), a journal dealing with foreign policy and enlighten- *nal,"*
ing the country on the ambition of the French king to domineer *" The*
Consoli-
over the Continent, and gave the first example of his genius *dator,"*
for describing, as if with the pen of an eye-witness, matters that *" Mrs*
he knew about chiefly by report, in *The Storm ; or, a Collection* *Veal "*
of the most remarkable Casualties and Disasters which happened
in the Late Dreadful Tempest, both by Sea and Land (1704). Two
subsequent works, among much writing of his usual polemical
kind, are of importance in the study of Defoe the future novelist.
The one was a volume entitled, *The Consolidator : or, Memoirs*
of Sundry Transactions from the World in the Moon. Translated
from the Lunar Language. By the Author of the True-born
Englishman (1705); the other a tract called, *A True Relation of*
the Apparition of one Mrs Veal, The next day after Her Death :
to one Mrs Bargrave At Canterbury (1706). The fourth edition
of the latter was published with Drelincourt's pious work, *The*
Christian's Defence against the Fears of Death, appended, and
these words added to the title, " Which Apparition recom-
mends the Perusal of Drelincourt's Book of Consolations against
the Fears of Death " ; but to suppose that Defoe wrote the book
to puff Drelincourt's tract is a mistake.

He derived the idea of his *Consolidator* from Cyrano de *The*
Bergerac, of whose satirical romance two translations had *" Consoli-*
appeared in the last half-century. For that amusing fantasy *dator "*
the original notion seems to have come from the Lucianic essay
of Francis Godwin, bishop of Hereford, *The Man in the Moone :*
or a discourse of a Voyage thither By Domingo Gonzales The speedy
Messenger, published posthumously in 1638, having probably
been written in Godwin's youth.[1] The story is based on the
theory that there is a regular passage by which locusts, birds,
and the like migrate between the two planets ; and Godwin's
adventurer, left on St Helena,[2] living a Crusoe life there, and

[1] It was translated into French by J. Baudoin (1648). The allusions in
Godwin's stories are to events in the fifteen-nineties.
[2] One of Mandelslo's desert islanders is left on St Helena (see below, p. 149),
and Hakluyt relates the experiences of John Segar alone on that island for a
year and a half (Secord, pp. 29-30).

afterwards a fugitive on Tenerife, escapes from savages by the agency of a team of swans which he has harnessed, and eventually is wafted to the moon. Defoe probably knew Godwin's tale, as well as the more serious work of another prelate, John Wilkins, bishop of Chester, whose treatise, *A Discovery of a New World in the Moone, with a Discourse Concerning the Probability of a Passage thither*, came out the same year. Wilkins states that he had finished his discourse when he lighted on the late Bishop Godwin's fanciful work. In a final chapter on the possibility of travel to the moon, he solemnly discusses Godwin's supposition of an air-track for birds and insects. His own fourteenth proposition runs, " That 'tis possible for our Posterity to find out a Conveyance to this other World, and if there be Inhabitants there, to have Commerce with them." No doubt, Robert Paltock had the Bishop of Chester's book in mind when he called his Utopian story of the winged folk *The Life and Adventures of Peter Wilkins* (1751). Defoe was acquainted with it. In *The Consolidator* he speaks of the " mechanic motions of Bishop Wilkins," [1] whose eleventh proposition, " That as their World is our Moon, so our World is their Moon," furnishes the basic principles of his own speculations and inventions. For this is a satire that, like Swift's *Gulliver*, shifts from one point of view to the opposite, now looking from the moon through a powerful telescope at the foolish squabbling of sects and nations on this earth, and now contemplating the wild struggles of Solunarians and Crolians, caricatures of the Anglicans and Dissenters, in the world of the moon. The pretence that he is abridging from the historiographer-royal to the Emperor of China indicates that Defoe saw the satirical value of the foreign observer, with his long-distance outlook on European affairs, even though he employs the device without skill or grace.[2]

Political satire

Defoe's narrative is, indeed, ill-proportioned and clumsy, and the humour heavy. His " Consolidator " is an engine consisting of a chariot carried on the backs of two vast bodies with extended wings, which are composed of 513 feathers, all of the same length and breadth, with the exception of a much larger

[1] *The Consolidator*, p. 280 (*Earlier Life and Works of Defoe*, ed. H. Morley, 1889).
[2] *The Turkish Spy* (1687-1693) was no doubt well known to Defoe, see below, p. 143.

one, " the presiding or superintendent feather," whose function it is " to guide, regulate, and pilot the whole body." This machine represents the English House of Commons, and in the account of its construction, its first voyages, and the accidents it sustained, Defoe allegorizes the history of the Civil Wars and the Revolution. He pleads for mutual understanding and moderation, and ridicules extremists of either party.

Methinks I begin to pity my brethren, the moderate men of the Church, that they cannot see into this new plot, and to wish they would but get up into our Consolidator, and take a journey to the moon, and there, by the help of these glasses, they would see the allegorical, symbolical heterodoxicality of all this matter ; it would make immediate converts of them ; they would see plainly that to tack and consolidate, to make exclusive laws, to persecute for conscience, disturb and distress parties—these are all fanatic plots, mere combinations against the Church, to bring her into contempt, and to fix and establish the Dissenters to the end of the chapter. But of this I shall find occasion to speak occasionally, when an occasion presents itself to examine a certain occasional bill transacting in these Lunar regions some time before I had the happiness to arrive there.[1]

This awkward mixture of argument and ridicule, direct and indirect description, can hardly be compared with the sustained irony of Swift. But there are obvious suggestions for the voyage to Laputa in *The Consolidator*, even if it be doubted whether the contrasted views of earthly and lunar affairs contributed anything to the first two books of *Gulliver*. Defoe gets some amusement out of two machines used on the lunar orb, the Elevators and the Cogitators. As to the former :

Possible suggestions for "Gulliver"

The mechanic operations of these are wonderful, and helped by fire, by which the senses are raised to all the strange extremes we can imagine, and whereby the intelligent soul is made to converse with its own species, whether embodied or not. Those that are raised to a due pitch in this wondrous frame have a clear prospect into the world of spirits, and converse with visions, guardian angels, spirits departed, and what not. And as this is a wonderful knowledge, and not to be obtained but by the help

[1] *The Consolidator*, pp. 306-307.

of this fire, so those that have tried the experiment give strange accounts of sympathy, pre-existence of souls, dreams, and the like.

The Cogitator or Chair of Reflexion is an engine into which a person is screwed, all his faculties are tightened up, every distracting object and the " thousand fluttering demons that gender in the fancy " locked out, and he is enabled to concentrate his brain through a series of glasses on whatever he desires to think upon.

There never was a man went into one of these thinking engines but he came wiser out than he was before ; and I am persuaded it would be a more effectual cure to our deism, atheism, scepticism, and all other -cisms than ever the Italian's engine for curing the gout by cutting off the toe.[1]

Later on he remarks:

Our Dissenters here have not the advantage of a cogitator or thinking engine, as they have in the moon. We have the elevator here, and are lifted up pretty much; but in the moon they always go into the thinking engine upon every emergency, and in this they outdo us of this world on every occasion.[2]

Defoe had his eye on blustering preachers of the doctrine of non-resistance, like Sacheverell, when he described his ecclesiastic engine, the " concionazimir," which makes a terrible noise when a clergyman gets inside and beats it, and is used in cases of alarm " as the Church's signal for universal tumult." He regrets that he is too bad a draughtsman to provide the reader with a diagram, but he describes it in detail as follows :

It is a hollow vessel, large enough to hold the biggest clergyman in the nation ; it is generally an octagon in figure, open before, from the waist upward, but whole at the back, with a flat extending over it for reverberation or doubling the sound ; doubling and redoubling being frequently thought necessary to be made use of on these occasions. It is very mathematically contrived, erected on a pedestal of wood like a windmill, and has a pair of winding stairs up to it, like those at the great tun at Heidelberg.[3]

---

[1] *The Consolidator, p.* 312.   [2] *Ibid.,* p. 377.   [3] *Ibid.,* p. 338.

The other very notable work *A True Relation of the Apparition of one Mrs Veal*, is not a work of fiction, as has often been supposed, but a piece of reporting ; yet it is no mistake to regard this as an early essay in those methods of winning credence in things exceeding the probable that Defoe afterwards brought to perfection in his fictitious narratives.[1] Having heard of Mrs Bargrave's story, Defoe, in his capacity of journalist, went down to Canterbury, investigated the case, and served it up with such a show of candour and of honest doubts irresistibly removed that the reader is almost compelled to believe, not only in Mrs Bargrave's good faith, but even in the reality of the apparition. The report is stated to have been sent by a justice of the peace at Maidstone, a very intelligent person, and to be attested by " a very sober and understanding gentleman, who had it from his kinswoman, who lives at Canterbury, within a few doors of the house in which the within-named Mrs Bargrave lived." Thus the brief preface, with an assurance that the report is given, as far as may be, in the actual words of Mrs Bargrave, a woman of much honesty and virtue, who had no reason to invent such a story, " her whole life being a course, as it were, of piety." Defoe, be it noted, here takes as much trouble to attest what he honestly believes to be true as he was often to take afterwards with downright fiction.

With the same object he inserts all those tiny irrelevant particulars that are so potent in lulling suspicion and convincing us of the artless veracity of a supposed witness ; such, for instance, as Mrs Bargrave's cheerful disposition, " notwithstanding the ill-usage of a very wicked husband " ; the little touches about Mrs Veal's and Mrs Bargrave's circumstances and the long break in their intercourse ; and the intimate household affairs discussed at Mrs Bargrave's tea-table in that most matter-of-fact conversation with the ghost—surely, the kindliest and gentlest of disembodied spirits ever called from the vasty deep ! Still more artful are the frank admissions of what might weigh against the story in the minds of the incredulous. Mrs Veal's

marginal notes:
" *The Apparition of Mrs Veal* "

Circumstantial realism

---

[1] Defoe's editor, Mr G. A. Aitken, showed that it was not fiction but a genuine piece of news, in an article in *The Nineteenth Century*, xxxvii., 1895.

brother, " a very sober man, to all appearance . . . now does all he can to null or quash the story."

Mr Veal does what he can to stifle the matter, and said he would see Mrs Bargrave ; but yet it is certain matter of fact that he has been at Captain Watson's since the death of his sister, and yet never went near Mrs Bargrave ; and some of his friends report her to be a liar, and that she knew of Mr Breton's ten pounds a year (this refers to an allowance paid to Mrs Veal, which was a secret and unknown to Mrs Bargrave till Mrs Veal told it her). But the person who pretends to say so has the reputation of a notorious liar among persons whom I know to be of undoubted credit.

But the most inimitable touch is that of the scoured silk dress.

Mrs Bargrave " took hold of her gown-sleeve several times and commended it. Mrs Veal told her it was of scoured silk, and newly made up." When she related her experience to Captain Watson's family, " and what gown she had on, and how striped, and that Mrs Veal told her it was scoured, then Mrs Watson cried out, ' You have seen her indeed, for none knew but Mrs Veal and myself that the gown was scoured.' And Mrs Watson owned that she described the gown exactly ; ' for,' said she, ' I helped her to make it up.' "

" To this crushing piece of evidence," observed Sir Leslie Stephen, who believed the whole story to be one of Defoe's inventions, " it seems that neither Mrs Veal nor the notorious liar could invent any sufficient reply." The " notorious liar " is, of course, Defoe. Another critic who held much the same opinion of Defoe, the late Sir Walter Raleigh, makes the general comment, that " the ordinary reader becomes so interested in the opinion that Defoe's characters have of one another's veracity that he forgets to ask whether they exist." [1] In the course of his journalistic labours Defoe had at times to relate things that are stranger than fiction, and in this way he learned how to pass off the less incredible products of an enterprising but not extravagant invention with a much stricter economy of evidence than he employed in his account of Mrs Veal's ghost.

After his release from Newgate, Defoe had accepted Govern-

[1] *The English Novel*, p. 130.

ment pay, and was now employed on secret services. When the *Further* Treaty of Union between England and Scotland was being *political* negotiated, he went as an emissary of peace and conciliation to *journal-* Edinburgh (1706), and did a great deal to allay national pre- *ism* judice by a continuous series of articles in his *Review*, by rejoinders to pamphlets airing Scottish grievances, and by his eulogistic poem *Caledonia*. His northern journey and his sojourn in Edinburgh were to help him later in the Scottish scenes of *Colonel Jacque* and other stories. He also published a *History of the Union with Scotland* (1709). Defoe's conduct as a Government agent, ready to throw in his lot with whichever party was in power, has often been impugned as a gross example of political temporizing. When Harley his first employer fell, with some demur he took service under Godolphin ; at the next crisis, with the same show of reluctance, he returned to his original protector Harley. In support of Godolphin and Marl-borough, he wrote to soothe the general impatience with the protracted French war. Later on, he was found on the same side as Swift, and a powerful advocate of peace. He changed sides, and, what was worse, he posed as a Tory whilst serving in the interests of a Whig administration. His most flagrant departure from the rules of correct behaviour was to have worked as the redactor of a Jacobite organ, Mist's *Weekly Journal* (1717-1724), for the surreptitious purpose of crippling its powers of mischief, spiking its guns in the interests of patri-otism. But although he was usually found on the side where his own interest lay, he probably always believed, even if he was not always aware of the motives that influenced him, that his interests coincided with those of his countrymen. A man of finer sensibility would have been loath to undertake jobs that laid him open to the charge of double-dealing. But Defoe never flinched from such questionable tasks. " It was not material to me," he said, " what ministers her Majesty was pleased to employ ; my duty was to go along with every ministry, so far as they did not break in upon the constitution and the laws and liberty of my country." [1] So, without a pang to his conscience, he collaborated with Mist in such a manner as to take " the

[1] *Appeal to Honour and Justice* (1715).

sting out of that mischievous paper," and " to keep it within the circle of a secret management," without letting Mist or any one concerned have the least suspicion of what was going on. In whatever he did, Defoe showed statesmanship and sagacity. By his own code he was both guiltless and deserving of his countrymen's gratitude in a time of perilous intrigue. Perhaps it is unreasonable to regret that a man of his intrinsic greatness was a law unto himself and not an observer of other men's rules.

Defoe's enormous fecundity Defoe's activity all this time was prodigious. Still publishing his *Review* single-handed, he contributed incessantly to other journals, and when it was politic to let this aggressive organ expire he became the editor or leading contributor to *Mercator*, which dealt with economic policy and supported Bolingbroke's treaty of commerce with France. He was probably the most industrious writer in the annals of literary production. The volume of his work,[1] a large part of which was of a fugitive kind, must have exceeded even the vast output of the literary factory run, a century ago, by the elder Dumas. He ran himself as a kind of publishing house, and was always ready with books, pamphlets, or articles, on any topic that happened to be engrossing public interest. It was indeed as a manufacturer of wares for the literary mart, or at least the mart for printed stuff, that Defoe, lineal successor of the old purveyor of chap-books, contrived in the end to become a novelist. Several of his diversified publications that had some little to do with his training for the part remain to be mentioned. In his journalism he was often called upon to relate incidents of interest as news, which gave him practice in the art of narrative and of bringing both the familiar and the strange graphically and strikingly before the eye. One section of his *Review*, which after the first year was issued separately as a monthly supplement, was entitled, *Mercure Scandale ; or Advice from the Scandalous Club.* Later it became the *Little Review.* In this he was continually dealing with social, moral, and practical topics, and dealing with them in a manner anticipating the *Tatler* and *Spectator*, if with much less delicacy

[1] A bibliography amounting to nearly fifty pages is given by Dottin (801-849); that of Professor W. P. Trent contains 370 titles (*Camb. Hist. of Eng. Lit.*, ix., 418-433).

and literary charm. This kind of writing he kept up for years after the *Review* had come to an end and he was busy with his novels and other substantial works ; his later essays and character-sketches, chiefly those contributed to the weekly journals of Mist (1717-1724) and Applebee (1720-1726), betraying that he had not read Steele and Addison in vain. He undertook historical narrative in his *History of the Wars of Charles XII.* (1715), written from the point of view of a " Scots Gentleman in the Swedish Service." He concocted spurious memoirs in his *Minutes of the Negociations of Mons. Mesnager . . . . Wherein some of the most Secret Transactions of that Time, relating to the Interest of the Pretender, and a Clandestine Separate Peace are detected and laid open. Written by himself. Done out of French* (1717). And at a time when he was compromised by his underhand political journalism and abused therefor by his enemies, when he was harassed by pecuniary embarrassments, at variance with some of his own family, and, to crown all, struck down by illness,[1] the veteran took in hand a book-making job in which his faculty for story-telling and his puritanic bent for moral admonition were both to find scope.

The Family Instructor in three parts. I. Relating to Fathers and Children. II. To Masters and Servants. III. To Husbands and Wives (1715), one of Defoe's most lucrative ventures, was an application of fictitious narrative and dialogue to the object of ethical teaching. It was designed, said the preface, " both to divert and instruct." He had at first intended to make it a dramatic poem, but found the subject too solemn. So, in his present contrite mood, he adopted the manner of a catechist, an innocent child, " with an air of mere Nature," asking questions on our origin, our state, our progress in the world, the reason of our being born into it, and, " which is the main cogitation," our condition beyond it. The first part is mainly taken up with the history of a family, the members of which, Defoe broadly hints, are living persons and may perhaps take offence at the freedom with which he treats them, although he has shown the civility of concealing their names. The father is a good man, who takes great trouble about his son's education, but impru-

" *The Family Instructor* "

---

[1] At any rate, so he makes out in his *Appeal to Honour and Justice* (1715).

dently gives him a tutor who has no regard for religion. Hence the boy and his sister are led astray by worldly temptations ; and, in the conclusion, the son runs away and joins the army, coming home a cripple and dying miserably. The daughter, however, is reformed by a religious aunt, and marries her cousin, a sober, god-fearing gentleman. There is a long discourse between the father and mother, lamenting the errors that have resulted in the demoralization of the children. The dreadful example of a father and family destitute of religion, and the horror experienced by a youth brought up in these surroundings when he comes to realize his forlorn condition, enforce the moral. Two boys are contrasted in the second part. The sober, pious lad is apprenticed to a rich shopkeeper who cares nothing for religion. The wild, profane lad is converted by the other, and to the surprise of his master, a religious clothier, attains a state of penitence and anxiety about his soul. The result of overhearing the colloquies between the boys is that the irreligious tradesman is brought to a sense of his own danger. All three parts are illustrated with instances of ill examples set by parents and superiors to children and servants, who ought to be provided with ghostly instruction and sedulously guarded from jeering and profane associates. Defoe's sincerity is not in dispute ; but the continual identification of goodness and self-interest is on no higher level than the Richardsonian ethics which were soon to receive a welcome from the same great body of middle-class readers and middle-class consciences.

Fiction before " Robinson Crusoe " Up to the date of *Robinson Crusoe* (1719), the first and best of what may be briefly described as his regular works of fiction, Defoe's invention had found employment, with the exception of the exemplary tales in his *Family Instructor*, only in irregular ways. In his pamphlets he often assumed a character and maintained opinions differing from his own, in which sense his *Shortest Way* might be counted among his works of fiction.[1] He had tried his hand at dialogue and satirical portraiture of bigoted and intolerant High Churchmen in the *Secret History*

---

[1] At a later period he takes on the personality of a " good old gentleman " in the *Memoirs* of Duncan Campbell ; and everybody knows his ways of impersonation in *Moll Flanders, The Plague Year*, etc.

of the October Club (1711). In all probability he was responsible, at least in part, for *The Continuation of Letters Written by a Turkish Spy at Paris* (1718), his portion treating of the period 1687-1693.[1] As a newsmonger, he had never been at a loss for picturesque detail, and had systematically posed as an individual possessed of unique information. All this was an invaluable apprenticeship for the series of fictitious biographies and histories, and fictitious narratives of travel and adventure, which were now to begin.

The Life and Strange Surprizing Adventures of Robinson Crusoe, Of York, Mariner : Who lived eight and Twenty Years, all alone on an un-inhabited Island on the Coast of America, near the Mouth of the Great River Oroonoque ; Having been cast on Shore by Ship-wreck, wherein all the Men perished but himself. With an Account how he was at last as strangely deliver'd by Pyrates. Written by Himself, appeared on 25th April 1719. By 8th August there had been four editions, besides an incorrect one probably pirated ; and on 20th August Defoe published a second part, *The Farther Adventures of Robinson Crusoe ; Being the Second and Last Part of his Life, And of the Strange Surprizing Accounts of his Travels Round three Parts of the Globe*. A third part, in which Defoe sought hopefully but unwisely to catch both the public who were enchanted by the adventures and the very different public who bought edition after edition of his *Family*

"Robinson Crusoe"

---

[1] *A Continuation of Letters Written by a Turkish Spy at Paris. Giving an Impartial Account to the Divan at Constantinople of the most remarkable Transactions of Europe, and Discovering several Intrigues and Secrets of the Christian Courts, especially of that of France : continued from the year 1687 to the year 1693. Written originally in Arabic, Translated into Italian, and from thence into English* (1718). This was supplementary to the English translation of Giovanni Paolo Marana's satirical work, *L'Espion turc* (1686), which was translated into English as *Letters writ by a Turkish Spy, who liv'd five and forty years . . . at Paris : giving an Account to the Divan at Constantinople of the most remarkable Transactions of Europe from 1637 to 1682* (8 vols., 1687-1693). In a series of pretended letters to the Sublime Porte, Marana gave an account of public affairs, the characters and doings of eminent personages, literary, scientific, and religious matters, social manners and private morals. The risks and misadventures of the spy and a rather tame love-affair help, not very effectively, to infuse a little narrative interest. The foreign point of view gives some piquancy to what would else have been a somewhat dull commentary. The *Turkish Spy* was immensely popular both in France and England, and was the precursor of Montesquieu's *Lettres Persanes* (1721) and Goldsmith's *Citizen of the World* (1762), to mention only the two most famous works of the kind in which the foreign observer is a medium for more philosophic criticism.

Instructor, was hurriedly compiled from his note-books and issued next year, with the formidable title, *Serious Reflections during the Life and Surprizing Adventures of Robinson Crusoe. With his Vision of the Angelick World* (1720), an abridgment of all three parts coming out almost simultaneously.

Outline of the main story

By *Robinson Crusoe* is ordinarily understood the first part, the story of the castaway's twenty-eight years of solitude on the island. The main portion of this is so well known to every one that there is no need to remind the reader of anything but the incidents that lead up to the shipwreck. These, however, are of considerable importance in regard to the question how Defoe made up the story. Crusoe begins with an account of his birth and parentage, and relates that in opposition to his father's advice he was determined to go to sea, and at last ran away from home, going on board a ship bound for London, on 1st September 1651. Dates, places, names and particulars of his relatives, and similar details, are given with great exactness : the method of a true and artless journal is followed with artful consistency. A violent storm was encountered off Yarmouth, and the vessel foundered, after those on board had been taken off in a boat. For this episode Defoe had done the preliminary study in his realistic monograph, *The Storm* [1] (1704): the relative particulars correspond exactly. They landed between Winterton Ness and Cromer, and Crusoe made his way to London. There he joined a vessel sailing for Guinea, earned a good profit on a stock of merchandise that he took with him, and on his return resolved to set up as a Guinea trader. But here his luck ended. On his second voyage to Africa the ship was captured by pirates from Salee, and Crusoe spent the next two years as a slave in that stronghold. Then he made his escape in a boat, with a black boy named Xury, and after some adventures on the west coast of Africa was picked up by a Portuguese ship and landed in Brazil, where he established himself as a planter. His restless disposition broke out again after four years of this remunerative but tedious occupation, and he induced some merchants and

---

[1] See above, p. 133, and Secord (76-85), who thoroughly examines the question whether Defoe borrowed from anyone but himself, as has been repeatedly alleged.

planters to fit out a ship to fetch slaves from Africa. The ship was carried out of its course by storms, and went ashore off an island near the mouth of the Orinoco, all on board perishing except Crusoe. He fought his way out of the water, and, more dead than alive, found himself alone on an uninhabited island on 30th September 1659, and there he remained till 19th December 1686.

Every schoolboy is familiar with the inimitable account of Crusoe's adventures on the island, the landing of stores from the wreck, the building of his fortified houses, the unexpected growth of the barley and rice, the domestication of his goats, the frequent mishaps that failed to daunt his courage, the making of a boat to carry him to the mainland and his ignominious failure to get her into the water, the shock when he discovered the footprint of a man, the arrival of the savages on his part of the island when he had been alone for eighteen years, his panic and then his scheme for capturing one of their prisoners, the fight with the cannibals and the rescue of Friday, and, later on, Crusoe's deliverance of the Spaniard and the mission for the rescue of the other Spaniards on the mainland, an enterprise unexpectedly interrupted by the advent of an English ship, the crew of which had mutinied and deposed the captain, the battle with the mutineers, recapture of the ship, and Crusoe's return to England with his man Friday : not *Hamlet*, not the *Pilgrim's Progress*, is better known than this immortal story. *Its general character*

No story, indeed, whether true or fictitious, has ever been told with such a combination of minute and inexhaustible realism and of the curiosity that keeps the mind on the stretch to the very end. There had been no fiction such as this from when literature began ; there has been nothing quite like it since. The matters recounted were all but incredible. The world had wondered at Selkirk's four years of solitude on Juan Fernandez : Crusoe lived alone for twenty-eight.[1] Other

[1] One of Defoe's latest critics remarks : "To exceed the experiences of Selkirk and the others, which are set forth as possible sources of *Robinson Crusoe*, Crusoe had no need of staying nearly a third of a century in solitude ; for the hero of Juan Fernandez was rescued after but four years, and Peter de Serrano after seven, and no other castaway is known to have survived so long as that. As Professor Trent has observed, Selkirk's island is not Crusoe's island, and I may add that Selkirk is not Crusoe" (Secord, A. W.,

unfortunates in a like situation had managed to exist : Robinson Crusoe made himself comfortable, and so secure that when marauders came on the scene he triumphed over them and was hailed as " Governor." His resourcefulness, his almost super-human feats of invention and endurance, his marvellous patience and self-sufficiency, needed powerful corroboration if they were to win poetic faith. Defoe meant them to be accepted as cate-gorical facts. Hence, he was driven to that untiring registration of the smallest incidents, the trivialities, the irrelevancies, the superfluities, which are the mark of honest, untutored narra-tive, and which became the trade-mark of Defoe's story-telling, though nowhere else was it necessary to carry it to such an extreme as in *Robinson Crusoe*.

The need for cogent realism

The essence of his method was to tell, not merely that some-thing was done, but how it was done. He was the man of practical genius, and his mind delighted in these minute details. The average narrator would, for instance, have mentioned simply that Crusoe made a sieve, and having no better material con-structed it of the stuff in a seaman's neckcloth. Defoe makes of this petty matter a whole paragraph, and we read it with absorption :

My next difficulty was to make a sieve, or search, to dress my meal, and to part it from the bran and the husk, without which I did not see it possible I could have any bread. This was a most difficult thing, so much as but to think on, for to be sure I had nothing like the necessary thing to make it ; I mean fine thin canvas or stuff, to search the meal through. And here I was at a full stop for many months, nor did I really know what to do ; linen I had none left, but what was mere rags ; I had goats'-hair, but neither knew I how to weave it or spin it ; and had I known how, here was no tools to work it with. All the remedy that I found for this was, that at last I did remember I had, among the seamen's clothes which were saved out of the ship, some neckcloths of calico or muslin ; and with some pieces of these I made three small sieves, but proper enough for the work ; and thus I made shift for some years. How I did afterwards, I shall show in its place.[1]

The Narrative Method of Defoe, p. 32). Nothing but Defoe's famous circum-stantial method could have made us stand the sheer improbability of *Robinson Crusoe*.

[1] *Robinson Crusoe*, ed. G. A. Aitken, 1895, pp. 135-136.

Who, after reading this, can doubt that Crusoe made that sieve, can help picturing that sieve, and the whole process of its manufacture ? The circumstantial method is justified of its pains. The mind is so impressed with the accumulated weight of detail, all coming as naturally as the unsifted jumble of facts poured out by an ingenuous witness, that it asks no questions and feels no mistrust. The parts are so weighty in the mass that the whole is accepted without challenge. And, what is more strange, we read all this with the same riveted attention, when he is describing the way he contrived a makeshift sieve, as if he were recounting the loss of a ship or a hairbreadth escape from the cannibals.

To trace Defoe's sources, to see how much he took from them and how he used it, is the right way to study his workmanship. For it was not simply rough material that he appropriated, but manufactured material ; in other words, he had perforce to simulate the manner and method of the travel-book as well as the facts it recorded. Defoe's editors and commentators have realized this, and research into his actual or supposed originals has produced a voluminous literature.[1] The sources from which he obtained his materials fall roughly into two lots : previous accounts, true or imaginative, of the life of a solitary in circumstances more or less like Crusoe's ;. and works of travel and adventure supplying the geographical and other detail. There were available in Defoe's time a number of works recounting what we may now denominate Crusoe experiences ; some of these he certainly used, some he may have used, the rest seem to have been unknown to him or at any rate to have furnished nothing of importance. To the travel literature of his day much the same remarks apply.

Defoe's sources for " Robinson Crusoe "

The original incentive to write *Robinson Crusoe* and the central idea of a man left by himself on a desert island, relying on his own resources for existence, and maintaining his courage and cheerfulness in spite of solitude and privation, came to

Previous accounts of solitaries living in desert places

---

[1] This has been rigorously examined by Professor A. W. Secord, to whose admirable monograph, *Studies in the Narrative Method of Defoe (University of Illinois Studies in Language and Literature*, ix., 1924, i.), with its bibliographical references, every one must go who wishes to pursue the subject further than the brief epitome given here.

Defoe from the actual experiences of Alexander Selkirk, the history of whose sojourn on Juan Fernandez was the great sensation of 1712-1713.[1] The several narratives of Selkirk's adventure must accordingly be considered first, although Defoe actually received more specific hints from the other works. For, with his usual audacity, he essayed to outdo at once the Selkirk story and all the other records of a similar kind extant. There was a variety of suitable material ready to hand. Five of these are discussed in a dissertation by Dr Friedrich Wackwitz : [2] Henry Nevile's *Isle of Pines* (1668), the accounts of a Mosquito Indian's solitary stay on Juan Fernandez in Ringrose's *Bucaniers of America* (1685), and Dampier's *New Voyage round the World* (1697), the story of the shipwreck of Peter de Serrano and his seven years on a desert island in the West Indies, found in *Royal Commentaries of the Yncas*, a professedly historical account of an ideal polity, translated by Sir Paul Ricaut from Garcilaso de la Vega (1688), and the life of Ebn Jokdhan, in several versions of a curious work originally written in Arabic by Ibn Tufail. Another German investigator, Max Günther,[3] suggested some other possible sources, particularly Grimmelshausen's picaresque romance *Simplicissimus* (1669), and two narratives of imaginary travels, *Les Avantures de Jacques Sadeur*, by Gabriel de Foigny, and the *Histoire des Séverambes*, by Denis Vairasse d'Allais, translated into English as *The History of the Sevarites or Severambi : A Nation inhabiting part of the third Continent, Commonly called, Terræ Australes Incognitæ* (1675-1679).[4]

It has recently been argued that Defoe gained more that was useful from Captain Robert Knox's relation of his long captivity in Ceylon, and a few incidents from Misson's fictitious account of Francis Leguat's struggle for existence on the island of Rodriguez (1707).[5] With one exception, the other possibilities are less important. Arber suggested, and Mr Aitken thought

---

[1] Alexander Selkirk (1676-1721) joined Captain Dampier's privateering expedition (1703), and he was left on Juan Fernandez (Sept. 1704–Jan. 1709).
[2] *Entstehungsgeschichte von Defoes Robinson Crusoe* (Berlin, 1909).
[3] *Entstehungsgeschichte von Defoes Robinson Crusoe* (Greifswald, 1909).
[4] This afterwards appeared with the new title *The History of the Sevarambians : a People of the South Continent* (1738). It had been made the basis of a bogus third volume of *Gulliver's Travels* (1727).
[5] Secord, pp. 92-93, etc. ; *ibid.*, pp. 119-123.

it likely, that the episode of Crusoe's deliverance by pirates originated in *A Relation of the great suffering and strange Adventures of Henry Pitman* (1689). Three short accounts of life on a desert island have been pointed out in Mandelslo's *Voyages and Travels*, included in *Voyages and Travels of the Ambassadors*, by Adam Olearius (1662).[1] Godwin's *Man in the Moone* was probably well known to Defoe, but would have yielded him little, though it had its share in the vogue of imaginary voyages and even of arduous experiences on an island.[2] The latest claimant to be the original of *Robinson Crusoe* is that portion of a Utopian romance, *Krinke Kesmes* (1708), by Hendrik Smeeks, which is concerned with the adventures of a Dutch cabin-boy left alone in a desert region and afterwards captured and well treated by savages.

But general accounts of travel helped Defoe as much as these closer anticipations of his more particular theme. Not only in the first part of *Robinson Crusoe*, but also in *The Farther Adventures*, he drew extensively upon the many accounts of travel and exploration current in his day. These furnished the geographical background and invaluable bits of actuality, and in the second part provided the entire groundwork of Crusoe's journeys to the Far East and back to Europe. He does not appear to have gone abroad himself since he was a young man, and to judge by his allusions to other people's sufferings on shipboard was a bad sailor [3]; but he was as intensely interested as any man of that

Defoe's indebtedness to the current literature of travel

[1] Dottin, ii. 319.

[2] The island is St Helena, which was the scene of a Dutchman's painful experiences of solitude, as related by Mandelslo, and of the equally trying eighteen months of John Segar, reported by Hakluyt (Secord, pp. 28-29). One of the busiest compilers of dubious compendiums of geographical and other information at that time, Nathaniel Crouch, who wrote under the name of R. Burton, embodied Godwin's narrative in a small book called *The English Acquisitions in Guinea and East India . . . with an account of the admirable voyage of Domingo Gonzales, to the world in the Moon* (1728). This is another offering to the voracious appetite for knowledge that had so much to do with the genesis of *Robinson Crusoe, Captain Singleton,* etc. Crouch or Burton was (1632?-1725?) both a writer and a publisher, and had a talent for melting down the contents of other people's books. His so-called histories and the like are compact of wonders, rarities, and curiosities, but have no literary value.

[3] " Cet intrépide navigateur en chambre goûtait fort peu les joies des traversées maritimes ; il n'avait pas le pied marin, et les heros de ses romans sont victimes d'un affreux mal de mer : il nous dépeint leurs souffrances par des détails et des images expressifs qui pouvaient seulement venir de ses propres expériences " (Dottin, *Daniel de Foe et ses romans,* i. 34).

exciting time in the progress of discovery and the exploits of the great navigators. Though himself an armchair explorer, no one was a better general authority on the subject. He knew more about the various regions of the globe than the hardiest explorer, whose knowledge might be more peculiar but was far less extensive. Defoe had a library full of books ; he kept himself abreast of the latest extensions of knowledge ; he studied the maps of recent explorers so intelligently that he was able to make conjectures about unknown seas and countries which time has confirmed.[1]

Defoe a compiler of fictitious travel-books

The great age of maritime discovery which had opened with the voyages of Columbus and his successors was not yet over. Large tracts of the world were still uncharted, and reports of travel in unknown or little known regions were read with avidity. The era of colonization had begun, and the popular interest in the voyages of English seamen was intensified by the sense of rivalry with other nations, who were competing fiercely for the richest territories. The record has been kept in an unrivalled series of journals, log-books, and other narratives, by the navigators themselves or by trustworthy chroniclers. But alongside of the authoritative literature there was a cheap, second-hand literature of travel, compiled from sound and unsound originals by such book-makers as Nathaniel Crouch.[2] Among these middlemen, Defoe was the best informed, and on the whole the most respectable ; at the same time, he was first and foremost a manufacturer of printed matter, with a watchful eye on the market, and a mind made up to give the public what they wanted, and to excite no distrust of his good faith. *Robinson Crusoe* and *Captain Singleton* have to be considered as fictitious narratives of travel, just as the *Memoirs of a Cavalier* and the *Journal of the Plague Year* have to be considered as fictitious historical works, and *Moll Flanders* and *Roxana* as fictitious biographies.

---

[1] As Secord observes (pp. 154-156), Defoe makes Singleton sail between South Australia and Van Diemen's Land, afterwards known as Tasmania, which was then supposed to be part of the Australian continent. Tasman, the discoverer, did not know it to be an island, nor was this ascertained till Bass sailed through in 1798, seventy-eight years after Defoe discovered Bass's Strait—on paper.

[2] See above, p. 149, n.

To describe life on a tropical island with apparently the same intimate knowledge as he described life in London, Defoe must have had behind him a vast fund of reading in the literature of travel. For this wide and miscellaneous erudition, not two or three but a whole library of books would have to be cited as his authorities. He had read them all, from Hakluyt and Purchas to his contemporaries, Captain Woodes Rogers and Captain Edward Cooke, the companions of Dampier. But there are some to which, patient investigation has shown, he was more particularly indebted. Dampier's *New Voyage round the World* (4 vols., 1696-1709), a sixth edition of which had appeared in 1717, probably gave him more material than any other book : it indicated the sea routes followed in *The Farther Adventures*, it furnished a wealth of incident and circumstance that Defoe utilized for the island story.[1] The facts and the local colour enabling him to recount Crusoe's life as a slave in Salee and his escape from that port with Xury have been traced to John Ogilby's *Description of Africa* (1670).[2] For the overland journey of his hero, in *The Farther Adventures*, Defoe went to Louis Le Comte's *Journey through China* (1697) and *Three Years Travels from Moscow overland to China* (1796) by E. Ysbrants Ides.[3]

Let us return to the island story. The sufferings of Alexander *Selkirk's* Selkirk, four years alone on Juan Fernandez, had been an old *experi-* story for some time when Defoe revived interest in the subject *ences* and turned it to account by writing *Robinson Crusoe*. There is no need to imagine that he visited Bristol and had a personal interview with Selkirk, as some biographers have gratuitously stated. The main facts were common knowledge. Woodes Rogers had described, in *A Cruising Voyage round the World* (1712), which was in a second edition in 1718, how the solitary man had been found on Juan Fernandez and to what shifts he had been reduced for existence ; and Captain Edward Cooke had likewise given an account of the affair in his *Voyage to the South Sea* (1712).[4] Among other notices of the famous episode,

[1] Secord, pp. 49-63.   [2] *Ibid.*, pp. 87-88.
[3] *Ibid.*, pp. 65-74, and Dottin, pp. 340-341.
[4] This portion of Woodes Rogers' book is reprinted by Aitken in his edition of Defoe's *Romances and Narratives*, iii. 317-324, and Cooke's account in the dissertation by Wackwitz. Steele's account is reproduced after that of Woodes Rogers by Aitken, pp. 324-328.

the best-remembered is Steele's article in the *Englishman*.[1]
Woodes Rogers relates the event with as much circumstance as
could be afforded in a seaman's narrative of an eventful voyage.
It gives the salient facts, but is naturally somewhat bare of
detail. There is as much about the first sighting of Selkirk's
fires, and the apprehensions that these might be the lights of
French ships anchored inshore, and about the business of landing men and searching the island, as about Selkirk himself. But
there is no mistaking where Defoe got many of his most telling
ideas : the lonely man clad outlandishly in goatskins, " who
looked wilder than the first owners of them," his tale of chasing
goats and hamstringing large numbers so as to have a supply in
case of illness, his escape from the Spaniards, his scanty outfit,
the two huts he built, his primitive method of making fire, the
providential crop of turnips, his reading, psalm-singing, and
praying, " so that he said he was a better Christian while in this
solitude than ever he was before, or than, he was afraid, he
should ever be again." Steele's is a brief and pithy article in a
periodical, adding little except judicious observations to the
terse reports of Woodes Rogers and Cooke, but dwelling on the
dramatic aspects of Selkirk's experiences, the mark they had
made on his character and his very appearance. Steele says that
he had frequently conversed with the man, and goes on :
" When I first saw him, I thought if I had not been let into his
character and story I could have discerned that he had been
much separated from company from his aspect and gesture ;
there was a strong but cheerful seriousness in his look, and a
certain disregard to the ordinary things about him, as if he had
been sunk in thought. . . . The man frequently bewailed his
return to the world, which could not, he said, with all its enjoy-
ments, restore him to the tranquillity of his solitude."

There were, no doubt, other contemporary versions of the
Selkirk affair, all based on the two genuine authorities.[2] These
would not escape Defoe's notice ; but he probably knew no

[1] 1st-3rd Dec. 1713.
[2] Secord cites, *e.g.*, an anonymous twelve-page pamphlet, *Providence Displayed :
or a very surprising account of one Mr Alexander Selkirk, Master of a Merchant-
man called the Cinque-Ports*, reprinted in *Harleian Miscellany*, xi., 1810, and in
Wackwitz.

more than appears in these documents. A very good case has *Probable* been made out for Captain Robert Knox as an inspirer of *debt to* *Robinson Crusoe*. Knox with his father and a number of men *the "Relation" of* from an English ship had been treacherously made prisoner in *Captain* Ceylon, two months after the date when Crusoe's ship was *Knox* supposed to have gone ashore (1659). The party were carried up-country, several of them died, including Knox's father; the others were kept in captivity, and when not in actual solitude were thrown on their own resources. After nineteen years, Knox and one comrade, by a long and adventurous flight, succeeded in escaping to the Dutch settlements. Defoe was well acquainted with Knox's story, which had been published in *An Historical Relation of Ceylon* (1681),[1] and gave a summary of it in *Captain Singleton*,[2] which came out after the second part of *Robinson Crusoe*, but before the third. There are many correspondences between the experiences of Robert Knox and those of Crusoe, and more between the two men's characters. Knox was not marooned on a desert island, but was held prisoner, with a small band of companions, in a populous country. Yet in many features of the deepest significance the situation of the two men was closely parallel. Knox had to solve for himself the problem of subsistence, of shelter, and of clothing. He built several houses, which like Crusoe he girt with hedges to secure privacy, though not for defence. He contrived a lamp; he captured and domesticated goats; he was forced to go in home-made garments and to let his beard grow till it was a quarter of a yard long. By an unexpected piece of luck he got hold of a Bible, and comforted his solitude by reading and religious meditation. He settled the question of unions with native women, when his fellow-captives grew restive, in much the same manner as Crusoe settled it when the number of his subjects was increased by the arrival of the English sailors, the Spaniards, and some natives. Further, Knox describes ways of making pottery, baskets, and other utensils, in vogue among the Sinhalese, which may have given hints to Defoe. There are other resemblances between the two stories, in the

[1] The relative portion is reprinted in *Voyages and Travels*, ed. G. Raymond Beazley (*English Garner*, 1903), ii. 285-429.
[2] *Singleton*, xvii.-xviii.

mode of narration, the method of recording the lapse of time, and even in the phraseology.[1] Further analogies have been detected in the additions to his original account found in the autobiographical manuscripts which Knox left unpublished ; [2] and it has been suggested that Defoe either knew and conversed with Knox or had access to these documents.[3] This is a speculation for which evidence is lacking.

Similarities of the two stories

But Defoe might well have had Knox's history at the back of his mind as one of the examples of trial and endurance with which he was to compete. There is a general parallel in character and career between the real and the imaginary hero. Knox had the same restless disposition, and went to sea likewise against his father's earnest desire. He also made one lucrative voyage, followed by a second that terminated in long years of captivity. He came back to England, and like Crusoe sought out his relatives, received a reward, and then spent several years in trading voyages to the East Indies, before settling down to his last days in London. Both men show the same mixture of practical sense and piety. Knox might well have been the author of the *Serious Reflections of Robinson Crusoe*.

Material derived from Dampier

But for concrete facts Defoe must be debited with a much longer account to Dampier's *New Voyage round the World,* recently republished (1718), the very title of which he was afterwards to appropriate in a book of his own.[4] Dampier had told the story of the Mosquito Indian left alone on Juan Fernandez and found there in 1684. In the account of his travels in the Western hemisphere, he had described innumerable features of life among the Portuguese of Brazil and the savages of the mainland and the West Indian islands, the natural products, the birds and beasts inhabiting the land, the turtles and fishes in the sea. He had depicted

[1] Secord, pp. 33-39.
[2] Printed with the *Historical Relation* (1911), part of it also at an earlier date by Arber (*English Garner*, i., 1887).
[3] Secord, pp. 39-49. The further details could hardly have aided Defoe materially. Knox had the same trouble as Robinson Crusoe over the problems of writing materials, his clothes, his hat, his hair, and the like, but solved them differently. His way of making planks was a better one than Crusoe's (p. 46), and it is difficult to see what Defoe could have owed to this.
[4] *A New Voyage round the World* (1724), in which Defoe makes special use of Dampier's last two volumes (1703-1709), dealing with the Australian voyage.

the manners and disposition of the natives, their ways of procuring subsistence, methods of building houses, of hunting, making canoes, fashioning articles of daily use, and so on. It is perhaps supererogatory to look in Dampier for the germ of such an incident as the finding of the footprint; but on the dramatic side, at any rate, his mention of the marks of trampling that might have been the tracks of hostile Spaniards, on the Isle of Pines,[1] is a more likely source, were one needed, than the tamer incident in Smeeks or that where Knox and his mate walk backwards on sandy ground to mislead pursuers.[2] In finding a scene for his hero's adventures, Defoe was naturally careful to place it a long way off from Selkirk's isle, without, however, falling under the spell of the mythic Terra Australis. Juan Fernandez is in the Pacific, off the coast of Chile. Defoe retained some of its features, but combined them with others culled from the various islands described by Dampier in the Atlantic, off the north-east coast of South America. One of these, the Isle of Aves, near Venezuela, has been pointed out as peculiarly suggestive.[3] If Defoe had that in mind, he transferred the main lines of its configuration to an island said to lie south-east of Trinidad and not far from the Orinoco. No such island exists; but Defoe may have followed Dampier's map which locates a small group at that point. There were goats on Selkirk's island, and Dampier mentions several islands overrun with goats.

From Misson's fictitious *Voyage to the East-Indies by Francis Leguat and his Companions* (1707),[4] aptly described as " a mosaic

Possible loans from

[1] Secord, p. 61. The Isla de Pinos, south of Cuba, is of course a totally different place from Nevile's fictitious island in the southern ocean (p. 159).
[2] See *Singleton*, xviii.
[3] Secord, pp. 55-56.
[4] *A New Voyage to the East-Indies by Francis Leguat and his Companions. Containing their Adventures in Two Desart Islands, and an Account of the most Remarkable Things in Maurice Island . . . and other Places in their way to and from the Desart Isles* (London, 1708), by François Maximilien Misson (actually published 1707, and simultaneously in French). Another French edition was printed in London (1720), and there were German and Dutch translations. The book was furnished with " maps and figures," and till recently passed as an unimpeachable record, the Hakluyt Society publishing an edition (transcribed from the English version by Captain Pasfield Oliver, 2 vols., 1891). But it has been shown to be a fabrication (see Geoffroy Atkinson: *Extraordinary Voyage in French Literature*, 1920, pp. 142-143, n., and *Publications of the Modern Language Association of America*, xxxvi., 1921, pp. 509-528, " A French Desert Island Novel of 1708."

Misson and Pitman

of observations of many travelers in both Africa and America," Defoe may have got the important incident of the growth of the corn, although Crusoe has more success than Leguat and his seven comrades on Rodriguez, whose repeated attempts to raise a crop are unavailing. Some resemblances have been remarked between the equipment of tools and stores supplied to Leguat and Crusoe's supply from the wreck. This work was afterwards reprinted as the *Robinson français* (1723). Some of the other narratives mentioned, if they yielded anything, at most gave Defoe the gist of some small episode or showed him how Crusoe might get out of some quandary or fabricate some article with improvised tools. Thus Pitman, the Duke of Monmouth's chirurgeon, and his companions, in *A Relation of the great sufferings and strange Adventures of Henry Pitman* (1689), having escaped from Barbadoes, whither they had been transported after Sedgemoor, land on Tortuga, build themselves huts, catch turtles and roast them, drying strips of the meat for storing, try in vain to make an earthenware vessel to boil them in, find a fragrant weed that they smoke in a crab's claw, and so on. (Crusoe found tobacco growing on the island.) Pitman describes exactly how they made everything; his plain, matter-of-fact style is very graphic. But the analogy pointed out by Arber and Aitken between his relation and *Robinson Crusoe* is that he eventually gets away through the arrival on the island of a ship with a mutinous crew. The way things turn out, however, in this episode is not the same as in the last act of Crusoe's tribulations, except that when Pitman departs he leaves Whicker and other comrades behind to undergo further hardships.[1]

The Adventures of Jacques Sadeur

The harrowing story of the Spanish Crusoe, Peter Serrano, thrown on a West Indian isle and joined after three years by another castaway, has still less in common with Defoe, though he may have read it.[2] Then there are two French stories of imaginary voyages which made some noise in the world, Gabriel de

[1] Pitman's *Relation* and the account communicated to him by Whicker are reprinted in *Stuart Tracts*, 1603-1693, ed. C. H. Firth (*English Garner*, 1903), pp. 431-476.
[2] See above, p. 148, and Dottin, ii. 520-521, who remarks that the book was not in Defoe's library, whilst Secord (pp. 30-31) claims to have found a reference to Garcilaso's work in *Robinson Crusoe* itself.

Foigny's history of the shipwrecked Jacques Sadeur and Vairasse d'Allais' *History of the Sevarites or Sevarambi*; either or both may have come in Defoe's way, that they gave Swift some ideas is certain. Both Foigny and Vairasse described an imaginary society in that Terra Australis which had by now entirely supplanted the western hemisphere as a plausible habitat for Utopias; in the former the element of fantastic adventure predominates, in the latter the speculative object leaves little room for such frivolities. Foigny's book first appeared as *La Terre australe connue . . . par M. Sadeur* (1676), and then with the new title, *Les avantures de Jacques Sadeur* (1692), and in English as *A New Discovery of Terra Incognita Australis, or the Southern World. By James Sadeur a French-man (Who being Cast there by a Shipwreck, lived thirty-five years in that Country* (1693). Sadeur relates his whole history, in the pseudo-historical way, and after a preposterous series of adventures in Central Africa and four shipwrecks brings us to his miraculous arrival in Australia, where he is saved by the inhabitants in a naked condition from the talons of gigantic birds. In these preliminaries, Foigny drew upon compendiums of travel, such as those of De Bry, but gave unlimited licence to a profligate fancy. Now comes the description of the Australian nation of hermaphrodites and their highly organized commonwealth, in which Foigny embodies his rationalistic philosophy and draws some satirical comparisons with Europe. Neither this nor the episode of Sadeur's escape on the back of one of the flying monsters, the urgs, could have been of much use to Defoe.[1]

The History of the Sevarites or Sevarambi : A Nation inhabiting part of the third Continent, commonly called, Terræ Australis Incognitæ . . . Written by one Captain Siden (2 parts, 1675-1679) appeared first in English, and then in French (1677-1678). The author of the first part, but perhaps not of the second, was Denis Vairasse, usually called d'Allais : Siden is an anagram for Denis, and Sevarias, the name of the Sevarambian law-giver, for Vairasse. Here too the tale is told in the first person. Captain

The Sevar-ambians

---

[1] For a full account of Foigny's novel, see Atkinson, G., *The Extraordinary Voyage in French Literature*, pp. 36-86. Günther cites it among the precursors of *Robinson Crusoe* (see above, p. 148).

Siden sails to the east, and is shipwrecked, landing with his crew and the passengers, including some seventy women, on the great south continent. The company establish themselves in a permanent camp, defended against wild animals by a stockade something like Crusoe's. In due time, Siden's colony become aware of the Sevarambians, the highly civilized inhabitants of Australia, and enter into friendly relations with them. The government and social system, the language and religion of this people are described in regular Utopian style. Like Foigny, Vairasse was a Deist, but he differed widely in the philosophical and social views illustrated in his ideal community. He followed a previous narration in the details of the voyage, shipwreck, and other incidents, and took some pains to substantiate his story, which was actually accepted as true. Defoe could hardly have owed anything to Vairasse, but *Robinson Crusoe*, when it appeared, was regarded by French readers as belonging to the same class as the accounts of imaginary voyages by Foigny, Vairasse, and several others. Swift, on the other hand, had read both *Jacques Sadeur* and the *Sevarambians*, there is little doubt, as most of his editors agree,[1] and the pretended third volume of *Gulliver* that appeared in 1727 was in the main taken from the *History of the Sevarites*.[2]

" Simpli-cissimus" another precursor

Grimmelshausen wrote a continuation to his romance *Sim-plicissimus* (1669), which at any rate was a forerunner of *Robinson Crusoe*, though Defoe may perhaps not have read it. The last of the hero's picaresque adventures is to be wrecked off Madagascar, and thrown with the ship's carpenter on an uninhabited island, somewhere towards " the unknown land of Australia," having a fertile soil, rich tropical vegetation, with abundance of citrons, pomegranates, and cocoanuts, and also birds, eggs, and fish in such plenty that they thought it a Land of Cocaigne or Monkeys' Paradise. The castaways have only an axe, a spoon, three knives, a prong or fork, and a pair of scissors ; but they find a powder-horn, and with the priming they make fire. A chest comes ashore from the wreck, and proves to contain the necessaries most urgently wanted; but unfortunately a woman is washed ashore

---

[1] *E.g.* G. R. Dennis, editor of *Gulliver* in Temple Scott's edition of the *Works*, Introduction, viii., xxiii.-xxiv., xxxi.

[2] Atkinson, pp. 87-139, *L'Hist. des Sévarambes.*

with it, who nearly persuades the carpenter to murder his comrade, but vanishes with the chest and its contents and a stench that betrays her diabolical origin. The carpenter drinks himself to death with palm-wine, and Simplicissimus continues to live on the island the life of a holy hermit. In an absurd sequel by Jean Cornelissen, the hermit is visited by plundering seamen, performs various miracles that bring them to their senses, but when they offer to take him home to Europe, elects to remain and die on his island. Some of the contrivances for making implements and earthenware, the marking of time by notches on a post, and suchlike, correspond roughly to Crusoe's expedients.[1]

Grimmelshausen was prompted to write his continuation, it *Nevile's* may be supposed, by reading Henry Nevile's curious story, *The* "*Isle of* *Isle of Pines, or, A late Discovery of a Fourth Island in Terra* *Pines*" *Australis, Incognita*, with the complementary narrative, *A New and further Discovery of the Isle of Pines in a Letter from Cornelius Van Sloetten* (1668). This short work is of little interest as regards Defoe, but claims attention on its own account. With a deceptive show of credentials and a detailed precision foreshadowing *Robinson Crusoe*, it is related that the Dutch East Indian fleet, arriving home from Java in 1667, reported that one of the ships sailing past the Cape of Good Hope towards the east was driven out of her course by storms towards the Antarctic Circle, and anchored off an unknown island, 28 or 29 degrees south latitude, where those on board found a people professing the Christian religion and speaking English who had been established there since 1589. Four English vessels had in that year been dispersed by a tempest, three perishing, and one, the *Indian Merchant*, going on the rocks. All took to the boats or threw themselves into the sea, except one man and four females. These the sole survivors, were washed up on pieces of wreckage, and found themselves on an island, uninhabited, but well-supplied with wild-fowl and fruit-trees, the river and sea abounding in fish. One tree bore fruit as large as the biggest apples, tasting like a walnut, and serving as bread.

All this was left on record by George Pines, the one man

---

[1] See *The Adventurous Simplicissimus*, by Hans Jacob Christoph Grimmelshausen, done into English, 1912, pp. 407-431.

surviving. Thirty years old at the time of the wreck, he unites himself first to the two English servants, next to the daughter of the captain, a girl of fourteen, and is then persuaded by the others to pay the Moorish handmaiden the same courtesy. He and his harem have thirty-seven children, who intermarry ; but in the next generation it is forbidden to brothers and sisters to unite. By 1650, when the patriarch dies, his sons and daughters and grandchildren number 1785 ; at the end of seventy-seven years the population of the island amounts to eleven or twelve thousand persons, though not a soul has arrived from the outside world. Nevile's object was to show a community living under a paternal system of laws apart from the rest of the world ; his achievement was a work of invention, substantiated with realistic particulars, that was accepted far and wide as a veracious record.[1]

"Ebn Yok-dhan"

Another philosophical study of a person dwelling apart from other men, the life of Ebn Yokdhan or the self-taught philosopher, is reputed also to be the oldest in origin of all Crusoe stories. The original *Hajji ibn Jakzân* or *Hayy ben Yaqdhân*, is said to have been written by Mohammed ibn Toefail or Tufail about the year 1169. An edition appeared at Oxford, with a Latin version by Edward Pocock, entitled *Philosophus Autodidactus* (1671), and it was thrice translated into English in Defoe's lifetime, first by a Quaker, George Keith, next by someone named Ashwell, and then by Simon Ockley. The long titles give the gist of the work. The first runs as follows :

An Account of the Oriental Philosophy, Shewing the Wisdom of some renowned Men of the East ; and particularly, the profound Wisdom of Hai Ebn Yokdhan, both in Natural and Divine Things ; Which he attained without all Converse with Men (while he lived in an Island a solitary life, remote from all Men from his Infancy, till he arrived at such perfection). (1674.)

The second translation is entitled :

The History of Hai Eb'n Yockdan, an Indian Prince : or, the Self-Taught Philosopher. Written Originally in the Arabick

---

[1] The book had more vogue on the Continent than here ; but Mr Montague Summers has shown me an allusion in Dryden's *Limberham*, iii. 1, where Pleasance says, " 'Tis a likely proper fellow, and looks as he cou'd people a new Isle of Pines." Which shows in what light Nevile's fiction struck his contemporaries.

*Tongue, by Abi Jaafar Eb'n Tophail, a Philosopher by Profession,
and a Mahometan by Religion. Wherein is demonstrated, by
what Steps and degrees, humane Reason, improved by diligent
Observation and Experience, may arrive at the knowledge of
natural things, and from thence to the discovery of Supernaturals ;
more especially of God and the Concernments of the other World*
(1686). The third title runs : *The Improvement of Human
Reason, Exhibited in the Life of Ebn Yokdham : . . . In which
is demonstrated by what Methods one may, by the meer Light of
Nature, attain the Knowledge of things Natural and Supernatural ;
more particularly the Knowledge of God, and the Affairs of another
Life* (1708).[1]

Among the Indian islands there is one, says the Arabian author, *Story of*
situated on the equinoctial line, where men are born without *Ebn*
father or mother, and on it grows a tree that bears women *Yokdhan*
instead of fruit, the which women are called Wakwaks. Some
say that Ebn Yokdhan was of this fatherless and motherless race;
others that he was the son of a beautiful woman who had committed him as a babe to the sea, near the Balearic Isles, and that
the coffer in which he lay was washed far among the trees on this
island by a tidal wave, which burst it open, and, the infant crying,
he was suckled by a wild goat. As the lad grows up he exhibits
a wonderful intelligence, examining all the objects he sees
around him and asking himself what they are for and how they
perform their allotted functions. The object of the book is to
show how a being, living from the first in solitude, would learn
to observe and to reason for himself, ultimately coming by natural
steps to the necessary conception of an infinite, eternal, wise
Creator and the immateriality and immortality of his own soul.
But incidentally it has to be shown how he would provide for
himself, finding out all sorts of useful devices by observation and
meditation on the causes of things. At first he clothes himself
in rushes; then, finding these too perishable, he makes garments
with the skins of beasts. He learns the art of building from the

---

1 A shorter version printed with Greene's *Dorastus and Fawina* (1696) is
simply entitled, *The History of Josephus the Indian Prince.* Cp. the title of the
bilingual edition : *Philosophus Autodidactus sive Epistola Abi Jaafar, Ebn Tophail
de Hai Ebn Yokdhan. In quâ ostenditur quomodo ex Inferiorum contemplatione ad
Superiorum notitiam Ratio humana ascendere possit. Ex Arabicâ in Linguam Latinam
versa Ab Edvardo Pocockio.* Oxonii, 1671.

swallows, and constructs a habitation surrounded with a barrier of canes. He tames wild horses and asses, and even birds of prey. Once, to his amazement, he sees the boughs of trees dashed together in a storm and producing fire. At first he gets burnt ; but he instantly perceives the pricelessness of this new element, kindles dry wood, and is careful never afterwards to let his fire go out. Ebn Yokdhan's solitude is at length interrupted by the arrival of a sage named Asal, who comes from a neighbouring island where the king, Salaman, is a philosopher. Asal holds long metaphysical colloquies with the solitary, and then takes him home to continue the discussion with the learned monarch. Defoe must have been acquainted with the book, though it obviously had little to offer that was useful. But it is a further proof, were one needed, that the theme of a man living in isolation from his species was a favourite one at that period, with the intellectuals as well as with the common reader who wanted wonders and excitement.[1]

Defoe's alleged plagiarisms from " Krinke Kesmes "   The question of Defoe's indebtedness becomes more acute with the last Crusoe story to be considered among the predecessors. A Utopian romance by Hendrik Smeeks, containing a long narrative of a Dutch boy's solitary existence on an island, was formerly believed to have been first published in 1721, the year of the second Dutch edition and of a German one frankly entitled, *Der Holländische Robinson Crusoe* ; in short, it was taken to be one of the numerous imitations of Defoe's work which began to swarm at that date. The similarities are so many and so obvious that this was inevitable. But when it came to light that the work had originally appeared in 1708, eleven years before *Robinson Crusoe*, the position was reversed. A problem arises

---

[1] Ibn Tophail, the original author of *Hajji Ibn Jakzân*, was born at Guadix, near Granada, in Spain, in the first decade of the twelfth century, and became secretary to the lieutenant of Granada, and afterwards physician and vizier to Abû Ja'qûb Jûsuf. He died in the year 1185. I am told by Baron F. E. Mulert, of Ommen, that he found in Morocco manuscript authority for the history of a boy who went to sea from Rabat-Salee about 1049 and was left on an uninhabited island. Baron Mulert supposes that this was the actual original of all the imaginary castaways, including Robinson Crusoe and the cabin-boy in the romance of Smeeks. He may well, at any rate, have been the original of the *Philosophus Autodidactus*. There is a life of the author, *Ibn Tophail, sa vie, ses œuvres* (1909), by Léon Gauthier, who had previously translated the work into French (1900) from a MS. found at Algiers.

which has been worked out in very different ways to almost opposite conclusions. The problem may be stated in the form of a double alternative. Is *Robinson Crusoe* based on this original, or are the resemblances accidental ? If the resemblances are so close and so numerous that they cannot have been purely fortuitous, are they sufficient to show, along with any other evidence that may exist, that Defoe was acquainted with the Dutch book and deliberately copied a great deal of it and made use of a great deal more in an indirect and disguised manner ; or do they merely show that this work of Smeeks was one of the many books, like those already reviewed, from which Defoe gathered hints and miscellaneous material for the composition of his story ? This last is the view adopted here. But the more extreme alternatives are those that have approved themselves to a number of critics.

Smeeks entitled his book, *Beschryvinge Van het magtig Koningryk Krinke Kesmes*—description of the mighty kingdom Krinke Kesmes. It described a fabulous country in the unknown Southland, situated under the tropic of Capricorn, which was said to have been discovered by a certain Juan de Posos, the book being put together from that person's writings. De Posos is driven by storms to the coast of Krinke Kesmes—the name is an anagram for Hendrik Smeeks—and so gains the knowledge of this Utopian community and its institutions which it is the main object of the book to unfold. Whilst there, he meets the Dutchman who as a boy had been left by his shipmates on a desert part of the Southland, and whose relation forms that section of the book, some sixty pages, which has roused so much interest.

Smeeks's book

The narrative begins with the same apparatus of dates, names, and other exact particulars as was afterwards to be customary with Defoe. The deponent was twelve years old, and a cabin-boy in the service of the Dutch East India Company, when his ship, the *Wakende Boey*, was sent from Batavia to bring home the crew of the *Goude Draak* which had been wrecked on the coast of the Southland. Whilst his comrades are searching the shore for the missing men, the lad wanders away into the interior, loses himself in the forest, and is left behind. After some days he finds his way back to the shore, and discovers that his shipmates have left him a chest full of useful articles ; this they have buried in the

Story of the castaway in " Krinke Kesmes"

sand, marking the spot with a stake, and telling him in a note that after nine days' searching and waiting they have been obliged to embark.

Resem-blances to Defoe's later story

From the very beginning, the lad's experiences have both a general and many minor resemblances to those of Robinson Crusoe. There is much in common between the localities. The little river, the hill with a look-out over the sea, from which both watch with their perspective glasses, the forest and the kindly fruits, the birds, beasts, and fish, and above all the friendly climate —these features correspond. When Smeeks's boy realizes that he is lost, his sensations are much the same as Robinson Crusoe's when he finds himself the sole survivor from the wreck. Crusoe's fits of gloom and despondency subside when he ruminates on the blessings that have been vouchsafed him. So too the boy finds tranquillity and contentment when he resolves to trust in God. He has a feeling as if he were being pushed in a certain direction ; and when he obeys this unseen guidance he is led out of the jungle and finds an apple-tree loaded with fruit, just as he is on the verge of starvation. Both castaways reflect on the valuelessness of money in such a situation as theirs.

All this, it may be said, was to be expected from the narrator of any such tale at a period when a moral or religious lesson always came in very seasonable as a gloss on either fact or fiction. But still more specific correspondences are numerous. Before he discovers the store left by his friends, the boy has nothing about him but his knife, tobacco-box, steel and tinder-box, a rusk, and some fish-hooks. Crusoe is in like case when he first gets ashore. But both soon have the immense good fortune of a bountiful supply of necessaries put within easy reach. The boy finds directions to another stake, beneath which a shovel is buried, and with this he digs up a second chest containing a much larger provision of all sorts of stores. He is now in a very similar condition to that of Crusoe when he had brought away all that could be moved from the wreck. But there is a still greater coincidence. In both cases a wreck is washed up with a further stock of useful articles and even luxuries. Smeeks, in truth, spoilt his story by furnishing his castaway with such a lavish collection of every comfort man could wish for, that there was no need for endurance or ingenuity. The inventory of his effects after the boy has looted the wreck is like the catalogue of a multiple store. He has so much brandy, for instance, that he pours away the contents of four cases, in order to bottle the French wine and mum which he prefers. Until, at the end of an unspecified number of years, the savages make their appearance, he is able to carry on housekeeping without stinting himself in anything. Defoe had the good sense to avoid this error. The great charm of his hero's story is in the ceaseless struggle with difficulties and the inventiveness that makes up for all that is lacking.

Both our adventurers find a dog on board the strange wreck and make friends with him. More important is the likeness between the elaborate residences which they construct. So well are these defended with palisades and entanglements of trees and osiers that the owners describe them as castles, fortresses, and the like. Both men have two houses ; the Dutch boy spends his leisure building others in various parts of his domain. Their methods of building are not very different. Everybody knows how Crusoe made his, half abutting on and half hollowed out of a convenient hill, and how he put a row of stakes in front. Later, he makes the fence a part of the dwelling, and uses a ladder to get over it, entering from above. The boy also makes a ladder with two straight limbs of a tree, but he has a doorway for entrance in the usual place. Calling to mind that he used to construct bird-cages of willow twigs, he fashions a door of wickerwork. It will be remembered that Crusoe likewise bethought him of having learned basket-making when a boy, and utilized the recollection to make hods. The boy leaves peepholes in the walls of his two castles, and plants harquebuses and guns ready for action. Here he stands siege when the savages come. But the event is entirely different from that of Crusoe's encounter. The boy foolishly ventures outside his stronghold, and is ignominiously seized in a defenceless state by the natives, who carry him off, but, not being cannibals, treat him gently, and before long he falls into the hands of the civilized people of Kesmes, who appoint him teacher of his own language.

Many other details could be pointed out in which it is hard to believe that the two men agreed without the one knowing the

*Value
of the
evidence*

other. There are many slighter resemblances ; but even these grow formidable by cumulation. Anyone describing the attempts of a castaway to maintain existence would hit upon many of the same ideas as Smeeks and Defoe, as our previous survey testifies ; but it is incredible that two lists of tools, utensils, opportune finds, shifts, and contrivances, should correspond so closely if they were quite independent. When Crusoe says he went fishing with a long line, but had no hooks, yet caught fish, and drying them in the sun ate them dry, it does look as if he had read of the Dutch boy's fishing, but had not troubled to think out the details. The boy had hooks and a line, and dried the fish he caught, but ate them boiled or roasted. On the other hand, some of the most memorable things in *Robinson Crusoe* cannot have been derived from Smeeks. The dramatic event of the shipwreck that left Crusoe stranded, the thrilling discovery of the foot-print,[1] the capture and education of Friday, and, finally, the life-like character of Robinson Crusoe himself, are of a totally different nature from anything in *Krinke Kesmes.*

*The
probable
extent of
Defoe's
indebted-
ness to
Smeeks*

It would be absurd to suppose that Defoe deliberately set himself to write a story like that of Smeeks, followed this original almost step by step, and where he departed from the path laid down did so in order to divert attention from his thefts. Such a view has, nevertheless, found advocates.[2] Read, as it used to be, as one of the progeny of imitations issuing from Defoe's book, *Der Holländische Robinson Crusoe* seems a feeble copy, in every way inferior to the supposed original. Now that the chronology has been corrected, it is evident that Smeeks deserves credit

[1] Mr L. L. Hubbard, to whom we are indebted for an English translation of the episode from Smeeks's book, finds what he thinks a parallel to the incident of the footprint. But he misses the entire significance of the incident in *Robinson Crusoe*, and in his eagerness to prove Defoe a plagiarist shows himself so myopic that he awakens the reader's suspicions even when he discerns a real similarity (Hubbard, L. L., *A Dutch source for "Robinson Crusoe"* . . . *Sjouke Gabbes,* Introd., xlvi.-xlvii. ; see also Secord, pp. 100-101.)

[2] Mr Hubbard is avowedly unable to appreciate the superiority of *Robinson Crusoe*, and with entire disregard of the immense disparity between Defoe and Smeeks, *Robinson Crusoe* and *Sjouke Gabbes*, tries by fair means and foul to make out an affirmative case in answer to the query, "Is it not the earlier story in fact, and ought it not of right to be considered, the pattern after which ' Robinson ' was molded? " (Preface to *Sjouke Gabbes,* xiii.). One of his reviewers, Julius Goebel, adopts the same uncritical attitude (*Journal of English and Germanic Philology,* xxii., 1923, pp. 302-313).

for having provided a suggestive sketch, a good deal of the raw material out of which Defoe created a masterpiece. Smeeks showed freshness, ingenuity, and life-likeness; Defoe's vivid imagination made this by far the best story of its kind, by imparting a peculiar greatness and dignity and making it as stable as a piece of history. Defoe's was an eclectic method; in all his fictions he used materials gathered from various sources, and he rarely missed any important work that would help him. It has been questioned whether he could read Smeeks in the original. It cannot be proved that Defoe had even a smattering of Dutch; but there was a Dutch grammar in his library, which was there presumably for some purpose, and his Dutch sympathies and connexions favour the supposition that he had at least a nodding acquaintance with the language. It seems reasonable to conclude that having made himself conversant with most of the Crusoe literature current in his day, he did not overlook an item so peculiarly serviceable. Probability and internal evidence alike indicate that *Krinke Kesmes* must be numbered among the sources of *Robinson Crusoe*.[1]

After reviewing all these available sources, we may conclude that Defoe assimilated the more important literature of travel, acquainted himself with most of the Crusoe stories already in existence, as previous authors of similar fictions had manifestly done before him, and then used what he borrowed as raw material, which he worked up in a manner entirely his own. There was nothing new or unique in this, except the manner in which he turned his loans to account, and this was due to the circumstance that he helped himself to other people's facts rather than to their characters and their stories. Dramatists had habitually made free with other men's plots. From Shakespeare to Dickens we can see the creative artist developing characters, which we can track to their origin in their personal experience or their reading, into finer and more complex representatives of human nature. Defoe was not a great creator of human character, but he was a fabricator

Defoe's way of using his material

---

[1] No stress has been laid above on the circumstance that both Smeeks and Defoe adopt the form of autobiography in these two fictions. But *Simplicissimus* and several of the true relations were written in this form, which was almost unavoidable in a narrative that aped matter-of-fact reporting, and was indeed the commonest form of fictitious narrative at the time.

of human histories, requiring somewhat different materials from those sought by a Shakespeare or a Dickens. He took these wherever he found them, and altered, amplified, and adapted to his own scheme, or merely utilized them to give concrete detail and realistic colouring to inventions of his own. This process he repeated in *Captain Singleton, Captain Carleton,* and the rest of his fictions.

How Defoe put himself into " Robinson Crusoe "

The tale of his sources, if it could be exactly determined, would show the datum-line for measuring his achievement. That achievement is to have applied innate artistry where others had merely spun a surprising yarn. He began *Robinson Crusoe* with the calculated purpose of writing a new sort of story that would pay, and knowing his public he expected it to pay well. But it cannot be doubted that this was the one of all his works that gave him most enjoyment in writing it. He put himself into the book, his delight in doing things ; he must have felt like a boy living and making himself snug on Crusoe's island, and occasionally like a man reflecting on the seriousness of the situation. He was more right than perhaps he sincerely felt when he decided later on to admit the impeachment that *Robinson Crusoe* was an allegory of his own life. For Robinson is unquestionably Defoe, and does exactly what Defoe would have done in the same position. That is why he is the most complete and life-like of Defoe's personages. Defoe's powers of delineating character were limited to this, that he could put himself in the situation assigned to a given individual and report accurately how he would have behaved. Such was to be his method again with Moll Flanders, such with Captain Singleton, Colonel Jacque, and the rest of them. These others, however, are Defoe in masquerade ; Robinson Crusoe is Defoe in the part that came most natural to him, the part that he would have sustained with entire credit. It might be said that Robinson Crusoe and his author are interchangeable characters. In relating the doings and experiences of his hero Defoe portrayed his idea of a man, the kind of a man he himself typified, a true-born Englishman of the most durable breed, strong, self-reliant, practical, winning through for the most part by dogged effort, though subject to rare fits of misgiving and despondency, in which the sense of forlorn self-dependence grew wellnigh unendurable. Such was Defoe, intrinsically a man of action, practical in all things, even in spiritual affairs, religion and morality, in which he valued principles by their results. Granted his religion and morality were sincere, inasmuch as he firmly believed them ; but they were hardly the religion and morality of the soul. Hence the moral sentiments which fall so ponderously in so many episodes of his novels have struck many readers as put in to conciliate the current prejudice against any literature that did not tend to edification. But it is wrong to question their sincerity or Defoe's earnestness ; these are his real sentiments, the applications of an ethical code which he held with conviction.

It was a strictly utilitarian code. Whatever he did and whatever he conceived his characters as doing was judged by its material effects. To Defoe even literature, or rather the practical operation of writing books, was a business, a useful job, not an art or an intellectual and spiritual activity. Pamphlets, poems, inquiries, collections of genuine or half-genuine facts, edifying memoirs of honest or dishonest persons, all had a similar justification ; they had the same productive value as his brick-and-tile works. From basket-making to conciliating opponents to a treaty, popularizing an economic policy, or recording the life of the solitary on his island, Defoe was always the man of action. Robinson Crusoe was himself : he had not the many-sided imagination to shape him otherwise.

This is the first novel in the complete modern sense, although it was not offered to the world as fiction, and differs considerably from the type ultimately established. The critic who laid it down that a novel must contain a love-story would have had to exclude *Robinson Crusoe* : there is hardly a woman in it. But it answers to our definition : *Robinson Crusoe* is not only a masterpiece of story-telling, it is also an interpretation of life. Man is shown in it at grips with Nature, not defending himself against a malicious foe, as in *Travailleurs de la Mer*, but wresting his livelihood from her churlish bosom. *Robinson Crusoe* is the epic of work. As a novel it has all the essential constituents : unity of theme, of action, and of style ; character, if not characters ; narrative that could not be bettered ; dialogue

" *Robinson Crusoe* " the first modern novel

not yet like that of the real world, but immensely nearer thereto than the belles and beaux of Mrs Behn and Mrs Manley had ever talked. In mere strength and solidity the fabric constructed by Defoe could not be excelled. Realistic fiction was established on granite foundations.

The second part, "The Farther Adventures"

Robinson Crusoe appeared on the 25th April, and its success was instantaneous, three legitimate further editions following, besides one that was evidently a piracy, before Defoe could make the most of such a favourable market by issuing a second part, *The Farther Adventures*, on the 20th August. In this supplement Defoe kept closer to certain first-hand accounts of travel. Crusoe revisits his island, and then goes on a trading voyage to the East Indies, reaching Pekin, and returning to his own country overland through Tartary, Siberia, and Russia. Home in 1705, he gives up roaming at the age of seventy-two. Critics have found it easier to identify Defoe's authorities for this than for the first part.[1] Numerous correspondences in the incidents of the eastward journey point to the second volume of Dampier's *New Voyage round the World* as his main source. For the account of the brief stay in China he relied chiefly on the Jesuit Louis Le Comte's *Memoirs and Observations Made in a late Journey through the Empire of China* (1697), a translation from the French, and perhaps also on John Nieuhoff's *Ambassade de la Compagnie hollondaise des Indes orientales au grand Khan de Tartarie* (1671)[2]; and for the transcontinental journey to Archangel he turned to a work translated from the Dutch, *Three Years Travels from Moscow overland to China* (1706), taking the route the opposite way.

In *The Farther Adventures* Defoe showed himself an expert compiler, so well grounded in geographical knowledge, and so careful in checking his hero's every move by the map, that he never went astray. But as this is merely a fictitious travel-book, with relatively little personal interest, there is no need to dwell upon it, except to point out that the study of Defoe's borrowings in this case helps to an understanding of the more complicated problem of his loans and his originality in the other.

[1] Dottin, pp. 339-342 ; Secord, pp. 49-53 and 63-74.
[2] Dottin, pp. 340-341.

His pen was busy meanwhile on other works, several of which are of interest as lives of notorious personages recounted with more or less admixture of fiction. But leaving these for the moment, let us glance at the third and last part of *Robinson Crusoe*, the *Serious Reflections*, in which he tried yet again, and this time without the success he met with in the second part, to exploit his hero's popularity.

It came out late in 1720, as a collection of moralizing essays enlivened with a few anecdotes, and met with the coldest of welcomes. Lovers of *Robinson Crusoe* did not want it, those who were not in love with him paid no heed. But, along with " Robinson Crusoe's Preface " and the publisher's introduction, the work is of prime importance in elucidating the question of Defoe's attitude towards his fictions and his readers. An envious denizen of Grub Street had brought out a pamphlet, just after the publication of *The Farther Adventures*, entitled *The Life and Strange Surprizing Adventures of Mr D . . . . . De F., London, Hosier, who Has liv'd above fifty Years by himself, in the Kingdoms of North and South Britain. The various Shapes he has appear'd in, and the Discoveries he has made for the Benefit of his Country. In a Dialogue between Him, Robinson Crusoe, and his Man Friday. With Remarks serious and Comical upon the Life of Crusoe* (1719). It was, of course, an open secret that the *Adventures of Robinson Crusoe*, though professedly written by himself, were by Defoe, who had many enemies in the scribbling tribe as well as elsewhere, and whose unparalleled success excited jealousy. He had personally offended Charles Gildon, who, it will be recollected, had officiated as a kind of literary executor to Mrs Aphra Behn,[1] and Gildon thirsted for vengeance.

The " Serious Reflections "

Gildon's attack on Defoe

He appears to have written part of his skit before Defoe's second part came out. There Defoe let fall a remark that the useful lessons which might be drawn from every part of his story " must legitimate all the part that may be called invention or parable in the story." [2] This hint of a parabolic meaning Gildon eagerly seized, and made it the basis for a ridiculous account of Defoe's life. It is a not ineffective piece of rough fooling, this pasquinade of Gildon's, though it would have been of the merest

[1] See above, p. 79.   [2] Author's preface, p. 1.

ephemeral interest had it not given Defoe the cue to assert in measured terms that *Robinson Crusoe* was in very truth an indirect autobiography. Gildon brings his butt upon the scene in the small hours of the morning in a great field near Newington, where Crusoe and Friday confront him and vent their reproaches for the scurvy way in which he had misrepresented their characters and made them look fools. They exact summary retribution by forcing their creator to swallow both volumes of the offending work, and finish by tossing him in a blanket. Gildon added an epistle in which he exposed numerous oversights, discrepancies, and sheer contradictions in the story ; but the poor man missed a good many more of these signs of haste and carelessness, for he was blind, and had to rely upon hearing the book read aloud. In a postscript, he told Defoe roundly that he was a liar.[1]

Defoe avows that " Robinson Crusoe " is an allegory

Gildon had really done his enemy a good turn. Defoe never avowed himself a writer of fiction. He had palmed off Robinson Crusoe as an existing person and his island as an existing place. Sharps were beginning to sell bogus relics of both the man and his non-existent domicile ; whilst the general public, zealous members of Defoe's own sect especially, were waxing suspicious and asking for more definite information. The pretence could not be kept up much longer. Hence, seeing a loophole of escape, Defoe gladly accepted the suggestion that *Robinson Crusoe* was simply an allegory, and declared that every material passage answered figuratively to some important episode in his own history. He, in the name of Robinson Crusoe, solemnly affirmed,

that the story, though allegorical, is also historical ; and that it is the beautiful representation of a life of unexampled misfortunes, and of a variety not to be met with in the world, sincerely adapted to and intended for the common good of mankind, and designed at first, as it is now farther applied, to the most serious uses possible.[2]

He goes on to recapitulate the most trying incidents of his hero's life, which, he says, taken together,

[1] Gildon's skit is reprinted by Paul Dottin, with an introduction, notes, and an essay on Gildon's life, in *Robinson Crusoe examin'd and criticis'd*, 1923.
[2] Preface (*Serious Reflections*, ed. G. A. Aitken, ix.).

are one whole scheme of a real life of eight and twenty years, spent in the most wandering, desolate, and afflicting circumstances that ever man went through, and in which I have lived so long in a life of wonders, in continued storms, fought with the worst kind of savages and man-eaters; by unaccountable surprising incidents, fed by miracles greater than that of ravens; suffered all manner of violences and oppressions, injurious reproaches, contempt of men, attacks of devils, corrections from Heaven, and oppositions on earth. . . . In a word, there is not a circumstance in the imaginary story but has its just allusion to a real story, and chimes part for part and stop for stop with the inimitable Life of Robinson Crusoe.[1]

Followed thereupon the publisher's introduction, probably by Defoe himself, endorsing this declaration in which " the riddle is now expounded," and advertising the ensuing observations and reflections as crowning the work and showing the application of the whole parable.

Nor, in discussing the multifarious casuistry of human life, *Defoe's* does Defoe shrink from stirring up the thorniest questions that *remarks* his enemies might have said were provoked by his juggling *on ficti-* with truth. He comes very near home in the section " On Talk- *tious* ing Falsely," where he condemns the telling of amusing stories *story-* in conversation, and asks us to consider whether the laughter *telling* which is the object is worth purchasing " at so great an expense as that of conscience and of a dishonour done to truth." " The supplying a story by invention," he continues, " is certainly a most scandalous crime, and yet very little regarded in that part." But, " the selling or writing a parable, or an allusive allegoric history, is quite a different case, and is always distinguished from this other jesting with truth, that it is designed and effectually turned for instructive and upright ends, and has its moral justly applied. Such are the historical parables in the Holy Scripture, such ' The Pilgrim's Progress,' and such, in a word, the adventures of your fugitive friend, ' Robinson Crusoe.' "[2] A disquisition " Of the Trial of Honesty," in which he begins by asserting that " Necessity makes an honest man a knave; and if the common world was to be the judge according to the common received notion, there would not be an honest poor man left

[1] Preface, *Serious Reflections*, ed. G. A. Aitken, xi.-xii.   [2] *Ibid.*, pp. 97-101.

alive," [1] contains an oblique apologia for his bankruptcy of years gone by.

But the most interesting and eloquent part of the *Serious Reflections* is the first chapter, " Of Solitude." Crusoe, reviewing his unparalleled experiences, tells his readers that he at one time wondered how absolute loneliness could be supported. But later he wondered " why it should be any grievance or affliction, seeing upon the whole view of the stage of life which we act upon this world it seems to me that life in general is, or ought to be, but one universal act of solitude." He touches upon profounder truths as he looks deeper.

Our meditations are all solitude in perfection ; our passions are all exercised in retirement ; we love, we hate, we covet, we enjoy, all in privacy and solitude. All that we communicate of those things to any other is but for their assistance in the pursuit of their desires'; the end is at home ; the enjoyment, the contemplation, is all solitude and retirement ; it is for ourselves we enjoy, and for ourselves we suffer.

And he concludes:

All the parts of a complete solitude are to be as effectually enjoyed, if we please, and sufficient grace assisting, even in the most populous cities, among the hurries of conversation and gallantry of a court, or the noise and business of a camp, as in the deserts of Arabia and Lybia, or in the desolate life of an uninhabited island.

[1] Preface (*Serious Reflections*, ed. G. A. Aitken, pp. 2-15).

CHAPTER VII

THE LATER FICTION OF DEFOE

Other works of Defoe at this period

BETWEEN the second and the third parts of *Robinson Crusoe*, in addition to his regular output of journalistic writing, Defoe published the following narratives, all professedly veracious histories, but all tricked out with some fictitious garniture, if only the pose of confidential information, and two of them fabricated from beginning to end in exactly the same manner as *Robinson Crusoe.* The first may be regarded as a piece of reporting ; but its subject, the loneliness of a person isolated from his kind through physical infirmity, chimed in with the greater work he had just finished on the same theme. *The Dumb Philosopher ; or, Great-Britain's Wonder* (1719), contained in its sixty-four pages an account of the life and death of the Cornish tinner's son, Dickory Cronke, who was born dumb and so continued fifty-eight years, till on the eve of his death he came to his speech, and delivered himself of various religious sayings and a string of prophetical observations on the affairs of Europe, more particularly of Great Britain, during the next decade. This was in October ; in December appeared a more pretentious biography, *The King of Pirates : being an Account of the Famous Enterprises of Captain Avery, The Mock King of Madagascar. With his Rambles and Piracies ; wherein all the sham accounts formerly published of him are detected.* This was dated 1720. Then came more reporter's work, *The History of the Life and Adventures of Mr Duncan Campbell, A Gentleman, who, tho' Deaf and Dumb, writes down any Stranger's Name at first Sight ; with their future Contingencies of Fortune. Now Living in Exeter Court over against the Savoy in the Strand* (1720); and subsequently two much more famous books, *Memoirs of a Cavalier* and *Captain Singleton.*

The kind of curiosity he indulged and the kind he exploited

in his account of the Cornish prodigy was the same as that which
was the object in *Duncan Campbell*. But besides the obvious
analogy between *The King of Pirates* and *Captain Singleton* there
is a more important connexion : the one book gave him the idea
and was unintentionally a first study for the other. For a score
of years the dare-devil pirate Captain Avery had enjoyed at
least as much popular renown as had been the lot for a briefer
period of Alexander Selkirk. Monstrously exaggerated rumours
were current of his exploits and the enormous wealth amassed
by him and his confederates ; most of these were retailed in a
Life and Adventures of Captain John Avery (1709), ascribed to
a Dutchman, Adrian van Broeck, who had been captured by
the so-called king of Madagascar and had got away. Avery had
also been the hero of a play, *The Successful Pirate*, which ran
for a short while at Drury Lane (1712). This was by Charles
Johnson, probably not to be identified with the Captain
Charles Johnson who afterwards gave a more sceptical and
prosaic account of the doughty rover in his *General History
of the Robberies and Murders of the most Notorious Pirate*
(1734).

The story pretends to be from Avery's own pen, and is cast
into the form of two letters, the first, a very long one, written
from Madagascar, the other after his departure. He protests
against the ridiculous misstatements of the *Life and Adventures*; he corrects the reports, widely circulated, about his
alleged army of 5000 men and the ten millions sterling said to
have been offered to the British Government for their free
pardon ; but he admits that he and his associates would gladly
have paid down a million pounds to be allowed to end their
lives in England. He adds that he, for his part, would have
liked to make restitution to those of his own countrymen whom
he had injured. These ostentatious corrections of other versions
of the story are the regular tricks of Defoe's narrative art : the
penitential assurances put in the mouth of the pirate king are
Defoe's regular way of finding sermons even in rogueries.
Captain Avery had no hand in either. Probably Defoe possessed
no material more authentic than the stigmatized book and the
popular legends ; but he was cautious enough to sift this

thoroughly and utilize only so much as sounded plausible. For realistic detail he resorted again to Dampier and no doubt to other authorities.[1]

The King of Pirates is, in short, a characteristic mixture of facts wrested from their proper place and fiction supplying circumstance and credibility. It really accepts many baseless reports, such as those of Avery's greatness as a Napoleonic buccaneer, which the historian of the pirates heavily discounted. Like *Captain Singleton*, it is an exciting narrative of fights, escapes, and miscellaneous exploits, but less enjoyable, since the incessant combats with Spanish and Mogul frigates tend to be as monotonous as the knightly encounters in old romance. Defoe put in his usual touches of actuality. Speaking of the notorious incident of the Mogul princess and the casket of jewels she was said to have handed over, Avery is made to affirm,

A mixture of some fact and more fiction

> I have them still in my keeping, and wish they were safe in England ; for I doubt not but some of them are fit to be placed on the king's crown.

When the story ends, Avery with his ill-gotten riches is stranded at Constantinople, hoping for an opportunity of making his way to France, and eventually settling down at some inland place in safe obscurity. In the story that was soon to follow, Singleton finds himself after his career of piracy in exactly the same predicament. Other correspondences will be noted when the later story is examined.

The History of Duncan Campbell (1720) is the memoir of a deaf-mute credited with supernatural powers who was much more prominent at that period than the humble Dickory Cronke. He was a Scotsman, born in Lapland, and was believed to be gifted with second sight. But even his dumbness, according to Addison, was assumed ; and Steele joins his colleague in deriding both his pretensions to mystical knowledge and the

" The History of Duncan Campbell "

---

[1] Dampier has been pointed out as his stand-by in recounting Avery's voyage from the West Indies to Juan Fernandez and his piracies in the South Seas (Secord, pp. 140-141). The incident of the piratical seizure of a vessel [in the Groyne (Corunna)], of which there is a different version in *Captain Singleton*, was also related by Johnson, and probably comes from a source common to Defoe and Johnson (*ibid.*, pp. 141-142).

fashionable persons who flocked to him for prophetic advice. Defoe was always interested in occult matters, apparitions, magic, astrology, and the like. But, with his wonted cunning, he makes his seer throw contempt on the ordinary run of conjurers and fortune-tellers. There is no reason to suppose that he regarded Campbell as a charlatan, his personal attitude towards all such questions being indicated by his open-minded discussions not only in this work but also in *The Second-sighted Highlander, The Friendly Demon ; or, the Generous Apparition* (1726), afterwards incorporated in his *Secret Memoirs of Duncan Campbell* (1732), and the half-serious *Political History of the Devil* (1726). Mrs Haywood, in her volume upon the Scottish thaumaturge, entitled *A Spy upon the Conjurer ; or, a Collection of Surprising and Diverting Stories, with Merry and Ingenious Letters* (1725), laid most stress, as would be expected, on his adventures among the fair who thronged to him for consultations ; hence she found a welcome with the mob of readers hungry for spicy anecdote. Her book may be put among her secret histories and collections of scandals.

This likewise a semi-fictitious work

Though the presentment of an actual celebrity, Defoe's *Duncan Campbell* is obviously the lineal successor of such works as *The Man in the Moone telling Strange Fortunes* ; it is also the grandfather of Smollett's episode of the hoaxing astrologer in *Peregrine Pickle*. Apart from the fictitious details which it would be difficult to disentangle, even if it were worth while, the story has one feature characteristic of Defoe's novels, that it is declared to be written by a good old friend of Campbell's, " now departed this life," and revised by a young gentleman of his acquaintance. Nor did Defoe omit the passages of officious moralizing which he always considered it his duty to append wherever convenient.

A predecessor of Defoe —Courtilz de Sandras

In the work that immediately followed, *Memoirs of a Cavalier* (1720), he turned from fictitious biography to a lively version of history in an autobiographical guise. In this, and the similar works that succeeded it, Defoe had a predecessor, if not a model, in Gatien de Courtilz (1646 ?-1712), chiefly remembered now as the author of the *Mémoires de M. d'Artagnan* (1700) on which Dumas based his *Trois Mousquetaires*. The

whole catalogue of the Frenchman's diversified writings bears
an astonishing resemblance to Defoe's more extensive list, both
consisting of histories, annals, memoirs, political revelations,
journals, and pamphlets, many of them so close an imitation of
straightforward history and so full of genuine or well-simulated
facts that they have frequently passed as true.[1] Courtilz, says
his biographer, was led to realism by his taste for history.[2] He
wrote lives which were largely fabrications, and romances which
he passed off as historical records. He drew his materials from
the gazettes and from common report ; he saved up anecdotes
and gossip ; he had a rich stock of personal reminiscences and
of his own experience of military life during the wars of the
Fronde. He filled out the picture from his ready imagination.
This is pretty much the same as Defoe was to do a little later.
Courtilz' largely apocryphal *Mémoires du Comte de Rochefort*
(1687) was just such another fabric woven of truth and invention as *The Military Memoirs of Captain George Carleton*, and
raised the same questions of authorship, of the historicity of the
hero, and the verity of the incidents avouched to be historic.
Courtilz was as little influenced by contemporary writers of
fiction as was Defoe ; both aimed at satisfying by the readiest
means at their disposal the prevailing appetite for knowledge,
or at least information, even more than the desire of entertainment. The satirical trend of the French writer's portraiture
may very reasonably be ascribed to the picaresque spirit bred by
personal disillusionment. His life had been a series of disasters,
through his taking the wrong side in the disturbances of the
Fronde. Courtilz and Defoe are the founders of historical
fiction, none the less so in that they passed off what they wrote
as history and not as fiction.[3]

---

[1] Woodbridge, B. M., *Gatien de Courtilz, Sieur de Verger : Étude sur un
Précurseur du Roman Réaliste en France* (Johns Hopkins' *Studies in Romance
Literatures and Languages*, v.), 1925, pp. 204-209, *Œuvres de Courtilz*.

[2] *Ibid.*, preface, ix.

[3] Defoe had read Courtilz de Sandras, that "specialist in pseudo-memoirs"
(Dottin, ii. 396). But the tendency was already implanted in England, as
the much-embroidered lives of criminals and other popular notabilities are
enough to show : see Bernbaum, E., *The Mary Carleton Narratives* (Harvard
University Press), 1914, and *Mrs Behn's Biography a Fiction* (*Publications of
the Modern Language Association of America*, xxviii.), 1913. Mme d'Aulnoy's
Relation du Voyage d'Espagne (1691), translated into English (1692) and

Defoe entitled the new book in full, *Memoirs of a Cavalier :
or a Military Journal of the Wars in Germany, and The Wars in
England ; From the Year 1632, to the Year 1648. Written Three-
score Years ago by an English Gentleman, who served first in the
Army of Gustavus Adolphus, the glorious King of Sweden, till his
Death, and after that in the Royal Army of King Charles the
First, from the Beginning of the Rebellion to the End of the War.*
To expand this synopsis a little, it need only be added that the
Cavalier is present as an active participant or a deeply concerned spectator at many of the most stirring events of the
Thirty Years' War, including the sack of Magdeburg, the battle
of Leipzig, the passage of the Lech, the siege of Nuremberg,
and the defeat of the Protestants at Nordlingen ; and, having
joined the Royalist forces in England, takes part in the battles
of Edgehill, Roundway Down, Marston Moor, the second battle
of Newbury, the ruinous battle of Naseby, and numerous
skirmishes, leaguers, and minor engagements. It is military history recounted from the point of view of an officer supposed to
be acquainted with the designs of his commanders, and with no
romantic interest to distract attention such as a modern novelist
would have introduced. There is no portraiture worth mention-
ing, but the Cavalier gives his impressions of the leaders on both
sides, and criticizes their generalship and their conduct towards
the civil population.

In the long title of the book Defoe claimed to have reproduced a journal contemporary with the events ; in the preface
he stated that the *Memoirs* had been discovered twenty years
before among the papers of one of King William's secretaries of
state. This specious assurance was generally accepted, and only
one question remained to be settled, who was the author ? The
publisher of the second edition, which appeared some years after
Defoe was in his grave, pretended to have solved this problem,
and identified the Cavalier with a certain Andrew Newport,
second son to the Royalist gentleman who afterwards became
Lord Newport. No other claimant to the honour has ever been

frequently reprinted in France during the following century, is an example of
the same apocryphal method applied to the literature of travel (see below,
p. 223).

put forward. But, when the facts that are known about Andrew Newport are scrutinized, it turns out that such an identification is impossible. Andrew was only eight years old at the time of the fall of Magdeburg, and neither his circumstances nor his career can be made to square with the history of our Cavalier. So the conclusion is obvious : Defoe, in order to add liveliness and personal interest to his recital of historic events, made these revolve about the doings of an imaginary person. He reveals nothing that was not public property at the time, no facts that could not be learned from the *Swedish Intelligencer* and other records of the war in Germany and from well-known authorities on the English Civil War.[1] He presents his facts with the realistic detail that has convinced generations of readers that they were perusing the actual journal of a combatant ; but this vivid detail, unless it was gleaned to some extent from survivors of those events with whom Defoe had conversed, must have been contributed by his own imagination. Glaring errors, many inaccuracies, and important omissions have been pointed out, which show that he was not even as careful as he might have been in reading up the subject in the historical works open to every one.[2]

Nevertheless, the *Memoirs of a Cavalier*, as a semi-historical narrative, cannot be surpassed for graphic and enthralling realism. Defoe's method is as unfailing here as in *Robinson Crusoe*. It is the same method exactly ; Defoe is not content to say that certain things occurred, he relates with the utmost particularity how they happened. In his account of battles and sieges, he shows himself conversant with the topographical features and possessed of a soldierly acquaintance with military tactics. His account of Marston Moor is not in accord with the authorities ; but as a lucid and moving narrative of a stricken field it could not be bettered. One example of his characteristic procedure must suffice. It is the account of the Swedish army's passage of the river Lech, under the guns of a powerful enemy. The Swedish king and his staff reconnoitred the position from

A realistic version of history

---

[1] The question is ably examined by Aitken (introduction to *Memoirs of a Cavalier*, 1895) ; see also Secord. pp. 207-212.
[2] Aitken, pp. 14-15.

a hillock overlooking the river, which ran almost straight till at the end of a reach it doubled short upon itself, making a round and very narrow point. " There's a point will do our business," says the king, " and if the ground be good I'll pass there, let Tilly do his worst." The difficulty was to find out the depth of the water between the banks. A reward of fifty dollars was offered for this information, and a sergeant of dragoons volunteered to bring it.

The king liked the motion well enough, and the fellow being very well acquainted with the country, puts on a ploughman's habit, and went away immediately with a long pole upon his shoulder. The horse lay all this while in the woods, and the king stood undiscerned by the enemy on the little hill aforesaid. The dragoon with his long pole comes down boldly to the bank of the river, and calling to the sentinels which Tilly had placed on the other bank, talked with them, asked them if they could not help him over the river, and pretended he wanted to come to them. At last, being come to the point where, as I said, the river makes a short turn, he stands parleying with them a great while, and sometimes, pretending to wade over, he puts his long pole into the water, then finding it pretty shallow he pulls off his hose and goes in, still thrusting his pole in before him, till being gotten up to his middle, he could reach beyond him, where it was too deep, and so shaking his head, comes back again. The soldiers on the other side, laughing at him, asked him if he could swim ? He said, " No." " Why, you fool you," says one of the sentinels, " the channel of the river is twenty feet deep." " How do you know that ? " says the dragoon. " Why, our engineer," says he, " measured it yesterday." This was what he wanted, but not yet fully satisfied, " Ay, but," says he, " maybe it may not be very broad, and if one of you would wade in to meet me till I could reach you with my pole, I'd give him half a ducat to pull me over." The innocent way of his discourse so deluded the soldiers, that one of them immediately strips and goes in up to the shoulders, and our dragoon goes in on this side to meet him ; but the stream took t'other soldier away, and he being a good swimmer, came swimming over to this side. The dragoon was then in a great deal of pain for fear of being discovered, and was once going to kill the fellow, and make off ; but at last resolved to carry on the humour, and having entertained the fellow with a tale of a tub, about the Swedes stealing his oats, the fellow being a-cold wanted to be gone, and he as willing to be rid of him, pretended to be very sorry he could not get over the river, and so makes off.[1]

The king having learned all he wanted has a portable bridge constructed out of sight of the enemy, digs trenches by night and plants cannon sweeping the other bank, which is twelve feet lower, and throwing the bridge across under cover of the guns, crosses with his army, Tilly, the hostile general, receiving a mortal wound in the heat of the conflict. That day's success, he often averred, " was every way equal to the victory of Leipsic."

Two weeks later appeared *The Life, Adventures, and Pyracies of the Famous Captain Singleton : Containing an Accot nt of his being set on Shore in the Island of Madagascar ; his Settlement there ; with a Description of the Place and Inhabitants : of his Passage from thence in a Paraguay, to the Main Land of Africa ; with an Account of the Customs and Manners of the People ; His great Deliverance from the Barbarous Natives and Wild Beasts : Of his meeting with an Englishman, a citizen of London, amongst the Indians. The great Riches he Acquired, and his Voyage Home to England. As also Captain Singleton's Return to Sea, with an Account of his many Adventures and Pyracies with the famous Captain Avery and others* (1720). Two great blocks of adventure are indexed in this summary ; first, the haps and mishaps of Singleton's early life, culminating in the great adventure of his journey across Africa, an exploit as unexampled as Crusoe's island sojourn ; and then the career of piracy in which he rivals the deeds and successes of Captain Avery. *" Captain Single-ton "*

Singleton was stolen in infancy, and in early boyhood was sent to sea. After three or four voyages he was taken by an Algerine rover, but his captor was retaken by a Portuguese vessel, and he found himself in Lisbon. Going as cabin-boy on a voyage to Goa, he learned from his dissolute and villainous shipmates to lie and steal and take his part in any mischief, and was suspected of being one of those who had plotted to murder the captain. He and twenty-six of the crew were put ashore in *Outline of the story*

[1] *Memoirs of a Cavalier* (Bohn's Library), pp. 73-74.

Madagascar, where the mutineers built a vessel out of a wrecked Dutchman, and reached the coast of Africa near Mozambique. There, hopeless of rescue by their own countrymen and fearful of falling into the hands of the Arabs and being sold as slaves, they " took one of the rashest, and wildest, and most desperate resolutions that ever was taken by man, or any number of men, in the world ; this was, to travel overland through the heart of the country, from the coast of Mozambique, on the east ocean, to the coast of Angola or Guinea, on the western or Atlantic Ocean, a continent of land of at least 1800 miles." After manifold adventures, they completed this daring project and, laden with considerable treasure, reached the Gold Coast, whence Singleton found his passage to England.

In two years Singleton squandered his money, and going to sea again speedily turned pirate. With a scoundrel named Wilmot he cruised in the West Indies, took the command of a captured frigate, and in Madagascar fell in with the redoubtable Avery. In one of his prizes he picked up the Quaker surgeon, William Walters, who in time becomes Singleton's closest friend, and is one of the most interesting characters in all Defoe's tales. Through a difference of opinion with Wilmot, the pirates separated, and Singleton, with a ship of forty-four guns and a sloop, cruised the eastern seas for years, preyed on trading vessels until he and his comrades were rolling in riches, and, induced by the representations of Quaker William to see the folly of continuing any longer in a career of crime, determined to repent and if possible settle down to a peaceable life in England. The two friends give their associates the slip, carrying off as much treasure as they conveniently can, and eventually reach this country. Singleton marries William's sister, and, living in retirement lest any should inquire too pointedly after their old friend " Captain Bob," he leaves off his story with the comment, " I am much more happy than I deserve."

Sonrces of " Captain Single- ton "

Singleton's story of his life thus consists of two contrasted parts : the first may be described as romance of travel, like Crusoe's *Farther Adventures,* which it far surpasses ; the second is a pirate romance, equally superior to the pretended history of Captain Avery. For both parts, Defoe rummaged far and wide for handy material, whilst relying for geographical correctness on his own unequalled knowledge of the literature of travel and the latest maps. He worked, that is to say, in the same eclectic manner as in writing *Robinson Crusoe*, and here again handled the borrowed materials so deftly and dovetailed so neatly that the narrative runs as smooth and limpid as if it were spontaneous. The bricks came from other buildings ; they were relaid and cemented together with Defoe's inimitable realism. The works of travel that stood him in most stead in his first great story, those of Mandelslo, Knox, Dampier, and Misson, were his foremost authorities in *Captain Singleton*.[1] Many minute correspondences make this plain. For the amazing journey across the dark continent he resorted again to Ogilby's *Description of Africa* (1670), and there were other works of a less general character available.[2] Internal evidence shows that he made continual use of the latest maps, including those of Herman Moll, afterwards collected into an atlas (1732). For the Madagascar episode he had on his shelves De Flacourt's *Histoire de la grande isle Madagascar* (1658). His main source for Singleton's further adventures was of course his own *King of Pirates* ; but he made additional levies upon Dampier, Exquemelin's *Bucaniers of America* (1678, translated, 1684-1685, continued by Ringrose 1685), on Knox, and probably on others, including recent reports of the doings of pirates. Besides Avery, he mentions Kidd, Harris, and Wilmot, notorious names in the annals of the black flag.[3]

It has often been said that the account of Singleton's journey

[1] " The adventures of Singleton are projected against the broad background of Defoe's reading in Hakluyt and Purchas. . . . More specifically Defoe made use of four writers of travel and foreign adventure, Mandelslo, Knox, Dampier, and Misson ; and a study of their influence upon *Captain Singleton* will be the principal task in the succeeding pages of this chapter." This is from A. W. Secord's admirable *Studies in the Narrative Method of Defoe*, ii. 114. The work is a landmark in the study of Defoe, and this second chapter traces the course of Singleton's journeys, showing how far they were suggested by the geographical knowledge or opinions then most advanced, and the source of numerous facts and incidents, with a painstaking research that makes further inquiry unnecessary. Even to summarize the chief points would be superfluous in a general study of the question of Defoe's place in the history of the novel. but the special student of Defoe cannot afford to neglect Dr Secord's results.

[2] See list in Dottin, ii. 631-632.
[3] Secord, pp. 116-147.

186 HISTORY OF THE ENGLISH NOVEL

Defoe's
supposed
anticipa-
tion of
later dis-
coveries

through Central Africa showed an insight or a faculty for probable conjecture unaccountably in advance of his time. But more
careful comparison of the imaginary route with the existing maps
proves that Defoe had good warrant for the position of the lakes
and rivers met with by his hero. When he trusted to his imagination, as he was bound to for considerable distances, he was
no nearer to the correct configuration of the region than the
geographers of his day, and as haphazard and hazy as in his
guesses about the fauna and flora. He actually showed rather
more prescience when, in the second part, he sent his pirate roaming in unexplored seas in the neighbourhood of what was still
Terra Australis Incognita. Speculations about such possibilities
as the North-West Passage haunted Defoe. William hears about
the remnant of a ship's crew, dwelling on the north side of Japan,
who had been wrecked after coming from Greenland and the
North Pole. Dampier was his pilot on the far eastern voyage,
but he went beyond Dampier in making Singleton sail between Australia and Tasmania, relying on his own theory that
Tasmania was an island.[1]

The
Quaker
William
Walters

Defoe drew very few characters that are memorable as individuals. If, besides those like Robinson Crusoe and Moll
Flanders who are spun out of his own substance, there is one that
stands out with uncommon distinctness, it is the Quaker William
Walters ; and he, or his less distinct original in *The King of
Pirates*, came to Defoe out of a book. We get only a glimpse of
the Quaker Skipper commanding a frigate-built ship captured
by Avery, who says, " It appeared by his countenance he would
not have been afraid of his flesh, or have baulked using the carnal
weapon of offence, viz., the cannon-ball." Invited to join the
pirates, he would not at first reply ; and when asked again he said
he did not know whether it was safe for him to answer that
question. Being reassured and given free option, he shrewdly
declined. Many claims to have found the original of the cautious

---

[1] Secord, pp. 147-160. Secord points out that Defoe's habit was, not to read
up the geography and then invent a series of appropriate incidents ; "more
frequently he picks up his geographical information and the suggestions for
his incidents side by side in the journals of actual travellers " (p. 118). The
identification of the incidents helps to the identification of the geographical
sources.

skipper and Quaker William have been put forward ; the likeliest
is that the latter was drawn from the Jacob Halsey commemo-
rated by Captain Alexander Smith, in Johnson's *History of the
Highwaymen*.[1] The genial truculence of Jacob, who addresses
his victims in such propitiating terms as " Dearly beloved, be not
surpriz'd at what I am going to say to thee ; for 'tis . . . only
to borrow what money thou hast about thee," is strongly
suggestive of Singleton's friend.[2]

This figure, with the more human interest that he brings into
the uningratiating Singleton's story, has a richer flavour of the
novel than anything else in the book. William was the surgeon
on a sloop captured on her way to Barbados, and he was bidden
to bring his instruments and come along with the freebooters.
" He was a comic fellow indeed, a man of very good solid sense,
and an excellent surgeon ; but, what was worth all, very good-
humoured, and pleasant in his conversation, and a bold, stout
fellow too, as any we had among us." Singleton found him not
averse to the proposal ; but the Quaker insisted on having a
certificate that he was taken away by force and against his will,
to ensure against accidents. Singleton falls in with this proviso,
signs the document, and makes a show of tying William's hands
behind him and carrying him aboard the other ship as a prisoner.
After this, none so bold yet wideawake and shrewd a pirate as
Quaker William. He refuses to meddle with cold iron, except in
the shape of his professional tools. But when the pirates hesitate
to grapple with a Portuguese ship of heavier build, it is William
who gives them the hint to shorten sail and take the enemy at a
disadvantage. In the thick of the action he is found lashing the
enemy's bowsprit to the corsair's mainmast. " The shot flew
about his ears as thick as may be supposed in such an action
. . . but there was William, as composed, and in as perfect
tranquillity as to danger, as if he had been over a bowl of punch,
only very busy securing the matter, that a ship of forty-six guns

A humorous character

---

[1] Secord, p. 144.
[2] The speech is quoted by Secord (*ibid.*). A less likely original has been
proposed in the Quaker mentioned in *George Fox's Journal* (ed. N. Penney,
1911, x.). He comes into the log of the Barbados voyage (1671), kept by
John Hall, and turned by Ellwood into a narrative in the first person
by Fox.

188 HISTORY OF THE ENGLISH NOVEL

should not run away from a ship of eight-and-twenty." The Portuguese slacken fire.

Presently comes William up to me. " Friend," says he, very calmly, " What dost thou mean? Why dost thou not visit thy neighbour in the ship, the door being open for thee? " I understood him immediately, for our guns had so torn their hull, that we had beat two port-holes into one, and the bulk-head of their steerage was split to pieces, so that they could not retire to their close quarters ; so I gave the word immediately to board them.

The Portuguese frigate is easily mastered : but William points out that fighting men-of-war was an unprofitable occupation when there were rich merchant-ships to capture. His advice is accepted. But, with his usual guile, he refuses to have anything to do with their plans. " Whether he made a piece of conscience of it, or whether he did not care to venture having it come up against him afterwards or no, this I know not ; but we concluded at last without him."

When, however, the pirates fall in with a shipload of slaves, who have murdered the captain and crew, the Quaker has no scruples about taking possession of the living freight ; he in fact undertakes to carry the ship into port and sell them privately, making up a plausible tale to outwit the Portuguese authorities. Except that he has taken his precautions against hanging, William throws in his lot with Singleton and his men ; he is a trusty partner in many emergencies, and holds himself entitled to a full share of the plunder. When this has swollen to a vast sum, and there is an ample competence for every man in the squadron, William considers it time to think of the future. He puts the question to Singleton, why should they go on thieving for the sake of thieving ? Surely, they are all rich enough to give over this trade, and retire to the bosom of their families. Singleton replies that he has not a friend or relation in the world. The Quaker is taken aback ; but he has another shot in his locker.

Says William (tears running down his face), " It is because men live as if they were never to die, that so many die before they know how to live. But it was not death that I meant when I said that there was something to be thought of beyond this way of living."

" Why, William," said I, " what was that? "

" It was repentance," says he.

" Why," said I, " did you ever know a pirate repent? "

William is startled at this plain speaking, but he will not let the argument drop. He weeps as he remonstrates with the phlegmatic Singleton ; but when Singleton gets really frightened, it is not the Quaker that suffers agonies of remorse, and dreams that the devil comes to him in the night to carry him off to hell.

They conclude that it is futile to " talk of repenting while we continue pirates." Abstaining from any further robberies, they deliberate how they shall secure the wealth which they have in their hands. By a stroke of craft they sell the captured goods, and lodge money and merchandise with trustworthy persons. The business of salving their consciences and their money is successfully concluded, and the moment arrives for leaving their shipmates in the lurch, for neither Singleton nor the Quaker remember that the other pirates have souls to save too. Trumping up a story to beguile their comrades, they pretend that they have fallen into the hands of the Turks, and so get off with their spoils. Singleton's conscience is still in trouble, as well it might be. "What then must be done with our wealth," he asks, "the effects of plunder and rapine?" William's answer is admirably temporizing : *Conclu-sion of the story*

To quit what we have, and do it here, is to throw it away to those who have no claim to it, and to divest ourselves of it, but to do no right with it, whereas we ought to keep it carefully together, with a resolution to do what right with it we are able ; and who knows what opportunity Providence may put into our hands, to do justice at least, to some of those we have injured ; so we ought, at least, to leave it to Him, and go on. As it is, without doubt, our present business is to go to some place of safety, where we may wait His will.

Defoe's editor, Aitken, rebuked those who questioned the sincerity of the Quaker's religion and the beneficent influence which he exercised over Singleton.[1] William is sincere enough,

[1] Introduction to *Captain Singleton*, xviii.

and Defoe had no thought of satirizing his moral attitude, though he almost seems to recognize the humour of such a comfortable identification of the interests of this world and of the next. Quaker William was a man after his own heart, and a candid embodiment of the ethics approved by himself and no doubt the majority of his readers.

" Moll Flanders"   A moral lesson was still more to the fore in Defoe's next story, *The Fortunes and Misfortunes of the Famous Moll Flanders, who was born in Newgate, and during a Life of continued Variety, for Threescore years, beside her Childhood, was Twelve years a Whore, Five Times a Wife (whereof once to her own Brother), Twelve years a Thief, Eight years a Transported Felon in Virginia, at last grew Rich, lived Honest, and died a Penitent. Written from her own Memorandums* (1721).[1] The preface expresses the hope that those who know how to read such a story " will be much more pleased with the moral than the fable, with the application than with the relation, and with the end of the writer than with the life of the person written of." Defoe's method of bringing about this ethical result is rather elementary. He says :

> Throughout the infinite variety of this book, this fundamental is most strictly adhered to ; there is not a wicked action in any part of it, but is first or last rendered unhappy and unfortunate ; there is not a superlative villain brought upon the stage, but either he is brought to an unhappy end, or brought to be a penitent ; there is not an ill thing mentioned, but it is condemned, even in the relation, nor a virtuous, just thing, but it carries its praise along with it.

Not a picaresque novel   Except in its autobiographical procedure, incidents succeeding each other with the chance disconnexion of real life, there is nothing of the picaresque in *Moll Flanders*. The heroine is a rogue, but not one rejoicing in her rogueries : quite the contrary. To the modern reader, her life is a serious study of the effects of heredity and environment in the making of criminals. "The offspring of debauchery and vice," " debauched from her youth," gives an account of " the particular occasions and circumstances by which she first became wicked, and of all

[1] It did not come out till 27th Jan. 1722.

the progressions of crime which she ran through in threescore years." Defoe was evidently conscious of the sociological significance of the book, though he stresses mainly the warning to evil-doers, and even the practical result of putting honest people on their guard against the snares of modern cony-catchers.

From the artistic point of view, Moll Flanders may be regarded as the female counterpart of Robinson Crusoe. His history was a great realistic epic of human courage and energy fighting a lonely battle in the most desperate circumstances. She is the lonely woman cast upon her own resources, fighting a world that has done its worst to destroy her, body and soul. Born in shame, outcast from the cradle, damned by her very nativity to more than her portion of original sin, the weaker nature of a woman rendering her a more inevitable victim of the bad blood she has inherited, Moll is cruelly betrayed, meets with the blackest misfortune, and falls into vice and crime, all through the force of circumstances and the defective ordering of society. But she keeps the reader's sympathy, because her weaknesses are human, and even his esteem, because of her courage, her self-reliance, and a certain good-nature that no external ills can utterly stifle. Defoe, however, probably did not regard the work in this light. He was merely writing another entertaining and saleable book, but felt it incumbent on him to make it an improving one, and to seize any opportune occasion for showing up the evils of the penal system and other parts of the social machine. Numbers of criminal lives were pouring from the press, most of them written with a levity that was far more mischievous to the classes who read them than the most unmoral of the picaresque novels. These glorifications of villainy lacked the caustic wit of the Spanish genre ; they were entirely without any intellectual appeal, with no appeal whatever except to the basest instincts. Defoe, on the other hand, felt the profound human interest of such a life as Moll's, and, whilst he relied upon situations and incidents to attract his readers, his own absorption in his theme and his penetrating insight made the book another masterpiece.

As usual, Defoe throws the story into the autobiographical form, and asserts that he has merely edited a genuine history, changing the names, and toning down language that had too

" Moll Flanders" a distant parallel to " Robinson Crusoe "

Pretence at historicity

much of Newgate in it for modest readers. But the assertion is rather perfunctory, and only the more credulous could be expected to accept Moll's opening statement :

My true name is so well known in the records or registers at Newgate, and in the Old Bailey, and there are some things of such consequence still depending there, relating to my particular conduct, that it is not to be expected I should set my name or the account of my family to this work ; perhaps after my death it may be better known ; at present it would not be proper, no, not though a general pardon should be issued, even without exceptions of persons or crimes.

It is enough to tell you, that as some of my worst comrades, who are out of the way of doing me harm (having gone out of the world by the steps and the string, as I often expected to go), knew me by the name of Moll Flanders, so you may give me leave to go under that name till I dare own who I have been, as well as who I am.

The pretence that might be taken seriously is on the way to becoming a mere device for securing imaginative acceptance. Still, there were people then who were ready to believe in Moll. She was identified with a Lætitia Atkins, of Galway; her parents, her "governess" or accomplice, and two of her husbands were provided with names, habitations, and other particulars. Aitken, Defoe's editor, took the trouble to test the authority of two catchpenny publications that in this way exploited the popularity of the disreputable heroine, and could trace no such person. Yet, he agreed, it does not follow that Defoe did not base his story on the life of some real unfortunate, or that his original will never be discovered.

Moll, the victim of her social environment

Moll Flanders is the history of a sinner, one who becomes a sinner through being sinned against. The illegitimate daughter of a thief, she is undone by the son of the house in which she is a servant, and is allowed by him to marry his young brother, who has fallen in love with her. Moll feels natural repugnance, but there is no other escape from the predicament in which her hot blood has involved her. With the death of this first husband, she takes another of her unlucky matrimonial ventures. This time a spendthrift husband runs away from his creditors and his wife. Passing herself off as a widow, she marries a sea-captain, and the pair go to Virginia, where it comes out that this husband is her half-brother. Returning to England, she lives as an adventuress at Bath and becomes the mistress of a well-to-do man, who repents and leaves her. Then she catches a supposed man of fortune, who turns out to be a fortune-hunter. Mutually deceived, they separate good-humouredly, and Moll falls back on a devoted lover, whom she marries and lives with five years, when he dies, leaving her with two children and nothing to maintain them. It is in this desperate strait that the temptation to steal becomes too much for her. She prospers in this profession for twelve years, but at length is caught and sentenced to death. In Newgate she meets the highwayman who had married her for her non-existent money, and when the death-sentence is commuted to transportation they go together to Virginia. Her half-brother is still alive, and so is her son by him. Moll makes herself known to the latter, and on the death of his father is able to live honestly with the reformed highwayman. They prosper and come back to England. Moll was now nearly seventy and lived to a great age, " and was not so extraordinary a penitent as she was at first ; it seems only that indeed she always spoke with abhorrence of her former life, and of every part of it." Such is Defoe's observation in the preface. Moll herself always speaks of her lapses with exemplary abhorrence.

Defoe, in truth, lays more stress on her pangs of conscience *Her* than strict analysis of her moral history would justify. This was *moral* the result of his dutiful observance of the ordinance that a story *reflections* which depicted evil must somehow make it repugnant and in- *are out of* culcate an edifying lesson. Moll's moralizations are not in tune *character* with her character. Her mind is engrossed with other interests altogether ; her throes of compunction, acute at first, had no chance against the demands of a hungry and destitute mother. Defoe was less consistent than Bunyan, the historian of Mr Badman, who did not let his wrong-doer meditate on the wickedness of his actions. If his main object was to frame an indictment of society, it would have been better to have shown her becoming simply unmoral through being driven to such a pass that she could no longer afford the luxury of distinguishing right from wrong.

In other words, Defoe's study of Moll Flanders is not entirely objective. Sometimes it is Moll that is speaking, sometimes her creator putting his comments and cautions in her mouth. Here, for example, we cannot mistake the voice of Defoe :

And this is the cause why many times men as well as women, and men of the greatest and best qualities other ways, yet have found themselves weak in this part, and have not been able to bear the weight of a secret joy or of a secret sorrow, but have been obliged to disclose it, even for the mere giving vent to themselves, and to unbend the mind, oppressed with the weights which attended it . . . such people, had they struggled longer with the oppression, would certainly have told it in their sleep and disclosed the secret, let it have been of what fatal nature soever, without regard to the person to whom it might have been exposed. This necessity of nature is a thing which works sometimes with such vehemency in the minds of those who are guilty of any atrocious villainy, such as a secret murder in particular, that they have been obliged to discover it, though the consequence has been their own destruction.[1]

Defoe it is again, intent on his demonstration that crime is the inevitable product of a heartless and improvident society, who cries out in the words of the deserted and destitute woman :

O let none read this part without seriously reflecting on the circumstances of a desolate state, and how they would grapple with want of friends and want of bread ; it will certainly make them think not of sparing what they have only, but of looking up to heaven for support, and of the wise man's prayer, " Give me not poverty lest I steal."

Where Defoe is objective and true to life

But the incident to which this was the proem shows a true imagination. The starving woman passing a shop sees a small bundle on a stool near the counter, the maid-servant to whom it belonged standing with her back turned away, and the shop-man on the counter reaching up to a top shelf, and his face also turned away.

This was the bait ; and the devil who laid the snare prompted me, as if he had spoke, for I remember, and shall never forget

[1] *Moll Flanders*, ed. E. A. Baker, p. 179.

it, 'twas like a voice spoken over my shoulder, " Take the bundle ;
be quick ; do it this moment." It was no sooner said but I
stepped into the shop, and with my back to the wench, as if
I had stood up for a cart that was going by, I put my hand
behind me and took the bundle, and went off with it, the maid or
fellow not perceiving me, or any one else.

It was her first theft, and it completely unnerved her.

It is impossible to express the horror of my soul all the
while I did it. When I went away I had no heart to run, or
scarce to mend my pace. I crossed the street indeed, and went
down the first turning I came to, and I think it was a street
that went through into Fenchurch Street ; from thence I
crossed and turned through so many ways and turnings, that I
could never tell which way it was, nor where it went ; I felt not
the ground I stepped on, and the farther I was out of danger
the faster I went, till, tired and out of breath, I was forced to
sit down on a little bench at a door, and then found I was got
into Thames Street, near Billingsgate. I rested me a little and
went on ; my blood was all in a fire ; my heart beat as if it was
in a sudden fright. In short, I was under such a surprise that
I knew not whither I was agoing, or what to do.[1]

What one can only describe metaphorically as a lack of atmos- *Defoe's*
phere in Defoe's stories, and especially in *Moll Flanders*, is due *lack of*
partly to his limitation of the interest to one central figure, *atmos-*
Robinson Crusoe, Moll, or Roxana, and, further, to his con- *phere*
centration of their attention and his on the matter in hand, on
what to do next, to the exclusion of everything else. The basic
problem of existence, how to exist, was so urgent in all Defoe's
books, that there was no room for the more trivial concerns
which were the main business of the average sentimental
novelist. His characters have no attention to spare for what
does not directly affect them ; they have no time to indulge in
emotion. Hence, though we may agree that Defoe puts his
characters in environments very familiar to himself, and that he
paints living realities,[2] the crowd killing time at Bath, the
debtors and bankrupts in the Mint, the inside of Newgate, the
animation of Bartholomew Fair, and other scenes typical of that
epoch, we also notice that he is far still from Fielding's power of

[1] *Moll Flanders*, p. 104.   [2] Dottin, p. 673.

impressing us with the sense of a whole world of crowded life. His social criticism is merely incidental, and so is his picturing of the world at large. His eye is by no means all-embracing. Through the eyes of his characters, through their direct contacts with their surroundings, we have glimpses which are vivid and authentic ; and we must build up for ourselves a realistic panorama from the materials so vouchsafed.

No doubt *Moll Flanders* and its pendant *Roxana* owe much of their strength to this simplicity and concentration ; but, at the same time, it is evident that Defoe's imagination was limited. There is nothing complex or subtle in either of these books, except perhaps in one episode in the latter where Roxana persuades her maid Amy to be ruined from an instinctive desire to drag her down to her own level. Defoe's cold-blooded matter-of-factness is as unvarying in the two novels dealing with women and affairs of gallantry as in those entirely engrossed in masculine themes. In *Robinson Crusoe* he never dwells on the imaginative significance of a situation, but sets down moving incident and meaningless detail with the same cool precision. Instances abound in his later stories of his curious lack of sensibility. Take one example, Moll's discovery that she is married to her half-brother. Here is material for tragedy, if you like ; to Defoe it is simply one of those unpleasant occurrences that dog a misspent life. He tells us that the heroine was horror-stricken, the husband fainted, and the mother was upset ; but he tells it with the same absence of emotional colour as he describes the monetary misfortunes that brought Moll Flanders to the gutter. The autobiographical form of all his stories, lending itself so readily to the free expression of feeling, makes the absence of it the more striking. The sordid, the horrible, the tragic never move a shudder in Defoe, though they may move him to preach, as a rule very superfluously. Impassibility to that degree, however, is a virtue compared with excess of sensibility. The reader finds a strength and grim impressiveness in this stark, phlegmatic realism which is to seek in the incurable sentimentality of most story-tellers.

It was apparently to Defoe's private interests in the occult that one remarkable exception is due, the touching account of

Moll's outbreak of grief and her experience of a supersensual   *An*
bond when she parts from her highwayman husband.   *occult*
incident

I sat down and looked upon these things two hours together,
and scarce spoke a word, till my maid interrupted me by telling
me my dinner was ready. I ate but little, and after dinner I
fell into a violent fit of crying, every now and then calling him
by his name, which was James. " O Jemmy ! " said I, " come
back, come back. I'll give you all I have ; I'll beg, I'll starve
with you." And thus I ran raving about the room several times,
and then sat down between whiles, and then walked about again,
called upon him to come back, and then cried again ; and thus
I passed the afternoon, till about seven o'clock, when it was near
dusk in the evening, being August, when, to my unspeakable
surprise, he comes back into the inn, and comes directly up
into my chamber.

I was in the greatest confusion imaginable, and so was he too.
I could not imagine what should be the occasion of it, and began
to be at odds with myself whether to be glad or sorry ; but my
affection biased all the rest, and it was impossible to conceal my
joy, which was too great for smiles, for it burst out into tears.
He was no sooner entered the room, but he ran to me and took
me in his arms, holding me fast, and almost stopping my breath
with his kisses, but spoke not a word. At length I began,
" My dear," said I, " how could you go away from me ? "—
to which he gave no answer, for it was impossible for him to
speak.

When our ecstasies were a little over, he told me he was gone
above fifteen miles, but it was not in his power to go any farther
without coming back to see me again and to take his leave of me
once more. I told him how I had passed the time, and how
loud I had called him to come back. He told me he heard me
very plain upon Delamere Forest, at a place about twelve miles
off. I smiled. " Nay," says he, " do not think I am in jest,
for if ever I heard your voice in my life, I heard you call me
aloud, and sometimes I thought I saw you running after me."
" Why," said I, " what did I say ? " For I had not named the
words to him. " You called aloud," says he, " and said, ' O
Jemmy ! O Jemmy ! come back, come back ! ' " I laughed at
him. " My dear," says he, " do not laugh, for, depend upon
it, I heard your voice as plain as you hear mine now ; if you
please, I'll go before a magistrate and make oath of it." I then
began to be amazed and surprized, and indeed frighted, and
told him what I had really done, and how I had called after him,

as above.   When we had amused ourselves a while about this, I said to him, " Well, you shall go away from me no more ; I'll go all over the world with you rather." [1]

" Due Preparations for the Plague "   The next issue of this wonderful year was an opportune work composed of useful information and illustrative anecdotes entitled, *Due Preparations for the Plague, as well for Soul as Body. Being some seasonable Thoughts upon the visible approach of the present dreadful Contagion in France ; the properest measures to prevent it, and the great work of submitting to it* (1722).   Defoe wrote no better example of domestic fiction with good characterization and dialogue, than in the part giving the history of a family of tradespeople who shut themselves up in a large house in Wood Street and lived there in retirement and godly exercises until the danger was past.   A month or two later the famous *Journal* dealing with the same subject was to appear, a work superior in unity and impressiveness, but having a similar object, to rouse and alarm, and to enforce the warning by a narrative that struck home.   This was quickly followed by a sociological treatise on a subject often ventilated in his novels ; it is entitled, *Religious Courtship : Being Historical Discourses on the Necessity of Marrying Religious Husbands and Wives only. As also of Husbands and Wives being of the same Opinions in Religion with one Another. With an Appendix of taking none but Religious Servants, and a Proposal for the better Managing of Servants.*   Defoe was very sure that the only happy marriages were those between pious persons holding the same religious views.   The book mingles instruction and exemplary fiction in the same manner as *The Family Instructor.*

" Journal of the Plague Year "   Next came *A Journal of the Plague Year : Being Observations or Memorials of the most Remarkable Occurrences, As well Publick as Private, Which happened in London During the last Visitation in 1665. Written by a Citizen, who continued all the while in London* (1722).   This, like the antecedent *Due Preparations*, was a literary venture suggested to Defoe by the Marseilles plague of 1720, which carried off a hundred thousand persons and excited apprehensions in this country of a similar visitation

---

[1] *Moll Flanders*, p. 82.

here. In obedience to a royal order, Dr Richard Mead published a *Short Discourse Concerning Pestilential Contagion* [1] immediately after the Marseilles news reached England. This was followed by several admonitory works by eminent physicians and others, including the translation by Dr John Quincy, under the title of *Loimologia : or, An Historical Account of the Plague in London in 1665 : with precautionary Directions against the like Contagion*, of a Latin work by Dr Nathaniel Hodges which had appeared in 1672. Defoe was late in the field : he had been busy with his other works, as we have seen. But he now followed the lead given him by these weightier authorities, well aware that books like *Due Preparations* or the *Journal*, spiced with anecdote and from the pen of a popular writer, would have at least as large a circulation. No doubt the cautionary attitude he assumed was something of a pose ; Defoe was always more interested in profits than prophecy. But he did not assume it without having faith in the practical advice that he offered.

The *Journal of the Plague Year* is a first-rate example of historical fiction, and, in spite of great and obvious differences in the character of the story told, was constructed on the same lines as those followed in *Memoirs of a Cavalier*.[2] Like the memoirs and histories of Courtilz de Sandras, it purports to be an authentic narrative. It is based on documents and recollections, and through the experiences of the imaginary narrator it paints a picture superior in its general truth and dramatic energy to that of any historian. The sources from which Defoe obtained his facts are not difficult to determine : they have been

Historical fiction : its sources

[1] In the revised edition of 1744 Mead referred to Defoe's popular account of the Plague in his *Journal*, a reference that has given rise to the absurd idea that Mead was indebted to Defoe instead of *vice versa* (Watson Nicholson, pp. 4-8).

[2] Dr Watson Nicholson, in *The Historical Sources of Defoe's Journal of the Plague Year* (1919), flatly asserts that it is history not fiction, after writing an excellent little book establishing the contrary. "The simple truth is, however, there is not a single essential statement in the *Journal* not based on historic fact." No doubt ; and the same may be said of any good historical novel, if not of the majority. He also points out that even the stories told by Defoe's imaginary narrator are founded on fact. Certainly, and that only goes to show how admirably Defoe wrote historical fiction. Merely basing a story on fact does not make it history. Dr Nicholson reminds us of the verdict of the Colonial judge: "On the arguments put forward by Mr Brandon, the decision is against him."

catalogued by his editor and others.[1] Hodges's *Loimologia* has
already been mentioned. This, short as it is, Defoe followed
closely and fruitfully. He even reproduced the errors.[2] There
was no end to his esteem for this wise and unselfish physician,
whose portrait is probably to be recognized in Dr Heath, who
gives such excellent advice to the journalist of the Plague.
Mead's *Short Discourse* was his manual in the frequent discussions on causes and remedies. The portents and prodigies may
have been borrowed from John Gadbury's tract, *Londons Deliverance Praedicted ; in a Short Discourse on Plagues in general*
(1665), written whilst the pestilence was raging. But Defoe was
so well versed in supernatural lore that this identification is
perhaps unwarranted. William Austin's poetical *Anatomy of the
Pestilence* (1665) may have furnished the legends of the diggers
who stripped the dead and that of the drunken piper who was
all but interred. One of the most grandiloquent and emotional
utterances of the time was the Nonconformist preacher Thomas
Vincent's jeremiad, *God's Terrible Voice in the City* (1667),
which deals with both the Plague and the Fire, regarding both
as the Almighty's chastisement of a wicked people. The terror
of the population, the vast numbers of the dead, the corpses
huddled into pits, the insane behaviour of many individuals, and
the moral effect during the visitation and after, are depicted
with a power less restrained than Defoe's.[3] Other possible
sources are Kemp's *Brief Treatise of the Nature, Causes, Signes,
Preservation from, and Cure of the Pestilence* (1665), George
Thomson's *Loimotomia, or the Pest Anatomized* (1666), and the
anonymous *Golgotha ; or, a Looking-Glass for London and the
Suburbs thereof, Shewing the Causes, Nature and Efficacy of the
present Plague, and the most hopeful Way for Healing* (1665).
Besides these, he had before him, as every reader of the *Journal*
sees at a glance, the weekly Bills of Mortality, the orders and
notices issued by the city and parish authorities, and the

Legends

---

[1] Aitken's introduction to the *Journal of the Plague Year* (1895), Watson
Nicholson's *Historical Sources of Defoe's Journal*, etc.

[2] Watson Nicholson, p. 71.

[3] Dr Watson Nicholson thinks it superior. "Not for one moment can his
[Defoe's] work be compared, in richness of materials, sincerity, and eloquent
pathos, with one of his chief sources, namely, Thomas Vincent's *God's Terrible
Voice in the City* " (*Ibid.*, pp. 76-77).

instructions circulated by the College of Physicians. Newspapers and other fugitive printed matter must have supplied him with many details, and there were also the recollections of survivors. Finally, there is no reason to doubt his own statement that he "very particularly" remembered the event,[1] though as he would have been only six years old his remembrance would be chiefly of the tales he had listened to in the years immediately following.

Here then, as elsewhere, Defoe was provided with masses of material, which he handled with his usual eclectic freedom. Here, too, as in *Robinson Crusoe*, he had a certain literary tradition behind him. For as there were Crusoe stories before *Robinson Crusoe*, so there were descriptions by earlier men of letters of famous visitations of pestilence in London and in other great cities. Defoe may perchance have read the account of the plague in Athens by Thucydides, of that in Jerusalem by Josephus, and of others hardly less celebrated; he may have been not quite unacquainted with the pamphlets in which Nashe and Dekker had expatiated with grim picturesqueness on similar catastrophes. His *Journal* is the last and finest of a number of powerful imaginative descriptions of a crowded city stricken with plague. For his facts we can see what records he had access to; to what extent he deliberately or unconsciously emulated the literary effects of his predecessors we can only guess.

The *Journal* unquestionably succeeds in giving the impression that it is by one who lived through that awful time. It is badly put together; it is fuller than Defoe's other books of inaccuracies, oversights, repetitions, and other signs of carelessness.[2] Though it would be absurd to suggest that Defoe introduced these on purpose, yet the apparent clumsiness and lack of literary skill only deepens the air of veracity in the homely record of his experiences by the Coleman Street saddler. Large parts of the book are cast into a statistical form; they read more like a Blue

General character of the "Journal"

---

[1] Defoe's introduction to the *Journal*.

[2] M. Dottin has counted up many of these. Defoe speaks sixteen times of persons stricken with disease who throw open their windows and shriek with agony; six times of those who, gone mad, run about the streets naked; fifteen times of persons who unwittingly carry about on them the germs of the plague; four times of the fatalism of the people; five times of the epidemic considered as a judgment of God, etc. (Dottin, iii., p. 611).

Book than anything else. This prosaic evidence, alternating with the descriptions of appalling events and corroborating their exactitude, are a large factor in the strange impressiveness of the book. For the rest, accounts of piteous or terror-striking incidents alternate with descriptions of the sights encountered by day and night, the desolate aspect of the city, the deserted streets with the shops closely shuttered, a few poor souls flitting by and shrinking from each other in deadly fear, plague-polluted bodies lying about the pavements, dreadful faces at the windows, the ghastly bell-man and his cry, " Bring out your dead! " and the dead-cart heaped with corpses to be shot indiscriminately into the public grave. There is no lack of atmosphere here. It is all invested with apocalyptic gloom. Defoe's fondness for tales of the supernatural served him well. The blazing star or comet that appeared several months before the plague, the poor wretches who ran about half-naked crying, by night and day, " O! the great and the dreadful God ! " the rumours of warning voices and of shapes and figures in the clouds, give to the *Journal* sensations of horror only to be matched in Bunyan's visions of destruction and the Book of Revelation.

Char-acter-drawing

The gloom is not all unrelieved ; the story told by the old Puritan saddler is a very human one. Compared with Defoe's previous historical novel, *Memoirs of a Cavalier*, the character-drawing is notably superior. The narrator himself is no mere figment nor a mere alias for Defoe. He is one of those sober, shrewd, God-fearing citizens whom Defoe regarded as the salt of the earth. He takes a man's part in the fearful emergency. He preaches earnestly to those who in their despair yield themselves to crime and debauchery ; he accepts the dangerous office of district inspector, and looks after the property of his fugitive brother. Curiosity and a sense of duty, reinforced by a firm belief that he is under divine protection, conduct him into the most hazardous situations. But he frankly admits his frequent misgivings : how he " generally came frighted and terrified home," yet could not restrain his desire to see what was happening in the town ; how he talked threateningly to the women whom he found plundering his brother's shop, but was afraid to proceed to extremities lest they should take the law into their own hands.

His doubts whether the official figures were to be trusted, his efforts to check every report, inspire confidence in his veracity.

Other life-like figures in the book are his friend Dr Heath, the under-sexton and gravedigger John Hayward, and the merry piper who is picked up dead-drunk, and only comes to when he finds himself in the cart among the dead bodies. Then there is the lively episode of the biscuit-maker, the sail-maker, and the joiner, who set out from Wapping—on a later page Defoe says Stepney—and try to escape into the country. After various accidents they are confronted by the watch at Walthamstow, but not to be turned back they arm themselves with muskets cut in the hedge and pretend to be a large force determined to make their way into Essex. Eventually they are allowed to settle down on the outskirts of Epping till the end of the plague. But the most picturesque of the many persons individualized is the Quaker Solomon Eagle, who went about denouncing judgment on the city. The Quakers were noted for these eccentricities, and Defoe either had some individual in mind or imagined a typical figure.[1] Pepys describes an incident in Westminster Hall, under date 29th July 1667 :

One thing extraordinary was, this day a man, a Quaker, came naked through the Hall, only very civilly tied about the privities to avoid scandal, and with a chafing-dish of fire and brimstone burning upon his head, did pass through the Hall, crying, " Repent ! repent ! " [2]

Parallels to this and similar characters and scenes have been pointed out in Austin's *Anatomy of the Pestilence* and George Wither's *Britain's Remembrancer*.[3]

Defoe's prose style has been variously judged.[4] There is no better example of the strength and versatility of his homespun than the journal attributed to the pen of the worthy saddler. Two passages are enough to quote; the first relates the *Defoe's prose*

[1] Watson Nicholson (pp. 14-15) identifies him or his original with a noted Quaker prognosticator, John Gibson.
[2] *Diary*, ed. H. B. Wheatley, vii., p. 44.
[3] Watson Nicholson, pp. 16-18.
[4] The extreme academic point of view is represented by Dr Watson Nicholson, who says, " Viewed from the point of style and art, the work is execrable " (*Historical Sources*, p. 90).

heart-rending incident of a mother's discovery that her daughter has caught the infection.

While the bed was airing, the mother undressed the young woman, and just as she was laid down in the bed, she, looking upon her body with a candle, immediately discovered the fatal tokens on the inside of her thighs. Her mother, not being able to contain herself, threw down her candle, and screeched out in such a frightful manner, that it was enough to place horror upon the stoutest heart in the world ; nor was it one scream, or one cry, but the fright having seized her spirits, she fainted first, then recovered, then ran all over the house, up the stairs and down the stairs, like one distracted, and continued screeching and crying out for several hours, void of all sense, or, as I was told, never came thoroughly to herself again. As to the young maiden, she was a dead corpse from that moment ; for the gangrene, which occasions the spots, had spread over her whole body, and she died in less than two hours. But still the mother continued crying out, not knowing anything more of her child, several hours after she was dead. It is so long ago, that I am not certain, but I think the mother never recovered, but died in two or three weeks after.[1]

The next (describes, as if by an eye-witness, a still more appalling incident. The saddler has obtained admittance to a churchyard, as the dead-cart enters, and sees " a man go to and again, muffled up in a brown cloak, and making motions with his hands under his cloak, as if he was in great agony."

When the buriers came up to him, they soon found he was neither a person infected and desperate, as I have observed above, or a person distempered in mind, but one oppressed with a dreadful weight of grief indeed, having his wife and several children, all in the cart, that was just come in with him, and he followed in an agony and excess of sorrow. He mourned heartily, as it was easy to see, but with a kind of masculine grief that could not give itself vent by tears ; and, calmly desiring the buriers to let him alone, said he would only see the bodies thrown in and go away, so they left importuning him ; but no sooner was the cart turned round, and the bodies shot into the pit promiscuously, which was a surprise to him, for he at least expected they would have been decently laid in, though indeed

1 Bohn's ed., pp. 42-43.

he was afterwards convinced that was impracticable ; I say, no sooner did he see the sight, but he cried out aloud, unable to contain himself. I could not hear what he said, but he went backward two or three steps and fell down in a swoon ; the buriers ran to him and took him up, and in a little while he came to himself, and they led him away to the Pye-tavern, over against the end of Houndsditch, where, it seems, the man was known, and where they took care of him. He looked into the pit again, as he went away, but the buriers had covered the bodies so immediately with throwing in earth, that though there was light enough, for there were lanthorns and candles in them, placed all night round the sides of the pit, upon the heaps of earth, seven or eight, or perhaps more, yet nothing could be seen.

This was a mournful sight indeed, and affected me almost as much as the rest ; but the other was awful and full of terror ; the cart had in it sixteen or seventeen bodies, some were wrapt up in linen sheets, some in rugs, some little other than naked, or so loose, that what covering they had fell from them in the shooting out of the cart, and they fell quite naked among the rest ; but the matter was not much to them, or the indecency much to any one else, seeing they were all dead, and were to be huddled together into the common grave of mankind, as we may well call it, for here was no difference made, but poor and rich went together ; there was no other way of burials, neither was it possible there should, for coffins were not to be had for the prodigious numbers that fell in such a calamity as this.[1]

This, it will be noted, is not the cold-blooded manner of *Moll Flanders* and other books. The narrator keeps his feelings under restraint ; he does not ignore them. But the prose is essentially the same as that of Defoe's other works. Literature has never gone more completely unadorned. Dryden had described his own plain style as derived from the refined conversation of Charles the Second's Court.[2] Defoe's style, which he too created for his own use, had a humbler origin, in the coarse but racy speech of the people. In both cases the colloquial language of the day was avowedly the foundation. The development of style, like the development of fiction, had started again, as it were, from the

Origin of his style

[1] Bohn's ed., pp. 47-48.
[2] *Defence of the Epilogue* (1672), see *Essays of John Dryden*, ed. W. P. Ker, i., p. 164.

beginning. The language was completely assimilated to the common currency, and it was accordingly possible to represent life as it actually is. Defoe's single aim was to tell his story plainly, to state the facts clearly, and let the manner of the statement go. He sought neither grace nor polish ; he let correctness wait upon clarity ; his pages bristle with the solecisms and slipshod phrases of everyday speech. But through this transparent medium we see life portrayed exactly as he saw it. He was one of those who achieved style by aiming at something beyond it.

"*Colonel Jacque*" Fictitious biography claimed Defoe again in his next work, published towards the end of the year. He gave a list of more than the contents in the title, *The History and Remarkable life of the truly Honourable Colonel Jacque, vulgarly called Col. Jack, who was born a Gentleman, put 'Prentice to a Pick-pocket, flourished six and twenty years as a Thief, and was then kidnapped to Virginia ; came back a Merchant, was five times married to four Whores, went into the Wars, behaved bravely, got preferment, was made Colonel of a Regiment, came over and fled with the Chevalier, is still Abroad completing a Life of Wonders, and resolves to die a General* (1722). The end of the book is not in accordance with the promise.

This life of an outcast related by himself in after years resembles *Moll Flanders* in portraying one led into dishonesty and crime through a bad upbringing, and the first part is a realistic and sympathetic study of manners and social conditions ; but the later career of the hero is a series of aimless and insipid adventures, in which Defoe betrays the recent influence of *Gil Blas*, which had been translated in 1716. Another difference from the story of Moll is that the hero, even in the midst of his misfortunes and the odium of his rascalities, aspires to be a gentleman and to retrieve his good name. Neither book is a picaresque story in the ordinary sense, though the Colonel's later career has touches of that style. In the preface Defoe declares that his object is twofold : to show the nation how thousands of unhappy youths are ruined through the lack of proper education, and to demonstrate that the only good end of a misspent life is repentance, which brings with it comfort and hope.

The illegitimate offspring of two persons of quality, the lad

THE LATER FICTION OF DEFOE 207

is brought up by a baby-farmer, who has a son of her own, also *Outline* called John, and presently receives another unfortunate child of *of the* the same name. Thus there are three Jacques, nicknamed the *story* Captain, the Colonel, and the Major. Colonel Jacque describes himself as a " poor, unhappy, tractable dog, willing enough, and capable too, to learn anything, if he had had any but the devil for his schoolmaster." The Captain was " sly, sullen, reserved, malicious, and resentful ; and, withal, he was brutish, bloody, and cruel in his disposition." But the Major was a most engaging lad, merry, facetious, pleasant, with a good share of wit, and " had something of the gentleman in him." He was also courageous, " and could look death in the face without any hesitation " ; his generous and compassionate nature was the opposite to the Captain's, and " he wanted nothing but honesty to have made him an excellent man." These three, by the death of their protectress, are left homeless and friendless in the East End of London. Colonel Jacque runs wild about the city, herds with thieves, and becomes an expert thief before he has learnt that stealing is not an honest trade. Defoe may possibly have had the career of an actual thief to work upon in writing *Colonel Jacque.* However that may be, his picture of the submerged world of London, and the particularity with which he describes the ways of the criminal classes, prove him to have been thoroughly familiar with the subject. No one was to depict the mean streets and the lower classes of the metropolis with such power and truth till the advent of Dickens. In this book, and occasionally in *Moll Flanders,* Defoe seasons the dialogue with thieves' slang.

The young street-arab has some success as a pickpocket, and after behaving very adroitly over a pocket-book stuffed with banknotes, which he steals and then pretends to recover from another member of the gang for a reward, finds himself in possession of a substantial sum. The dialogue with the owner and still more the episode of his losing the money are scenes that led Charles Lamb to praise this part of *Colonel Jacque* as " the most affecting, natural picture of a young thief that was ever drawn."

Never having had such an amount of money before, the boy is *A* at his wits' end where to bestow it. He cannot sleep in his usual *touching* lair on the warm ashes of the glass-house, in Rosemary Lane or *incident*

Ratcliff Highway, for fear of being robbed by the other boys. At last he thinks he will hide it in some hole in a tree. He finds a likely one near a footpath across the fields to Bethnal Green, climbs up and drops his treasure in. But the tree is hollow. His money slips away, and do what he will he cannot reach it. He climbs up again and again, and tries to reach the packet of money with a stick ; but all to no purpose. Then, happening to come down on the other side, he suddenly sees his money, for the tree had a great open place in it, and the package had fallen down close to the ground. He goes on :

I was but a child, and I rejoiced as a child, for I hollo'd quite out aloud when I saw it ; then I run to it, and snatched it up, hugged and kissed the dirty rag a hundred times ; then danced and jumped about, run from one end of the field to the other, and, in short, I knew not what, much less do I know now what I did, though I shall never forget the thing, either what a sinking grief it was to my heart, when I thought I had lost it, or what a flood of joy overwhelmed me when I had got it again.

While I was in the first transport of my joy, as I have said, I run about, and knew not what I did ; but when that was over I sat down, opened the foul clout the money was in, looked at it, told it, found it was all there, and then I fell a-crying as savourly as I did before, when I thought I had lost it.

In due course he takes to the road, and narrowly escapes with his neck as a highwayman. He finds himself in Edinburgh ; but kilts do not favour pickpockets, nor did the magistrates, and he enlists. But Jacque deserts when the troops are ordered to Flanders, and at Newcastle is kidnapped and carried to Virginia, where for a time he works as a slave on a plantation. But he is given his freedom and appointed overseer, a job he hates, for discipline was maintained by a cruel use of the lash. Jack prospers and becomes the owner of a plantation. He sends to England for the money he had deposited in safety, the proceeds of his robberies. But the ship is wrecked, and his awakening conscience sees in this loss the just punishment for his misdeeds. As a nameless waif he had been told that he was of gentle parentage, and he determines to live up to the standard of virtue due to his descent.

But from this point the interest is not equal to Defoe's good intentions. Jacque decides to revisit England, but is captured by *Conclu-* the French, enters the service of Louis XIV., goes through the *sion of* Italian campaign of 1701-1702, and making the acquaintance of *the story* the Pretender takes part in the Jacobite attempt of 1715. Later he receives a pardon from George I. The latter half of his story is concerned with his military and trading adventures and also his adventures in gallantry and wedlock, which are as unfortunate in their result as they are uninteresting to read about. In the military portions of Colonel Jacque's history, Defoe followed the authorities in the same way as he had done in *Memoirs of a Cavalier* and was shortly to do again in *Captain Carleton*.[1] Divers well-known personages of the time, such as Sir William Turner, president of Bridewell, the goldsmith, Sir John Sweetapple, and the military leaders in the various campaigns, appear incidentally. Major Jacque is declared to be the same as the bandit Anthony who was broken on the wheel at Paris, after a notorious career. It is noteworthy that when he comes to England incognito, before the 'Fifteen, the Colonel adopts the name of Charnock, that of the Jacobite executed in 1696. But these are the easier tricks of realism, and mere trifles in comparison with the meticulous care with which Defoe had studied the topography of Virginia, where he had never been, and the historical details into which his hero's adventures fitted as if he had really taken part in them as he alleged.

He adopted the methods of Courtilz de Sandras in the semi- *"Rox-* historical parts of *Colonel Jacque* ; in his next work of fiction he *ana"* drew a flashy adventuress who cuts a figure in London society outrivalling the celebrated impostor Mary Carleton, whose memoirs may have given him his cue. But he also had before him as popular examples of the novel of gallantry the various histories and semi-fictitious memoirs of Mrs Aphra Behn, Mrs Manley, and Mrs Haywood. There is a very close analogy

[1] It is my opinion that not a great deal of research would be required to show that the continental adventures of the Cavalier and of Colonel Jacque are based upon public histories and newspapers just as the Carleton story is. . . . The three narratives, those of the Cavalier, Colonel Jacque, and Carleton, are alike in substance, giving attention chiefly to the larger features of the campaigns which could be found in printed records, and setting forth their hero's adventures in the same style and with similar details (Secord, p. 211).

between the novel called for short *Roxana* and *The Adventures of Rivella*, in which Mrs Manley embellished fact with fiction in the supposed memoirs of a courtesan, identified more or less with herself. Defoe's preface announced that the foundation is laid in truth of fact, " and so the work is not a story, but a history." He adds that the scene is laid so near where the events actually took place that it was essential " to conceal names and persons, lest what cannot be yet entirely forgot in that part of the town should be remembered," and the actors recognized. Thus the book must be put among the secret histories, personages both living and deceased being hinted at discreetly. Defoe changed his plan more than once before he cut the story short rather than concluded it, and so he made havoc of the chronology. Roxana could not have been the mistress of Charles II., as suggested, since she was only twelve years old when he died. The latter and more engrossing part of the book is so carelessly constructed that the reader has to cast about to pick up the threads. Defoe related twice over how his heroine left England and was established in Holland, the scene of her final experiences, harking back in between to set forth at length the sensational events before her departure. In the best of the continuations, the one added in 1745 by an unknown but very skilful writer, much of this ground has to be gone over again.

Defoe, the journalist in a hurry, was always happy-go-lucky in his methods of composition. He evidently never troubled to work out a scheme beforehand. It has been seriously contended that the most interesting portions of both *Robinson Crusoe* and *Captain Singleton*, the adventures on the island in the one and the crossing of Africa in the other, were not foreseen at the beginning, but that their great possibilities dawned upon him as he wrote.[1] Such a speculation in the latter case is not unlikely, however incredible it may seem in the other. At all events, the best things in *Roxana* have every appearance of being afterthoughts. Had Defoe realized at an earlier stage the immense opportunities latent in the situations which Roxana's improbity was sure to bring about, had he made due provision for seizing the opportunities and developing the situations, he

[1] Secord, p. 162.

might have achieved something as great in a different way as his masterpiece, *Robinson Crusoe*. For, by accident instead of foresight, he happened in this case to produce a story having the complications, the dilemmas, the surprising, pathetic, and ironical crises that are usually prepared long ahead by means of a symmetrical plot. But, unfortunately, he had not thought out a plot. Through faulty workmanship, this is not one of Defoe's best novels ; but it is the one in which he took his longest stride forward in the art of dramatic narration.

In full it is entitled, *The Fortunate Mistress : Or, A History of the Life and Vast Variety of Fortunes of Mademoiselle de Beleau, Afterwards Call'd The Countess of Wintelsheim, in Germany, Being the Person known by the Name of the Lady Roxana, in the Time of King Charles II.*[1] (1724). Born in Poitou about 1673, Roxana—she was hailed by that heroic name later on in her days of splendour—was brought to England by her parents, who were Huguenot refugees. At the age of fifteen she was married to a wealthy brewer, to whom she brought a dowry. He was an easy-going, extravagant person, who ran through her money and his, and going bankrupt absconded, leaving her penniless, with five children. These she managed to plant upon his reluctant relatives, and she now prepared herself to face a world that had wronged her by arbitrarily depriving her of her little fortune.

Roxana's story

Being now without encumbrances, she first enters into an alliance with a prosperous jeweller, and goes with him as his wife to France ; she finds herself much admired at Paris and Versailles, but is again left in the lurch through the murder of her lover. The murderers are disappointed of their booty, for Roxana has his case of diamonds, which she unscrupulously keeps, together with all the sums of money she can lay hands on. She also sends to England for her devoted servant, Amy, who brings over all that is of value in the jeweller's house. Roxana is now set up with a fortune of at least £10,000: she is a woman after Defoe's own heart in the miserly exactitude

[1] Wintelsheim may stand for Windesheim, three or four miles from Zwolle, capital of the province of Overyssel. The castle of Windesheim, built about 1690, on the remains of an old monastery, has interesting archives which await investigation.

with which she keeps account throughout of her ill-gotten gains. She grows famous as the pretty widow of Poitou, and attracts the attentions of an amorous prince. For two years she enjoys a brilliant life as his mistress ; then the prince, summoned to his wife's deathbed, vows to reform, and Roxana is again cast adrift. But this time her nest is well feathered. She still has the jeweller's diamonds ; the prince's generosity has loaded her with gifts. But avarice is almost her undoing. In an attempt to dispose of them the diamonds are recognized, and Roxana is threatened with prosecution. In this perilous emergency she is rescued by a Dutch merchant, who follows her to Holland, where she has found a safe market for her spoils, and offers to marry her. But Roxana has learnt to prize her freedom ; she is a believer in women's emancipation. She accepts the man, but declines wedlock ; has a son by him, and rather than change her mind about marriage, lets the Dutchman go.

Now comes the most garish period of Roxana's career. Beautiful and rich, but still ambitious, she fulfils her fond dream of returning to England. She sends Amy in advance to procure and furnish a large house in Pall Mall, where she gives herself out to be a French lady of high rank, and is visited by all the fashionable world. Noblemen and royalties appear at her gaming-tables ; she lives apparently with the utmost prodigality, but farming her capital under the guidance of the financier Sir Robert Clayton, and adding to it by the sale of her person. In seven years she finds herself a wealthy woman, but still insatiable. The tale of her gallantries need not be dwelt on ; it is to a reader nowadays only the dull prelude to the real drama. But in the course of this episode, which was of course much savoured by Defoe's public, he inserts some incidents that are afterwards to have momentous consequences. Roxana, as the fruit of her many amours, has had a number of children. Apparently she, and certainly the reader, fails to keep count of them. But those of her first marriage whom she had left in charge of their relations now come to light. She makes a fairly generous provision for each, without disclosing her identity. One of her sons is a servant in the next-door mansion in Pall Mall ; a daughter is cook-maid in her own household. Both are witnesses to the brilliance and profligacy of the Lady Roxana, and are destined to bring fatal evidence against her in years to come.

After further vicissitudes, Roxana realizes that her day is over. She meets the Dutch merchant again, who once more offers marriage, rather in order to legitimate their son than out of affection for the now faded beauty. She keeps him for a while in suspense, for there is a momentary hope of a more magnificent alliance. But when the merchant figures up his possessions, and promises to buy a title of nobility in Holland and a baronetcy in this country, she can no longer resist. It is at this moment, when she has before her the prospect of a dignified and opulent refuge for her latter days in another land, far from any whisper of infamy, that her past arises, like an avenging ghost, menacing complete disaster. Her children had accepted their portions, and all but one were content to live in obscure stations without inquiring after their parents. But the girl who had been a domestic in Roxana's own establishment refused to be hoodwinked. At first she thinks that Amy, the dispenser of the mysterious bounty, must be her mother; and when Amy denies it she scents more behind, and at length gets on the right track. Like a sleuth-hound, like a vindictive fury, she pursues the terrified Roxana, who expects every moment that all will come out, the desertion of her children, her fame as a noted courtesan, and that the Dutchman will contumeliously withdraw his offer. She hides herself in the back streets of the City; she takes lodgings with a Quaker lady whom she makes her friend by half-divulging her secret and loading her with presents. Married to the honest Dutchman, she prepares to sail for Holland, and goes aboard the vessel to see her cabin. What is her dismay to meet her daughter, who is an intimate friend of the captain's wife! The daughter is hot on the scent, but has not yet identified her mother. Roxana cannot avoid saluting her.

Dramatic complications inadequately resolved

I cannot but take notice here, that notwithstanding there was a secret horror upon my mind, and I was ready to sink when I came close to her to salute her, yet it was a secret inconceivable pleasure to me when I kissed her, to know that I kissed my own child, my own flesh and blood, born of my body, and who I had

214 HISTORY OF THE ENGLISH NOVEL

never kissed since I took the fatal farewell of them all, with a million of tears, and a heart almost dead with grief, when Amy and the good woman took them all away, and went with them to Spitalfields. No pen can describe, no words can express, I say, the strange impression which this thing made upon my spirits. I felt something shoot through my blood, my heart fluttered, my head flashed, and was dizzy, and all within me, as I thought, turned about, and much ado I had not to abandon myself to an excess of passion at the first sight of her, much more when my lips touched her face. I thought I must have taken her in my arms and kissed her again a thousand times, whether I would or no.[1]

A powerful situation

All nearly comes out when the two women call upon Roxana at the Quaker's, and there is mention of a famous Turkish robe which she had worn in her palmy days and danced in before half the Court. The mischief was that the Quaker had seen the robe among the belongings of the disguised Roxana. The visitors admired her morning vest.

This gown or vest put the girl's tongue a running again. . . . " This is just such a thing as I told you," says she, " the lady danced in." " What," says the captain's wife, " the Lady Roxana that you told me of ? Oh ! that's a charming story," says she, " tell it to my lady." I could not avoid saying so too, though from my soul I wished her in heaven for but naming it ; nay, I won't say but if she had been carried t'other way it had been much as one to me, if I could but have been rid of her, and her story too, for, when she came to describe the Turkish dress, it was impossible but the Quaker, who was a sharp, penetrating creature, should receive the impression in a more dangerous manner than the girl, only that indeed she was not so dangerous a person ; for if she had known it all, I could more freely have trusted her than I could the girl, by a great deal, nay, I should have been perfectly easy in her. However, as I have said, her talk made me dreadfully uneasy, and the more when the captain's wife mentioned but the name of Roxana. What my face might do towards betraying me I knew not, because I could not see myself, but my heart beat as if it would have jumped out at my mouth, and my passion was so great, that, for want of vent, I thought I should have burst. In a word, I was in a kind of silent rage, for the force

[1] *Roxana*, p. 358.

I was under of restraining my passion was such as I never felt the like of. I had no vent, nobody to open myself to, or to make a complaint to, for my relief. I durst not leave the room by any means, for then she would have told all the story of Roxana, that is to say, of myself, and not know at the same time whether she was in earnest or in jest, whether she knew me or no ; or, in short, whether I was to be exposed or not exposed.[1]

The Quaker is a very taking creature. She might have been own sister to Singleton's William Walters. She is not strongly individualized—Defoe's characters seldom are—but at any rate she always speaks in character. Too shrewd not to see there is something behind all this fuss, too discreet and aware which side her own interests lie to give her friend away, she behaves very jesuitically. " Says the kind Quaker, ' if she had any view towards thee, that's no business of mine ; and I should be far from desiring thee to inform me.' " And when the persistent Susan comes again to cross-question her, and asks what has become of her perfidious mother and whether she has not a favourite servant called Amy—Amy who had acted as her go-between ?—

" Why, truly," says the Quaker, with a very happy turn of wit, " I do not like to be examined ; but lest thou shouldest take up any mistakes by reason of my backwardness to speak, I will answer thee for once, that what her woman's name is I know not, but they call her Cherry."

Roxana observes, " My husband gave her that name in jest on our wedding-day, and we had called her by it ever after ; so that she spoke literally true at that time."

The girl goes on to tell the whole story of the notorious Lady Roxana, which she knew at first-hand as a servant in the house. " My good friend the Quaker," Roxana relates, " though terribly shocked at the story, and not well knowing what to say, yet was too much my friend to seem convinced in a thing she did not know to be true, and which, if it was true, she could see plainly I had a mind should not be known." And when cornered, she was far too cautious to tell a downright lie, but always managed to be non-committal, and to assert something that was true if taken in the most favourable sense.

Abrupt end of the story

Leslie Stephen, who on the whole treated Defoe very unkindly, was impressed by the fever of suspense and apprehension in which Defoe leaves us on the eve of Roxana's departure for Holland.[1] Panic-struck by the tireless pursuit, and expecting full exposure at any moment, she wishes for anything that would relieve her from her tormentor. Amy, in spite of her mistress's half-hearted remonstrances, swears that she will put her enemy out of the way. Amy disappears. In a day or two the girl also is missing ; and the conscience-stricken mother is left in doubt whether Amy has carried out her threat to murder the girl, or whether the girl has escaped to expose her to her husband. Defoe left the question obscure, and perfunctorily wound up the story with the brief statement that Roxana arrived in Holland, where, " After some years of flourishing and outwardly happy circumstances, I fell into a dreadful course of calamities, and Amy also ; the very reverse of our former good days. The blast of Heaven seemed to follow the injury done the poor girl by us both, and I was brought so low again, that my repentance seemed to be only the consequence of my misery, as my misery was of my crime." [2] Defoe's readers would not leave it thus, and a number of sequels were provided, the only one of which worth considering is that of 1745, which reconstructs the whole episode on rather different lines.

Defoe's failure to prepare for his crises

Not till Godwin wrote *Caleb Williams* was there to be another story exciting the same emotional tension, the same sensations of mystery and suspense, distracted flight and relentless pursuit. But Godwin prepared his climax by calculated steps. Defoe ran his head against it. The haphazard way in which he lighted upon a situation and his inability to perceive the inherent drama are illustrated by his failure to make anything out of other promising conjunctures. Earlier in the same novel, for instance, Roxana, flaunting it with her prince in the gardens of the palace of Meudon, is thunderstruck and terrified to see her husband the brewer, who had left her years ago but still has the

---

[1] " Defoe's Novels " (*Hours in a Library*, ii. 174-176).
[2] *Roxana*, p. 389.

right to call her his wife. He is now one of the guards at the palace. It is like Defoe's carelessness to have said, many pages earlier, that she never saw him again after his flight from his creditors. But the point now is that if he should recognize his deserted wife all her prosperity and splendour would crumble into ruins. He passes by, without a sign of recognition. The incident is over ; Roxana's fears are assuaged : Defoe is content to mention it as an occurrence entirely without consequences. It is one of the loose ends that give such an air of artlessness and candour to his pages. Similarly, in *Moll Flanders*, he had treated the discovery that Moll is cohabiting with her own brother. He might have made of it grimmest tragedy ; he might have woven a dramatic romance out of Moll's tardy recognition of her son and her long-deferred reunion with her highwayman husband, the only lovèr she had doted on. A plot would have put these things in a very different perspective. It would have aroused our sense of expectation and fulfilment by linking up disconnected events into a chain of causes likely sooner or later to have certain effects. To Defoe they are simply the curious accidents of life. He excites the sensation of surprise without appreciating the higher emotional value of suspense. And, after *Roxana*, he did not go on to make capital in further novels out of the artistic secrets on which he had had the good luck to stumble ; he was content to let his successors profit by them. It remained for an inferior hand to provide the truncated story with a logical conclusion, to complete the broken climax, without, however, thrilling us as when we are left wondering whether the too-faithful Amy has carried out or not carried out her diabolical threat.

Among other works of the same year, besides the first volume of his pleasant and instructive *Tour thro' the Whole Island of Great Britain* (3 vols., 1724-1725), in which he recounted his own journeyings with customary indirectness, he published a full account of a recent murder case in France,[1] two separate histories of the criminal exploits of Jack Sheppard, and the most ambitious of his narratives of imaginary travels. This was

"A New Voyage round the World"

[1] Reprinted as *An Account of the Cartoucheans in France* (in Aitken's ed. of the *Romances and Narratives*, xvi., 1896).

entitled, *A New Voyage round the World, By a Course never sailed before. Being a Voyage undertaken by some Merchants, who afterwards proposed the setting up an East-India Company in Flanders.* It was dated 1725, but actually appeared in November 1724. Defoe had always been a potential traveller. As a young man he had toured on the Continent, evidently having been sent to Spain on business, but travelling into other countries with eyes wide open for everything of practical interest.[1] Since then his life had been too much occupied for peregrinations outside Britain. At last, in old age, when the hope of realizing his inveterate desire was extinguished, he betook himself to the kind of exploration for which continual reading and much thought had qualified him better than any man alive, the account of an imaginary journey in which he might give his speculations on regions still untravelled the fullest fling. In its genesis, *A New Voyage* belongs to the same order of books as *Robinson Crusoe* and *Captain Singleton.* But it is not a novel. It is too empty of personal interest, although there is no lack of incident—unexpected and formidable difficulties, mutinies, pirates, finds of gold and pearls, misadventures in strange places. The book was not only a labour of love, but also a patriotic work. With the journals of all the navigators behind him, Defoe worked out an itinerary of his own, and drew attention to routes that he thought should be exploited for commercial purposes. This practical object is especially in view in the crossing of South America, in the second part, where the adventurers traverse the Andes, to show a way by which the riches of Chile might be tapped without interference from the Spaniards established farther south. In the earlier part, the expedition is prevented by stormy weather from entering the Straits of Magellan, and sailing past the Cape of Good Hope into the South Seas makes various landfalls in that Terra Australis which was still an unknown land of promise. Defoe's autobiographical narrator is a London merchant, said to be commissioned by a rich amateur to make observations in the interests of science. His sources were Dampier, Sir John Narbrough, who had ex-

[1] In the years between 1678 and 1683 (Professor Trent, in *Cambridge Hist. of Eng. Lit.*, ix. 6).

plored the Straits of Magellan, Drake, Woodes Rogers, and
Frobisher, Le Maire and Van Schouten, Frezier, author of a
Voyage to the South Sea, and along the Coasts of Chili and Peru,
Alonzo de Ovalle, whose account of Chile had been included in
Churchill's *Collection of Voyages,* and possibly Shelvocke, whose
Voyage round the World, however, was not yet out.[1]

Two other books of travel show fairly certain marks of Defoe's
handiwork ; but the extent to which he was merely an editor
or to which he made his own contributions has yet to be
determined. The *Four Years Voyages of Capt. George Roberts ;
Being a Series of Uncommon Events, which befell him in a Voyage
to the Islands of the Canaries, Cape de Verde, and Barbadoes,
from whence he was bound to the Coast of Guiney*—this amounts
to only a small fraction of the descriptive title—is stated to be
" Written by Himself " ; but it borrows from authorities used
habitually by Defoe in a manner that points to that expert
compiler. He probably dealt still more arbitrarily with the
journal given him or the account orally related by the piratical
Captain Drury, and made them up into a book that would go
down with his readers, in *Madagascar : or, Robert Drury's
Journal, during Fifteen Years captivity on that Island* (1729).[2]

Adventures of Captain Roberts and Robert Drury

During his connexion with *Applebee's Journal* (1720-1726)
Defoe wrote a number of articles and pamphlets on recent
criminal cases and the exploits of illustrious malefactors, which
are applications of his usual mixed methods to what professes
to be straightforward reporting. *The Highland Rogue : or, the
Memorable Actions of the Celebrated Robert Mac-gregor, Commonly called Rob-Roy* (1723), is a feeble life attributed to Defoe
on the slenderest evidence. Aitken also declines to accept the
ascription to Defoe of *The Life and Actions of Lewis Dominique
Cartouche : Who was broke Alive upon the Wheel at Paris.* . . .
Translated from the French (1722) ; but he admits the later
piece, *A Narrative of the Proceedings in France, for discovering
and detecting the Murderers of the English Gentleman . . . near*

Criminal biographies

---

[1] See G. A. Aitken's Introduction to *A New Voyage* (1895), ix., and Dottin,
iii. 752-753.

[2] See Secord, p. 207, and Dottin, iii. 793-794. Dottin thinks that Defoe's
part was to touch up and make presentable the rude narrative of Capt.
Roberts (*Ibid.*, p. 777).

Calais (1724), which deals with two members of Cartouche's gang, Bizeau and Le Febvre.[1] On the formidable Jack Sheppard, whose daring escapes from Newgate made him a hero to the mob, Defoe wrote two tracts in 1724, besides sixteen articles in *Applebee's Journal*. The sketchy *History of the Remarkable Life of John Sheppard, Containing a Particular Account of his Many Robberies and Escapes*, was superseded in a month by *A Narrative of all the Robberies, Escapes, &c., of John Sheppard, Giving an Exact Description of the Manner of his Wonderful Escape from the Castle in Newgate, and of the Methods he afterwards took for his Security. Written by himself during his Confinement in the Middle Stone Room, after his being retaken in Drury Lane*.[2] Defoe, no doubt, had interviewed the prisoner, and to palm off this graphic account of his achievements as a true dying confession, arranged for the condemned man on his way to the gallows to hand what was supposed to be the manuscript to a messenger, possibly Applebee himself, who published it next day. After all, such a trick was on all-fours with the literary deceptions Defoe had practised in *Moll Flanders, Roxana*, and other books. Seven editions of the tract were called for within a month.

Another eminent scoundrel, Jonathan Wild, came to a well-deserved end the following year. He too was interviewed in gaol by Defoe, who celebrated him in *Applebee's Journal*, and in *The True, Genuine and Perfect Account of the Life and Actions of the late Jonathan Wild* (1725), which is declared to be partly from his own mouth and partly from his writing. Immediately after there appeared *An Account of the Conduct and Proceedings of the late John Gow, alias Smith, Captain of the late Pirates, executed for Murther and Piracy* (1725).[3] Gow, who was the original of Captain Cleveland in Scott's *Pirate*, committed his atrocities on the high seas, was apprehended in the Orkneys, and executed in London. This narrative is written in the third person, and describes the trial of Gow and his men and their hanging. The doings of a gang of desperadoes who infested the

---

[1] See note, p. 217.
[2] Both are reprinted by Aitken (*Romances and Narratives*, xvi.).
[3] Both the Wild and the Gow pamphlets are reprinted (*Ibid.*).

streets of London, recounted in *A Brief Historical Account of the Lives of the Six notorious Street-robbers who were executed on Wednesday, April 6, at Kingston* (1726), is reminiscent of Cartouche and his followers.[1] Defoe returned to the subject, proposing to cure the evil by lighting and policing the metropolis, and by providing charitable institutions, hospitals, schools, and academies, in *Augusta Triumphans : or, the Way to make London the most Flourishing City in the Universe* (1728), and, the same year, *Second Thoughts are Best : or, a Further Improvement of a late Scheme to Prevent Street Robberies*, and *Street Robberies Consider'd*.[2] One of his last works was *An Effectual Scheme, for the immediate Preventing of Street Robberies, and suppressing the other Disorders of the Night* (1730). A vast deal of literature was provoked by the intolerable condition of the London streets, Swift, Bernard de Mandeville, and several writers not so well remembered, taking up the cause of the public welfare.

Defoe's industry in these latter years hardly relaxed, though his powers were evidently failing. A monumental treatise, *The Complete English Tradesman, In Familiar Letters, Directing him in all the several Parts and Progressions of Trade* (1725), and a batch of works dealing in a half-credulous, half-critical fashion with a favourite subject, *The Political History of the Devil* and *A System of Magick ; or, a History of the Black Art* (1726), followed by *An Essay on the History and Reality of Apparitions* (1727), are most noteworthy. One work alone comes in for a little closer consideration. *The Military Memoirs of Captain George Carleton* (1728), which according to the voluminous sub-title covers the period from the Dutch war of 1672 to the end of the war in Spain in 1713, has been alternately ascribed and denied to Defoe, but is now in a fair way of being finally admitted to the list of books written throughout by him. Like *Memoirs of a Cavalier* and the *Journal of the Plague Year* it has been accepted by such able critics as Dr Johnson, Sir Walter Scott, Lord Stanhope, historian of the War of the Succession

" Memoirs of Captain Carleton "

[1] Reprinted. *Ibid.*, xvi. 345–381.
[2] Professor Chandler finds considerable traces of Quevedo's or some other picaresque writer's influence in this last work (*Literature of Roguery*, ii. 321–322), but admits that it is the only place in his " fiction " where it can be detected (*Ibid.*, p. 288, n.).

in Spain, and Sir Leslie Stephen, as a brilliant fragment of history and undoubtedly authentic. The discovery that there was a real officer of the name serving in the operations described seemed to Stanhope and others ample warrant for pronouncing the *Memoirs* a reliable authority. Even were it admitted that Defoe had a hand in their fabrication, they argued, he must have worked upon a rougher diary kept by the supposed author. But traces of characteristic pilfering from other books, numerous departures from the facts of Carleton's career set down in the official records, and the stamp of manner, style, and method, are conclusive grounds for rejecting belief in Carleton's and recognizing Defoe's authorship.[1]

Outline of Carleton's story   At about the age of twenty, Carleton is said to have taken part as a volunteer in the naval engagement of Solebay (1672). Enlisting two years later in the service of the Prince of Orange, he fought in the Netherlands, and won his ensigncy in Fenwick's regiment (1676). His regiment came to England to help to put down the Monmouth Rebellion (1685) ; after which Carleton served in Scotland, and then, promoted to captain in Tiffin's regiment, took part in the battle of Steenkerke (1692). He exchanged to another regiment, and was given a post on Peterborough's staff with the expedition to Spain (1705), being present at most of the important actions until he was made prisoner at Denia (1708), not being liberated till the end of the war. As a history of the times, seen through the eyes of a participant, there is nothing seriously amiss with the *Memoirs*. Even the account of the supposed writer's career is approximately correct; but in matters of detail it is patently wrong. Carleton could not have been present at several of the more famous actions that are described, as, for example, the battle of Solebay and of Steenkerke and the siege of Namur. He did not land at Ostend till after Steenkerke was fought. During the siege of Namur he was engaged in operations of minor note. In short, the book is composed in the same manner as the semi-historical memoirs written by Courtilz de Sandras and by Defoe himself, notably

---

[1] The question is thoroughly thrashed out by Secord (pp. 165-229). Defoe's claim is admitted by Professor Trent (*Camb. Hist. of Eng. Lit.*, ix. 23). My own hesitating attitude of twenty years ago is now out of date.

the *Memoirs of a Cavalier* and the military portions of *Colonel Jacque*. Many facts are there, but essential facts of Carleton's real life are ignored and many are distorted. Taken as a whole it is a work of fiction.

The general outline of the events has been shown to be founded on Abel Boyer's *History of William III.* (1702-1703) and *Life of Queen Anne* (1721), and John Freind's *Account of Peterborow's Conduct in Spain* (1707). The *London Gazette* (1672-1700) and other public prints supplied further particulars, and for the Spanish portion Defoe drew extensively upon the Countess d'Aulnoy's *Ingenious and Diverting Letters of the Lady —— Travels into Spain* (seventh edition, 1708), a rich account of the manners and peculiarities of the people, and of the most famous sights of Madrid and other places of interest. This work, itself the history of a tour that never took place, " is the origin of approximately the last half of the *Memoirs*." [1]   These were the chief authorities ; but there were many more, and innumerable passages have been traced to their place of origin in works accessible to every one at that period. It is most unlikely that Carleton himself went wrong so many times in an account of his own career. The obvious deduction is that someone else was the author, and who could that author be but Defoe ? That it must have been Defoe, the resemblances of method to his fictitious biographies of the Cavalier and Colonel Jacque, amounting sometimes to almost verbal repetition, and the continual reappearance of his ideas and sentiments, his idiosyncrasies of wording, favourite allusions and anecdotes of strange occurrences, not to mention his inveterate errors and inconsistencies, prove beyond reasonable doubt.

Sources for "Captain Carleton"

When Defoe is acclaimed as the founder of the modern novel, the begetter of a new literary species, his title can be admitted with some reservations. As we have seen, others had already practised his peculiar method of composition, though not his peculiar realism. Stories had been made up out of veritable facts, and skilful combinations of fact and fiction had been passed off as valid history or biography, by both native and foreign writers.

Defoe's part in the foundation of the modern novel

---

[1] Secord, pp. 202-203 : "A strict comparison of the pretended observations of Carleton with those of the Countess reveals that a negligible part remains to attribute to Carleton or to the real author."

But their work lacked many of the chief constituents of fiction. *Robinson Crusoe*, although it was the outcome of similar modes of composition, surpassed them so far in the strength of the human element, in the quality of a history that had been lived and lives again before us, that it may reasonably be regarded as a different kind of work, as the first complete example of the modern novel. And beside it may be placed *Moll Flanders*, *Colonel Jacque*, *and Roxana*. *Captain Singleton* also stands apart from mere counterfeit works of travel, like *A New Voyage round the World*, by virtue of its personal thread. The memoirs of the Cavalier, of the Plague, of Captain Carleton, are historical fiction of a kind transitional between pseudo-history or pseudo-biography and the historical fiction that pretends to be nothing else. A large part of *Colonel Jacque* belongs to the same category.[1]

His "lying"

The difficulty in appraising his achievement and honouring his claim is that Defoe would not have put it forward himself. He uniformly pretended that he was not writing fiction. It is futile to urge that later novelists have blamelessly employed similar deceptions.[2] They have used them openly and above board as literary devices to assist the imagination. Illusion, the temporary suppression of disbelief, is a necessity in all kinds of fiction, by whatever means it may be sought ; delusion is an offence. For the benefit of some, at any rate, of his readers, Defoe said what was not, and meant it to be taken as it was said. But there were extenuating circumstances. His elaborate misstatements may be excused on the ground that the writing of fiction was not yet recognized as a legitimate art, or even as a reputable occupation. Defoe performed yeoman service in helping to elevate it to that dignity, though the honour was conceded only after he was no more. Defoe, however, did not think of novel-writing as an art. He never, we may be sure, tried to evolve a new theory of the novel. The difference between his solid and serious work and the futilities of the Behn and Manley school was, first of all, the difference between the hard, strong, puritanical man of affairs, intent on realities and deeply versed in the facts of life, and the effeminate voluptuaries of the post-Restoration period.

[1] See Dottin, ii. 487.
[2] Aitken makes this plea (Introduction to *Robinson Crusoe*, 1895, lx.).

Secondly, it was the difference between shallow cleverness and intrinsic genius, genius that saw what was to be done and found the way to do it.

His mistake was not to have distinguished between life and art, between the materials and the product. When he showed himself a true artist it was, as it were, unintentionally, through unconscious instinct, his conscious aim being to satisfy the demands of a lively but indiscriminate curiosity. Out of his multifarious knowledge and his keen interest in the remotest phases of life, he wrote his circumstantial account of what a man would do in such a position as Robinson Crusoe's. He went on to depict with the same knowledge and exactness various aspects of the contemporary world, and to portray representative types, such as Moll Flanders, Colonel Jacque, the pirates and Quakers in *Captain Singleton* and other books, the reprobates and courtesans of *Roxana*. These people had no charm of personality, except that he endowed them with a share of his own doggedness and independence. He preferred to delineate extreme cases, and to be plausible he had to be realistic, in his own extreme fashion. In spite of the exceptional nature of his stories, he knew that he had to mirror life as it is, and his craftsmanship in this respect was surpassingly patient and conscientious, even though as a salesman describing his goods as genuine in the literal sense he showed such a singular lack of integrity. As Leslie Stephen put it, "One is left in doubt how far Defoe was conscious of his own merits."

His services exceed his deliberate intentions

He set out to tell exciting stories. But the result of Defoe's immense knowledge of contemporary life in all its shapes, and of the untiring research he undertook when he told a story of times past, is that his books are not only stories of doings and experiences, but presentments of life in its fullness. Whether he was describing the existence of the solitary on his island, the hard lot of the rogue and the criminal, the ways in which prostitutes and courtesans are made and how they drive their trade, or the terrible plight of a great city in the grip of pestilence, there was always this not mere duality of interest but identification of the personal drama and the entire mundane scene. Even where his concentration on the individual tends to shut off part of the view, and we complain of a lack of atmosphere, the external world is

His stories are a portrayal of life

shown by flashes of intense realism. In the *Journal of the Plague Year* the story is purely subsidiary and instrumental, and in his other historical fictions it tends to disappear at times in the generalities. In *Robinson Crusoe* the personal and the general aspects are perfectly fused; we cannot dissociate the man and his environment, the actions and the whole range of circumstances : hence the greatness of the book.

The immense difference between the old fiction and the new

The immense gap between the fiction with which this history began and the fiction ushered in by Defoe is forcibly brought home to us if we compare the opening of Sidney's *Arcadia* with that of *Robinson Crusoe*, the fine type of the old poetical fiction with the prototype of the novel whose necessary vehicle is prose. This is how Sidney begins his recital, in his final version :

" It was in the time when the earth begins to put on her new apparel against the approach of her lover, and that the sun running a most even course becomes an indifferent arbiter between the night and the day, when the hopeless shepherd Strephon was come to the sands which lie against the island of Cithera, where, viewing the place with a heavy kind of delight, and sometimes casting his eyes to the isleward, he called his friendly rival Claius unto him ; and setting first down in his darkened countenance a doleful copy of what he would speak, ' O my Claius,' said he, ' hither we are now come to pay the rent for which we are so called unto by overbusy remembrance; remembrance, restless remembrance, which claims not only this duty of us, but for it will have us forget ourselves.' "

Sidney appeals entirely to the imagination, Defoe steadily addresses himself to our sense of the actual.

" I was born in the year 1632, in the city of York, of a good family, tho' not of that country, my father being a foreigner of Bremen, who settled first at Hull. He got a good estate by merchandise, and leaving off his trade, lived afterward at York, from whence he had married my mother, whose relations were named Robinson, a very good family in that country, and after whom I was called Robinson Crusoe, and so my companions always called me.

" I had two elder brothers, one of which was lieutenant-colonel to an English regiment of foot in Flanders, formerly commanded by the famous Col. Lockhart, and was killed at the battle near Dunkirk against the Spaniards : what became of my second brother I never knew, any more than my father and mother did know what was become of me." [1]

Defoe's work in the reconstruction of prose fiction was to bring the novel down from the region where the plastic imagination roams at large, and fix it firmly in the solid earth. His immediate precursors felt vaguely that this wanted to be done, but did not know how to do it. He showed, more fully than any novelist before or since, the irresistible cogency of the circumstantial method. In fact, he overdid the thing, and took it upon him to hoodwink his readers. Even now, as we have seen, it is not settled beyond all shadow of doubt whether certain works are fictions by Defoe or narratives of other men's actual experiences. But the speedy result of this realism was that the novel, which had hitherto been a hybrid and nondescript affair, a sort of by-product of poetry, was at last differentiated as an independent art-form.

Popular literature revived in Defoe; the lower middle classes, *Defoe's* and orders still humbler, saw their lives and circumstances, their *revival of* interests and ideals, represented with a sympathy and a serious- *popular* ness that had hitherto been accorded only to their betters in the *literature* social scale. Their great-grandfathers had narrowly escaped this good fortune ; Deloney had almost succeeded in establishing the bourgeois novel. But the whole strength of Puritanism had been in opposition, the time had not come for literature and the democratic spirit to be wedded. The fiction in which the lower orders delighted was unworthy of the name of humane letters. Mrs Behn, Mrs Manley, and Mrs Haywood, like the romancers before them, wrote for an upper-class public: the airs and graces of their style, as well as the social position of the majority of their characters, show that they were not writing for plain folk. We shall find Richardson continuing the tradition of writing for the quality. His Pamela is indeed a maidservant ostensibly drawn by herself; but she is in reality depicted by an obsequious middle-class person, with the feelings of an upper servant in a great house; she is an admiring votary of rank, like her creator; in short, she is a snob. But Defoe brought into the novel the popular

---

[1] *Cp.* the opening of *Moll Flanders* (see above, p. 192).

vernacular strain of Deloney and Bunyan. Dickens alone, in the history of the English novel, struck another such blow for the common people. The two strains coalesce again in Fielding's catholic presentment of English society. They run side by side in Scott ; in spite of his aristocratic proclivities, the popular strain, in truth, is the stronger. It would be instructive to trace them further, and show how essential was the element recovered by Defoe to the full vitality of the novel, which like an effete aristocracy must be restored to health from time to time by an infusion of peasant blood.

His strength and his weaknesses

There is no evidence that Defoe imitated picaresque fiction, even though Moll Flanders, Captain Singleton, Colonel Jacque, Roxana, and many others are rogues and adventurers. His attitude was entirely different from and antagonistic, except in rare moods, to the spirit of the picaresque.[1] It is also a mistake to suppose that he trained himself for fiction by writing biography, and after relating genuine lives began producing spurious ones. Most of his biographical work was done after the best of his novels were finished. But his own diversified career and all his miscellaneous occupations were a training than which he could have had no better for the kind of fiction we have found his to be. Of special value as a technical preparation was his reporting, more particularly in the journalism in which he assumed a factitious pose, and his retailing of edifying stories, whether true or invented, in such didactic compendiums as *The Family Instructor*.

Defoe is not among the great creators of character. So far as any of his figures come to life, it is through their being chips of himself.[2] His two Quakers are perhaps an exception, and they probably originated in other heads. The subtleties of personal disposition, the arcana of temperament, the inner world of the feelings, were to him a sealed book. All his men and women are extremely simple and strikingly bare of idiosyncrasy. He certainly did not exhibit any remarkable intuition of feminine character in Moll Flanders or Roxana, both admirably

---

[1] F. W. Chandler (*Lit. of Roguery*, passim) persistently classes him with the picaresque writers. Dottin considers *Moll Flanders* a picaresque novel (*Vie et Aventures de Daniel de Foe*, pp. 211-216).
[2] See Dottin on the Defoean personality (iii. 795-798).

commonplace women. The art of life-like and expressive dialogue he never mastered. It cannot be mastered without a finer psychology than he knew. The conversations in his *Journal of the Plague Year* are more natural than his average, perhaps because the theme had gripped him ; but, as a rule, he failed to get out of the old rut, and remained stiff and conventional. It is, above all else, in his superlative excellence as a story-teller that his power consists ; it is in the shape of narrative that he presents his view of the world. Nothing holds the imagination like straightforward narrative. Defoe gave us human histories, not galleries of human characters. He put the interest not in personal traits, but in what the people of the story do and undergo, and what effect it has upon their lives. And since he always seems to be speaking the unvarnished truth, his people, what they do and what befalls them, and the world in which they move, seem as actual as the world of our own sensations.

CHAPTER VIII

SWIFT

Jonathan Swift THE name of Jonathan Swift (1667-1743),[1] who was eight years Defoe's junior, does not bulk so large in the history of the novel as in the general annals of literature. A number of his writings have the outward form of fiction, but like Bunyan's stories, though they depict life and character with great insight and power and in narrative art are unsurpassable, they are not novels and were never meant to be. As Bunyan used fiction for the practical purpose of converting the ungodly, so Swift wrote it for controversial purposes or to express his contempt and abhorrence for the great mass of humankind. Satire is the prime motive in all of his work that can be classed as fiction, from the withering *Tale of a Tub* to the trivial but masterly *Genteel Conversation* and *Directions to Servants*. *A Tale of a Tub* is one of those few works that can without qualification be described as inimitable. *Gulliver's Travels*, though it hardly falls short of it in greatness, has been the model and ultimate criterion for satirical Utopias down to the latest competent example of the kind, Butler's *Erewhon*. Defoe in his fictitious memoirs and histories was really writing novels. Swift, according to his own oft-cited declaration, lacked something that is probably indispensable to the novelist, kindly regard or even sympathetic tolerance for the rest of his species. He could tell a story as brilliantly and convincingly as Defoe. He could not have written a novel had it occurred to him to attempt it.

Swift and Defoe Swift on more than one occasion somewhat gratuitously expressed his contempt for Defoe—" the fellow that was pilloried, I forget his name "—who was in a certain sense his rival. Both of them critics of social, political, and religious thought

---

[1] The biographies of Swift are collated and corrected by Emile Pons (*Swift : Les Années de Jeunesse et le " Conte du Tonneau*," Université de Strasbourg, 1925).

and action, they were often engaged in the same controversies, and not invariably on different sides. Swift was a publicist and pamphleteer like Defoe, but of a superior class; better educated, of a more liberal, acute, and subtle intellect; one who examined every problem from a more comprehensive viewpoint, and always looked beyond superficial aspects to the deeper realities. Swift withal had more artistic genius, a finer style, an infinitely keener humour. The trained scholar, accurately and widely read in ancient and modern learning, the churchman of proud ambitions, the familiar friend of secretaries of state, the polished and versatile wit of the drawing-rooms, would not relish having anything in common with the hackwriter, the demagogue, the self-taught polymath of Stoke Newington. But in one respect there was a good deal in common; and Swift in his most popular book, *Gulliver's Travels*, was, perhaps involuntarily and unconsciously but none the less undeniably, a borrower of Defoe's methods. By the same devices as Defoe had made the extraordinary, Swift made the impossible actual to the imagination, and told a story that stands beside *Robinson Crusoe* as a classic of realism.

Besides a mass of controversial writings, in which he frequently adopted Defoe's ruse of assuming a character,[1] Swift was the author of two considerable pieces of fiction, *A Tale of a Tub* and *Gulliver's Travels*, and of two collections of notes of things said and comments on things done, his *Genteel Conversation* and his *Directions to Servants*, which are by no means irrelevant to the history of the novel. *A Tale of a Tub* was written in the prime of his manhood, the main portion probably by 1696, and was published in 1704 with the shorter *Battle of the Books*, written probably in 1697.[2] To examine it merely as a specimen of his story-telling is of course to do injustice to a great masterpiece of philosophical and satirical literature, in which the story is a minor and relatively

Swift's works of fiction

---

[1] E.g., *An Argument against Abolishing Christianity; Mr Collins's Discourse of Free-thinking*, and the *Proposal for the Advancement of Religion*, written by "A Person of Quality."

[2] The digressions were probably added later, in 1697 and even as late as 1700-1703 (see Pons, especially pp. 222, 243, 245, and 253). *The Battle of the Books* and the *Tale* were both in hand together: "Le Conte et la Bataille sont deux phases de la même lutte" (*Ibid.*, p. 253).

unimportant feature [1] ; but that is all we are called upon to do here.   In chapters alternating with the wittiest digressions on folly and pedantry in general, Swift propounds an allegory, the object of which is to expose one colossal instance of the same, the pedantic, pretentious, and overbearing dogmatism of the Roman Catholic and the Dissenting Churches. Anglicanism, the *via media* of the sane man, is defended ; but Swift's handling of the theological problem involved is too disrespectful not to excite suspicion of its friendliness.

"A Tale of a Tub" The well-known story is very ingenious and fulfils its purpose brilliantly. The three brothers who, after living a free-and-easy life in blissful oblivion of their father's will, suddenly find themselves pulled up by its stern provisions, stand for the three hostile creeds : Peter and Jack represent Rome and Geneva, Martin the Church of England. Led away by the pleasures of the world, they have run after loose women, Pride, Wealth, Ambition, and have bedizened the plain coats bequeathed by their father in gross violation of his commands. The will is rediscovered ; the prohibitions can no longer be ignored. But the brothers act each in his proper character. Peter, who has been the ringleader, continues unreformed. The sensible Martin removes all the finery that can be unsewn without damage to the garment. Jack, in a violent fit of revolt from Peter's bullying, strips off the trimmings and great pieces of the coat at the same time.

The story-telling Peter, Martin, and Jack are not so much living characters as figureheads ; but the tale goes with a wonderful swing. The account how they find pretexts for their shoulder-knots, gold lace, and silver fringe, by twisting the clauses of their father's will or adding codicils ; the way Peter insists that he is the sole heir and browbeats Martin and Jack—all this is narrated with an infectious vigour. The dialogue is not less trenchant. Peter has heard a city magnate remark that beef is the king of meat, and he takes the fancy of applying the notion to his brown loaf.

[1] This is not to subscribe to the strange remark of Sir Henry Craik : " The account of Martin, Jack, and Peter, the names under which the Church of England, the Dissenters, and the Romish Church are typified, is the poorest piece of the whole " (*Life of Swift*, i. 140).

" Bread," says he, " dear brothers, is the staff of life ; in which bread is contained, inclusive, the quintessence of beef, mutton, veal, venison, partridge, plum-pudding, and custard. . . . Come, brothers," said Peter, " fall to, and spare not ; here is excellent good mutton ; or hold, now my hand is in, I will help you." At which word, in much ceremony, with fork and knife, he carves out two good slices of a loaf, and presents each on a plate to his brothers. The elder of the two, not suddenly entering into Lord Peter's conceit, began with very civil language to examine the mystery. " My lord," said he, " I doubt, with great submission, there may be some mistake." " What," says Peter, " you are pleasant ; come then, let us hear this jest your head is so big with." " None in the world, my lord ; but, unless I am very much deceived, your lordship was pleased a while ago to let fall a word about mutton, and I would be very glad to see it with all my heart." " How," said Peter, appearing in great surprise, " I do not comprehend this at all." —Upon which, the younger interposing to set the business aright ; " My lord," said he, " my brother, I suppose, is hungry, and longs for the mutton your lordship has promised us to dinner." " Pray," said Peter, " take me along with you ; either you are both mad, or disposed to be merrier than I approve of. If you there do not like your piece, I will carve you another : though I should take that to be the choice bit of the whole shoulder." " What then, my lord," replied the first, " it seems this is a shoulder of mutton all this while ? " " Pray, sir," says Peter, " eat your victuals, and leave off your impertinence, if you please, for I am not disposed to relish it at present." But the other could not forbear, being over-provoked at the affected seriousness of Peter's countenance. " By G——, my lord," said he, " I can only say, that to my eyes, and fingers, and teeth, and nose, it seems to be nothing but a crust of bread." Upon which the second put in his word ; " I never saw a piece of mutton in my life so nearly resembling a slice from a twelve-penny loaf." " Look ye, gentlemen," cried Peter in a rage, " to convince you what a couple of blind, positive, ignorant. wilful puppies you are, I will use but this plain argument ; by G——, it is true, good, natural mutton as any in Leadenhall market ; and G—— confound you both eternally, if you offer to believe otherwise." Such a thundering proof as this left no farther room for objection. The two unbelievers began to gather and pocket up their mistake as hastily as they could. " Why, truly," said the first, " upon more mature considera- tion——" " Ay," says the other, interrupting him, " now I

have thought better on the thing, your lordship seems to have
a great deal of reason." "Very well," said Peter, "here, boy,
fill me a beer-glass of claret : here's to you both, with all my
heart." The two brethren, much delighted to see him so
readily appeased, returned their most humble thanks, and said
they would be glad to pledge his lordship. "That you shall,"
said Peter, " I am not a person to refuse you anything that is
reasonable : wine, modestly taken, is a cordial ; here is a glass
a-piece for you ; 'tis true natural juice from the grape, none of
your damned vintner's brewings." Having spoke thus, he presented to each of them another large dry crust, bidding them
drink it off and not be bashful, for it would do them no hurt.
The two brothers, after having performed the usual office in
such delicate conjunctures, of staring a sufficient period at Lord
Peter and each other, and finding how matters were likely to
go, resolved not to enter on a new dispute, but let him carry
the point as he pleased ; for he was now got into one of his
mad fits, and to argue or expostulate farther, would only serve
to render him a hundred times more intractable.[1]

Apart from the deadly satire of popish claims and observ-
ances, this is incomparably good narrative, and so in a rather
different way is the pithy sketch of English history setting the
Anglican compromise in a simplified perspective.[2] For clear,
forcible, expeditious narration, and for the ironies and paradoxes of a derisive argument, Swift's style was now at its best.
It is the plain style purged of slovenliness, and made precise, a
perfect instrument for either narrative or reasoning. Swift was
no superstitious observer of grammatical rules. But he was
never careless or slipshod, like Defoe. When he committed
irregularities, it was because he preferred the clear and telling
to the merely correct, or because he wanted to be racy and
colloquial for the sake of point. There was no need for him to
repeat anything, or put it again in another way; he always had
the right and adequate expression at the outset. Defoe's
actuality in narrative and description has never been surpassed,
unless by Swift, and Swift had the advantage of a terse and
frugal precision hardly sought and never attained by Defoe.
He also had the advantage of a sense of order and shapeliness;
hence, not only his sentences and paragraphs, but also his works

[1] *Tale of a Tub*, ed. Temple Scott, pp. 85-87.   [2] *Ibid.*, pp. 147-149.

as wholes, have a symmetry of arrangement and finish beyond the reach of Defoe's teeming and hasty pen. The neatness with which the episodes and the digressions alternate, in *A Tale of a Tub*, and the admirable fitness and point of the allegory, show the artist in Swift ; the ease and aplomb with which he handles incident, dialogue, solemn absurdity, and cool invective, show it not less conclusively.[1]

Compared with this satire of deep-seated and ineradicable follies, the diverting fable called *The Battle of the Books* is an ephemeral toy ; but, though a mere fantasy in the hackneyed mock-heroic style, this piece has the same adequacy, fitness, and proportion. The long title runs, *A Full and True Account of the Battel Fought last Friday, between the Antient and the Modern Books in St James's Library*. It is a burlesque of the famous controversy on the relative merits of the ancients and the moderns, in which Swift's patron, Sir William Temple, had taken up blunted weapons against Bentley and Wotton, champions of modern learning, or, as Swift would have it, modern arrogance, futility, and pedantry. The allegory of the Bee and the Spider, the creature that sits in one place and spins noxious matter out of its own entrails, and the busy harvester who, ranging through every corner of nature, furnishes mankind with "the two noblest of things, sweetness and light" ; and the epical recital that follows of the pitched battle between the ancient and the modern authors : both show the same ease and address. Books and men and allegorical figures mingle and melt into each other without surprising or confusing us. His narrative skill is equal to any task that Swift's audacity can put upon it. Take the passage in which Criticism, that malignant goddess, issue of Ignorance and Pride, enters the fray in support of her beloved Wotton :—

"The Battle of the Books"

But here, the tender cares of a mother began to fill her thoughts, and move in her breast. For, at the head of a troop of Modern Bow-men, she cast her eyes upon her son W–tt–n ; to whom the Fates had assigned a very short thread. W–tt–n, a young hero, whom an unknown father of mortal race begot

[1] Possible sources of the allegory are discussed in the edition by Guthkelch and Nicol Smith (Introduction, xxix.-xl.). On Swift's reading at Moor Park, see Emile Pons: *Swift: Les Années de Jeunesse et le "Conte du Tonneau,"* 1925, pp. 211-219.

236 HISTORY OF THE ENGLISH NOVEL

by stolen embraces with this goddess. He was the darling of his mother, above all her children, and she resolved to go and comfort him. But first, according to the good old custom of deities, she cast about to change her shape ; for fear the divinity of her countenance might dazzle his mortal sight, and overcharge the rest of his senses. She therefore gathered up her person into an octavo compass ; her body grew white and arid, and split in pieces with dryness ; the thick turned into pasteboard, and the thin into paper ; upon which her parents and children artfully strowed a black juice, or decoction of gall and soot, in form of letters ; her head, and voice, and spleen, kept their primitive form, and that which before was a cover of skin, did still continue so. In which guise she marched on towards the Moderns, undistinguishable in shape and dress from the divine B–ntl–y, W–tt–n's dearest friend. " Brave W–tt–n," said the goddess, " why do our troops stand idle here, to spend their present vigour and opportunity of this day ? Away, let us haste to the generals, and advise to give the onset immediately." Having spoke thus, she took the ugliest of her monsters, full glutted from her spleen, and flung it invisibly into his mouth ; which, flying straight up into his head, squeezed out his eyeballs, gave him a distorted look, and half overturned his brain. Then she privately ordered two of her beloved children, Dullness and Ill-manners, closely to attend his person in all encounters. Having thus accoutred him, she vanished in a mist, and the hero perceived it was the goddess his mother." [1]

Swift always knew how to begin a story and when and how to finish ; the symmetry of this piece is not impaired by the aposiopesis.

His contributions to periodicals, etc.

Criticism of life and society, unerring insight into human foibles, and a humour only at times more tolerant, more tempered with sweetness and light, than was habitual to the author of *A Tale of a Tub* and *Gulliver's Travels*, characterize his contributions to the *Tatler* and *Examiner*, and his other miscellaneous essays. We discern more of Bacon than of Steele and Addison in the strings of acute observations and pithy aphorisms. There is, however, more nimbleness and grace in the transitions from the story to the digressions in *A Tale of a Tub* and in the raillery in the first two books of *Gulliver* than in most of his essays. What an eagle eye he had for the weaknesses of his contemporaries,

[1] *Prose Works,* i. 176-177.

especially of the fair sex, is evident in such pieces as the "Treatise on Good Manners and Good Breeding," "Hints towards an Essay on Conversation," and "Of the Education of Ladies." Swift was a charitable and kindly man towards his intimates, whether equals or inferiors, as many anecdotes of his good nature evince. He loved John, Peter, Thomas, he said, but "I heartily hate and detest that animal called man." So, whenever he took pen in hand he dipped it in the gall of satire, occasionally diluted to a less corrosive raillery. His famous hoax on the unfortunate almanack-maker Partridge, whose death he predicted on a certain date and duly recorded, calmly refuting the wretched victim when he protested that he was still alive, urbane as is the tone of the benevolent Mr Bickerstaff throughout, must have been torture for Partridge.[1]

At what date Swift began writing portions of what he called his "travels," which he afterwards expanded into his best-known satire, the four books of *Gulliver*, is a question still unsettled. At any rate, considerable parts of the first and third books were composed some years before he finished the work in 1725. It has been conjectured that he began it as a playful wonder-tale of strange adventures in the style of Lucian's *True History* and the more philosophical though not less extravagant satire of Cyrano de Bergerac, with a view to contributing it to the *Memoirs of Martinus Scriblerus*, projected by Swift, Arbuthnot, Pope, Gay, and their friends, about 1714.[2] If this was so, he put the manuscript aside when his hopes were dashed by the fall of Oxford, quickly followed by the death of Queen Anne (1714), after which he retired into uncongenial exile in Dublin. Then, about 1720 or

" Gulliver's Travels "

[1] *Predictions for the Year 1708.* By Isaac Bickerstaff, Esq.; *The Accomplishment of the first of Mr Bickerstaff's Predictions, being an Account of the Death of Mr Partridge, the Almanack-maker, upon the 29th instant;* and *A Vindication of Isaac Bickerstaff, Esq.; against What is Objected to Him by Mr Partridge, in his Almanack for the present Year 1709* (*Prose Works*, ed. Temple Scott, i. 297-324).

[2] The first book of the *Memoirs of Martinus Scriblerus*, a medley of satires on pedants and projectors, eventually appeared in the second volume of the *Works of Pope, in Prose* (1741). Sir C. H. Firth believes that Swift began the work at this early date (*Proceedings of the British Academy*, ix., "The Political Significance of 'Gulliver's Travels'"). Swift's latest editor, Mr Harold Williams, thinks that nothing equivalent to a first draft of *Gulliver*, in however fragmentary a form, was in existence in 1720. The satire is mainly concerned with the years 1720-1725 (*Gulliver's Travels: the Text of the First Edition, with introduction, bibliography, and notes*, 1926). Most modern editions reproduce the second edition.

1721, when he was a little easier in mind, he picked up the threads of the story, and gradually finished it. He revised and transcribed the whole in 1725, as he reported in letters to his friends, Charles Ford and Pope. There is a good deal of satire in the third book, " A Voyage to Laputa," which might well have been conceived in the first instance as a contribution to the satirical symposium on pretentious men of learning. On the other hand, the many political and personal allusions in the first two books refer to the period 1721-1725. All that is certain is that Swift did not write *Gulliver's Travels* at one heat, but was at work upon it at intervals for years. This accounts for the very different attitude of mind evident in the different books, and in different parts of the same book.[1]

Swift's debt to Defoe's realism

Travels into several Remote Nations of the World, In Four Parts, By Lemuel Gulliver (1726), is a work that invites comparison with many of the accounts of imaginary voyages, the Utopias, and suchlike, that have been described as forerunners of *Robinson Crusoe*. Besides Lucian and Cyrano de Bergerac, Swift had before him the tale of Bishop Godwin, Vairasse d'Allais' *Sevarambians,* Gabriel de Foigny's *Journey of Jacques Sadeur,* Defoe's *Consolidator,* and, we must not forget, *Robinson Crusoe* itself.[2] He would no doubt have disclaimed any indebtedness to Defoe. But it is hard to believe that the close resemblance between the two men's realistic methods was accidental or merely due to the very practical and matter-of-fact mentality prevailing at that time. On the face of it, the relation between the two books seems to be that Defoe invented the circumstantial method and the various artifices for making a story sound like the honest statement of a man repeating his own experiences, and Swift adopted and perfected the method by giving it more precision. He seems to copy even the lapses and carelessnesses of Defoe, in order to give verisimilitude to the recital as well as to the matters recited.

Further, there are great and obvious resemblances between the stories, despite their greater differences. *Gulliver's Travels*

[1] Books I. and III. show such inconsistencies.
[2] For an account of his sources (including Ablancourt's translation of Lucian's *True History*, with a supplement curiously suggestive of *Gulliver*) see W. A. Eddy: *Gulliver's Travels: A Critical Study,* 1923, also Pons, pp. 211-219.

is another tale of an imaginary seaman's experiences. It is full of nautical adventures, wanderings in unknown regions, and various accidents that result in leaving the hero in a place whence he cannot escape without extreme difficulty. The shipwreck through which Gulliver finds himself in Lilliput inevitably reminds the reader of Crusoe's shipwreck on his island. Gulliver arrives in the country of the Brobdingnagians in circumstances more like those in *Krinke Kesmes*. But in Laputa it is pirates, and in the land of the Houyhnhnms a mutiny on board ship, that are the agency; and again *Robinson Crusoe* is called to mind. On the other hand, it may be alleged that Swift acquired the requisite knowledge from the same sources as Defoe, and at the same time studied the homely but effective manner of the untutored scribes. Thus Captain Gulliver avers that he is a cousin of Dampier's, and that he gave him the advice, which was accepted, to let a young gentleman from one of the universities overlook and correct his *Voyage round the World*. Swift places his wonderlands not in the Western hemisphere but in the neighbourhood of the mysterious Terra Australis Incognita ; but this does not help to solve the problem how far he was influenced by Defoe.[1]

Defoe might well have been responsible for all the preliminaries ushering Mr Gulliver upon the scene. First there is a notice headed " The Publisher to the Reader," signed by Richard Sympson, who claims to be an old and intimate friend and also a sort of cousin of Gulliver, who has left the papers in his hands to be published. A deft touch is that the editor has thought fit to strike out innumerable passages about winds and tides and the management of the ship in storms, in the style of sailors, but is willing to let any curious person inspect the original manuscript at large. Then comes a letter to Sympson from his cousin Captain Gulliver, who takes him to task for many vexatious shortcomings. The whole object of this is, of course, to evoke that air *Swift's realistic method*

---

[1] Twice Swift announced a book (in the 1711 and the 1734 editions of *A Tale of a Tub*) entitled *A Description of the Kingdom of Absurdities—A Voyage into England by a Person of Quality in Terra Australis incognita, translated from the original*. The book has not been traced, and was probably never written. In *A Tale of a Tub*, Lord Peter buys a large continent in Terra Australis Incognita, with a view to colonizing it—*i.e.*, establishing Purgatory there (*Tale of a Tub*, p. 79).

of authenticity which Defoe conjured up for fraudulent purposes but which Swift used more legitimately, at the same time revelling in the ingenuity with which he mimics truth and ingenuousness.[1] *Gulliver* is partly burlesque of travellers' tales, and partly realistic wonder-book with a very different satirical aim.

If the essence of Defoe's peculiar realism is its practical character, its showing how things are done as well as telling about them, then we have the same in *Gulliver*. Take this page of Gulliver's life in Lilliput : it almost seems as if Swift had mastered Defoe's secret and was trying what was the utmost that could be wrung out of it.

And here it may perhaps divert the curious reader, to give some account of my domestic, and my manner of living in this country, during a residence of nine months and thirteen days. Having a head mechanically turned, and being likewise forced by necessity, I had made for myself a table and chair convenient enough, out of the largest trees in the royal park. Two hundred sempstresses were employed to make me shirts, and linen for my bed and table, all of the strongest and coarsest kind they could get ; which, however, they were forced to quilt together in several folds, for the thickest was some degrees finer than lawn, their linen is usually three inches wide, and three foot make a piece. The sempstresses took my measure as I lay on the ground, one standing at my neck, and another at my mid-leg, with a strong cord extended, that each held by the end, while the third measured the length of the cord with a rule of an inch long. Then they measured my right thumb, and desired no more ; for by a mathematical computation, that twice round the thumb is once round the wrist, and by the help of my old shirt, which I displayed on the ground before them for a pattern, they fitted me exactly. Three hundred tailors were employed in the same manner to make me clothes ; but they had another contrivance for taking my measure. I kneeled down, and they raised a ladder from the ground to my neck ; upon this ladder one of them mounted, and let fall a plumb-line from my collar to the floor, which just answered the length of my coat : but my waist and arms I measured myself. When my clothes were finished, which was done in my house (for the largest of theirs

---

[1] As he enjoyed his parody of a sailorman's technical jargon in the account of the ship's plight in a storm, before Gulliver is landed in Brobdingnag.

would not have been able to hold them), they looked like the
patchwork made by the ladies of England, only that mine were
all of a colour.[1]

Defoe often walks very uncertainly on the dividing-line of art
and reality. Swift knows better. What in Defoe is a dodge, or a
makeshift, or a lucky intuition, is conscious art in Swift. He
employs Defoe's deceptive sleights for a lawful result ; he knows
exactly what he should aim at, and hits the mark unerringly and
with expert ease. His command of strong, racy, concrete terms,
terms that instantly bring up sensible, visual, tactile images, is
astounding in a bookish man. Swift solves triumphantly all the
problems of verisimilitude in his dealings with the improbable
and the impossible.

Where he is less consistent is in the attitude assumed in the *In-*
different books and in the same book; and this was due, no doubt, *equality*
to the piecemeal way in which the work grew. The first begins *of the*
as amusing make-believe, with some suggestions of an idealistic *work*
Utopia, and then becomes a satirical caricature of England under
George I. and its relations with France. The Utopian idea is
dominant in the second book, the object of which is to satirize
by the method of contrast. This again is the scheme of the
terrible fourth book, in which, however, Swift's wrath and indignation carried him beyond the bounds of any logical scheme.
But the third book suffers most from piecemeal composition,
Swift's prejudices flying out in all directions, at theorists, projectors, and innovators of whatever stamp. In all but the third
book he postulates some striking change of nature or environment
that enables us to contemplate the actual world from an abstract
point of view.

How he does this, by showing man through the telescope in *Changes*
Lilliput, and through the microscope in Brobdingnag, and lastly *of*
by inverting the relation between man and the commonest *attitude*
domestic animal in the Houyhnhnms, is too well known to need
repetition. The changes introduced in the third book are not
so revolutionary and disturbing, and hence not so successful in
making us see things in an absolutely new light. This portion
wavers between allegory and direct caricature ; it suffers from

[1] *Gulliver*, ed. Temple Scott, pp. 64-65.

a lack of unity and consistency. It is in the first two books
that Swift makes the heaviest drafts upon our imagination,
and proceeds with the most methodical and indefatigable pains
to compel us to honour them. All Defoe's artifices for securing
plausibility are reduced to a system: tone of matter-of-fact
reporter, abundance and superabundance of petty detail, lucid
explanation of the way things happen and the way things are
done, bits of corroborative evidence slipped in as if by accident
to set our minds at rest. Finally, Swift works out the equation,
as it were, to the last decimal point. The mathematical minute-
ness with which everything is proportioned to the original
change of scale has evoked endless admiration. At the same
time he invites us to make merry at this foible of exactness,
which the contemporary pedantic geographer made a fetish.

The reader may please to observe, that in the last article for
the recovery of my liberty, the Emperor stipulates to allow me
a quantity of meat and drink sufficient for the support of 1728
Lilliputians. Some time after, asking a friend at court how
they came to fix on that determinate number, he told me
that his Majesty's mathematicians, having taken the height
of my body by the help of a quadrant, and finding it to exceed
theirs in the proportion of twelve to one, they concluded from
the similarity of their bodies, that mine must contain at least
1728 of theirs, and consequently would require as much food
as was necessary to support that number of Lilliputians. By
which, the reader may conceive an idea of the ingenuity of that
people, as well as the prudent and exact economy of so great a
prince.[1]

This is as far from the clumsy buffoonery of Defoe's *Consolidator*, on the one hand, as it is from Cyrano de Bergerac's
flippant and Munchausen-like disregard of realism, on the
other.[2]

[1] *Prose Works*, viii. 45; *cp.* the amusing exactness with which he gives the
latitude and longitude of the fabulous countries, the provision of dates, hours,
dimensions, etc.

[2] Mr Walter de la Mare, in a lecture on Swift a little while ago, delivered
himself of the opinion that there is no great significance in the change of
dimensions in *Gulliver*. But some such wholesale change of nature or environment had to be contrived to enable us to abstract. It is not merely that the
telescope brings distant things near, or that the microscope enables us to
perceive the infinitesimal; the instrument provides a new form of vision: we

As the tale proceeds, Lilliput becomes a diminutive copy of *Lilliput* Hanoverian England, the cherished greatness of the nation, the *a satire* majesty that doth hedge a king, the grandeur of titles and *on con-* decorations, the glory of war and conquest, appearing ridi- *temporary England* culous as the attributes of a race of pygmies. Swift quickly realized what opportunities were here for particular as well as general satire. Many of his hits were patent then, though not so easy to make out at this distance of time; others, for pru- dential reasons, were surreptitious, and are now difficult to detect. At first Lilliput and its institutions are a model for England; afterwards the political disputes and intrigues be- come a caricature of those at home. The continual hostilities with Blefuscu typify the long-standing feud with France. The two rival parties, Tramecksan and Slamecksan, high-heels and low-heels, represent the Tories and Whigs, the High Church and the Low Church parties. The emperor favoured the low- heels, just as George I. inclined to the Whigs, and as the Prince of Wales adhered to the opposite party, so did the heir to the throne in Lilliput. Then there are the Big-Endians and the Little-Endians, Roman Catholics and Protestants : it was like Swift's irreverence to dismiss the distinction between them as worth about as much as whether one's egg should be eaten from the large or the small end. When Gulliver has brought over the fleet of Blefuscu but refuses to crush that kingdom altogether, it is one of the articles of impeachment against him that he would not put to death the Big-Endian exiles who had taken refuge there. The reference to the French policy of giving countenance to Jacobite and other refugees is obvious.

All this, and the ridicule of the orders of the Thistle, the Bath, *Particu-* and the Garter, in the green, red, and blue threads awarded *lar allu-* to those courtiers who cut the highest capers—that is, who *sions* showed the greatest dexterity in political intrigue—are easy

see differently. A general change of size in itself is nothing ; Gulliver, how- ever, does not change his size. Other story-tellers have adopted other devices ; but some such device is essential. The celestial observer, the observer from China, Persia, the land of the Redskins, etc., or even a non-human and even an inanimate observer, were much in vogue for a time, and bear witness to the need for some violent alteration of the usual conditions, if the reader were to be enabled to see the things around him in a new way.

to recognize. A great many more allusions are discernible to students of the contemporary history. Gulliver himself, who at the commencement is no one in particular, seems later on to denote Swift's unfortunate friend Bolingbroke, who had been criticized for concluding peace too soon and on terms too favourable to the enemy, and was now in exile. Flimnap, the prime minister, is, of course, Walpole : he cuts the highest caper on the tightrope. Bolgolam, Galbet or Admiral of the realm, has been identified with Swift's enemy Nottingham, who had been First Lord of the Admiralty, and plumed himself on his naval sagacity. Gulliver's friend Reldresal is probably meant for Carteret.[1]

Brobding-nag : change of method in the satire In the next book Swift changes the method of his satire. The Brobdingnagians are not a ridiculous people, although Swift characteristically shows how horrible even such a harmless thing as a lady's skin can look when magnified many dimensions. They are a simple, clean-minded, clear-sighted race, who despise political squabbling and have made legal chicanery a capital offence. Like the Houyhnhnms of Book IV., they are beings of a higher civilization who look down with contempt on the pettiness and foolishness of *homo insipiens*. Swift's irony here is at its best. The allegory is a perfect fit, and the indignant king's explosion comes with a more devastating force through being kindled by Gulliver's vaunts of his country's superiorities :

But, I confess, that after I had been a little too copious in talking of my own beloved country, of our trade, and our wars by sea and land, of our schisms in religion, and parties in the state ; the prejudices of his education prevailed so far, that he could not forbear taking me up in his right hand, and stroking me gently with the other, after an hearty fit of laughing, asked me, whether I were a Whig or a Tory. Then turning to his first minister, who waited behind him with a white staff, near as tall as the mainmast of the *Royal Sovereign*, he observed how contemptible a thing was human grandeur, which could be mimicked by such diminutive insects as I : and yet, said he, I dare engage, these creatures have their titles and distinctions of honour, they contrive little nests and burrows, that they call houses and cities ; they make a figure in dress and equipage ;

1 Sir C. H. Firth, *The Political Significance of " Gulliver's Travels,"* pp. 4-10.

they love, they fight, they dispute, they cheat, they betray. And thus he continued on, while my colour came and went several times, with indignation to hear our noble country, the mistress of arts and arms, the scourge of France, the arbitress of Europe, the seat of virtue, piety, honour, and truth, the pride and envy of the world, so contemptuously treated.[1]

The third book is a patchwork of satirical outbursts in which Swift indulged from time to time, perhaps during the period from when he first thought of contributing to *Martinus Scriblerus* till when he sat down to finish off his " Travels." His hatred of theorists, scientists, projectors and innovators of all kinds is expressed in a series of caricatures that are but loosely connected together. The Flying Island seems a cumbrous invention, none the less clumsy when we are told that its method of hovering over the subject land and keeping it obedient by the threat of cutting off the sunshine and rain or taking the extreme measure of crushing a rebellious city with its adamantine bottom, is an allegory for the systematic maltreatment of Ireland by the English Government. All the time Swift was completing *Gulliver's Travels* he was obsessed by the persistent injustice that had reduced his adopted country to the condition of Balnibari, and had made Dublin a city of decay like Lagado.[2] Swift was that unusual combination, a conservative and an impassioned lover of liberty. He was conservative by habit and prejudice rather than principle. He clung to all that was ordered and firmly established, and hated projects, because they were projects. Innovations and all that was regarded as progress are condemned indiscriminately in *Laputa*. Yet in the vindication of human rights, he was as dauntless a champion as any Harmodius and Aristogeiton. The later phrase of his epitaph, *Strenuum pro virilitate libertatis vindicem*, is less quoted than the tragic *saeva indignatio* ; but it gives the secret of his bitterness and anguish, of his indignation that folly and greed should hold down a large part of mankind in misery, nakedness, and degradation.

"Laputa" a hotch-potch of random satire

[1] *Prose Works*, viii. 109.
[2] For the details of Swift's application of the Laputa episode to England and Ireland see Firth, pp. 16-23, as also for his hits at other contemporary grievances of his.

*The
Houy-
hnhnms*

In the fourth book Swift again contemplates man from the point of view of a superior civilization, and this time his denunciation is more misanthropic, though not more biting, than in the second. This book has been judged very unfavourably, and Swift has been condemned for an almost insane hatred for everything human. Artistically, it is almost as unsatisfactory as the preceding book. With all his elaborate realism, he cannot make the idea go down of his horses riding about in carriages and training men as their beasts of burden : it is too clumsy a fiction for even a Swift to render plausible. But the chief criticism has been aimed at his conception of the bestial Yahoos. It is a moral objection to his libel on humanity. Yet, after all, the Yahoos are but the king of Brobdingnag's "most pernicious race of little odious vermin " left to themselves in a state of nature, without even the pretence of social or moral control. Swift, during the last few years, had had his soul embittered by the continual sight of the " savage old Irish," the dispossessed natives, who had been reduced by abject poverty, total lack of education, and the barbarity of English-made law to the state of outcasts. As things were, he saw no hope for such a race, and vented the wrath that inflamed his soul in this ghastly picture of the Yahoos, and later in his *Modest Proposal,* for ending their wretchedness in the next generation by encouraging parents to sell off their children to be eaten by the gentry. The irony of such a proposal, it has been argued, could come only from a person whose feelings were utterly callous. But Swift was anything but a heartless man ; it was the fury and despair to which the constant spectacle of injustice drove him that found this vehement expression.

*—the
Yahoos
suggested
by the old
Irish*

*The two
kinds of
Yahoo*

Gulliver, but not Swift, distinguishes between the two kinds of Yahoo, the debased wretches who infest the country of the Houyhnhnms and the European Yahoos who enjoy the benefits of culture and the arts of civilization. It would be to miss his irony if we put the wrong stress on the difference between the two races. No doubt, he was impelled to paint the savage and bestial Yahoo by his experiences among the poor Irish ; but they gave him also his whole idea of Yahoodom. The civilized Yahoos are not less, but on the contrary far more, deserving of reprobation because they have acquired sciences and arts and have made nothing better of these than to utilize them with the same selfishness and brutality and a more refined ingenuity to satisfy their lusts. It is as if Swift were saying, in another Irish pamphlet, " Look at these abandoned wretches, and see what you have made of them ! You are of the same species, your nature is the same ; but you are baser than they, for you have committed the infamy of making them worse than the brutes." [1]

The obscenity of so much of Swift's work was probably due to the same vehemence of repulsion as drove him to these misanthropic outbreaks. He was continually obsessed with images of the filthy and the nauseating, through his hatred of uncleanness and the continual presence of it in the life around him. His impatience and loathing for the animal side of man's nature, his revolt from the uncleanness and degradation that cannot be escaped—such was the morbid attitude to which it drove him —was perhaps the reason why he never lived with the woman he loved, the true motive of his hideous picture of the Yahoos, and one of the main causes of his madness. Swift adored " sweetness and light "; he longed above all things for order, temperance, tranquillity. But he found them so unattainable under mortal conditions that he lapsed into the uttermost despair and misanthropy. His pessimism was complete : there was no place on earth for the values he cherished. *Swift's obscenity*

Both *Genteel Conversation* and *Directions for Servants* were collections of jottings made by Swift over a long period of years. In spite of his contempt, he was a close observer of mankind. Anecdotes are extant of his watchfulness, both as a priest, dispensing a bounty beyond his narrow means and doing his charitable deeds by stealth, and as the master of a household, knowing a servant's duty and whether he did it or neglected it, and not ignorant of the personal characters and private affairs of those in his employ. He spoke of these two " great works " together as being in hand at the same time ; the one was " to *"Genteel Conversation"*

---

[1] See Firth, pp. 12-16, for a résumé of the evidence that Swift drew the Yahoos upon the model of the old Irish. It seems to me that this critic misreads the difference between the two kinds of Yahoo, and fails to perceive Swift's ironical intention.

reduce the whole politeness, wit, and style of England into a short
system, for the use of all persons of quality, and particularly
the maids of honour. The other is of almost equal importance ; I may call it the whole duty of servants, in about twenty
different stations, from the steward and waiting-woman down

Swift's
intro-
duction

to the scullion and pantry-boy." He says, with regard to the
former work,[1] " I always kept a large table-book in my pocket ;
and as soon as I left the company, I immediately entered the
choicest expressions that passed during the visit." He adds,
" he can faithfully assure the reader, that there is not one single
witty phrase in this whole collection, which hath not received
the stamp and approbation of at least one hundred years, and
how much longer, it is hard to determine ; he may therefore
be secure to find them all genuine, sterling and authentic." [2]
He took the further trouble to arrange this vast collection of
colloquial tags into three dialogues forming a sort of play.[3]
The dialogue is unquestionably the nearest to the give-and-
take of would-be vivacious conversation that had yet seen the
light.

Lady Smart's Antechamber—Miss Notable comes in.

Neverout. Miss, your slave : I hope your early rising will do
you no harm. I hear you are but just come out of the cloth-
market.

Miss. I always rise at eleven, whether it be day or no.

Col. Atwit. Miss, I hope you are up for all day ?

Miss. Yes, if I don't get a fall before night.

Col. Miss, I heard you were out of order ; pray, how are you
now ?

Miss. Pretty well, Colonel, I thank you.

Col. Pretty and well, Miss ! that's two very good things.

Miss. I mean, that I am better than I was.

Neverout. Why, then, 'tis well you were sick.

[1] *A Complete Collection of Genteel and Ingenious Conversation, According to the Most
Polite Mode and Method Now used at Court, and in the Best Companies in England.
In three Dialogues.* By Simon Wagstaff, Esq. (1738).

[2] Another and still more enterprising Irishman, the dramatist Synge, also
played the eavesdropper outside cabins and shebeens, and so collected the racy
phrases out of which he made his wonderful tessellated dialogue.

[3] It was actually presented as a play in Dublin, at the time the book was
published, the proceeds of both the book and the play being ample enough to
relieve the immediate necessities of his friend Mrs Barber, to whom he had
given the manuscript when she was in difficulties.

Miss. What, Mr Neverout; you take me up, before I'm down.

Lady Smart. Come, let us leave off children's play, and come to push-pin.

Swift kept *Directions to Servants* by him in the same way, and left the collection to be published posthumously in 1745. His irony must be discerned in the former book in the pretended seriousness with which he writes down the silliest witticisms. It is shown more after his own manner in this exposure of " the villainies and frauds of servants to their masters and mistresses," which is stamped with his characteristic coarseness. A quotation or two will suffice to show that Swift surveyed the servants' hall with the same vision as he surveyed more august haunts and the world at large, and that there was no corner of the universe that escaped his irony.

" Directions to Servants"

If you see your master wronged by any of your fellow-servants, be sure to conceal it, for fear of being called a tell-tale : however, there is one exception, in case of a favourite servant, who is justly hated by the whole family ; you therefore are bound, in prudence, to lay all the faults you can upon the favourite.

If it be possible, never tell a lie to your master or lady, unless you have some hopes that they cannot find it out in less than half an hour.

When you find that you cannot get dinner ready at the time appointed, put the clock back, and then it may be ready to a minute.

Had Swift but known the warm appreciation of humanity that is the novelist's main incentive to write, he assuredly possessed the other qualifications. But, instead of rejoicing in the infinite variety of human life, he perceived only its littleness, and lumped all together as examples of the vices and follies of a species that had gone bankrupt. His stories take little count of individual character. The figures in *A Tale of a Tub* and *The Battle of the Books* are only marionettes who are at the same time embodiments of hated absurdities. They are not even caricatures. Those in *Gulliver* are either myths, representing his moral aspirations, or again generalized embodiments of vice and folly, even when they are personally identified with

Con-clusion

particular enemies. He is not interested in individual traits but
only in general truths.[1] Thus he has at easy command much of
the technique of the novelist, yet not the one thing needful.
But, as it is, the form Swift chose for his chief polemical and
satirical works, and especially the overwhelming force of his
realism, which stamps even wild improbabilities on our
imagination and renders them for ever ineffaceable, is further
evidence that the appointed hour had come, and that whatever
shape the contemporary novel took, it would have to be a
truthful and cogent study of realities.

[1] Pons, p. 183.

SELECT READING AND REFERENCE LIST

GENERAL

BAKER, E. A. *A Guide to the Best Fiction in English.* 1913.

CHANDLER, F. W. *The Literature of Roguery*, vol. i. 1907.

ESDAILE, ARUNDELL. *A List of English Tales and Prose Romances printed before 1740.* 1912.

GOSSE, SIR E. *Seventeenth-Century Studies.* 4th ed. 1915.

MORGAN, CHARLOTTE. *The Rise of the Novel of Manners.* 1911.

RALEIGH, WALTER. *The English Novel.* 1904.

SAINTSBURY, GEORGE. *A History of the French Novel*, vol. i. 1917.

TIEJE, S. J. *The Theory of Characterization in Prose Fiction prior to 1740.* (University of Minnesota Studies in Language and Literature. 1916.)

WARD, A. W., and WALLER, A. R. *The Cambridge History of English Literature*, vols. vii.-ix. 1911-1912.

CHAPTERS I.-V.—THE REVIVAL OF ROMANCE

(a) TEXTS

ALCOFORADO, MARIANNA D'. *The Letters of a Portuguese Nun.* Translated by Edgar Prestage. 1900.

AUBIN, PENELOPE. *A Collection of Entertaining Histories and Novels.* 1739. (Contains the following and others :)
Adventures of the Lady Lucy. 1726.
Life of the Count Albertus. 1728.
Life of Madam de Beaumont. 1721.

BARCLAY, JOHN. *Barclay his Argenis.* Translated by Kingsmill Long. Second edition, 1631.

BARKER, JANE. *The Entertaining Novels of Mrs Barker.* Third edition. 1736.

BEHN, APHRA. *Works*. Edited by Montague Summers. 6 vols. 1915.
>   *Novels*. Edited by E. A. Baker. 1905.
>   *Love-Letters between a Nobleman and his Sister*. 1694.
>   *Lycidus, or The Lover in Fashion*. 1688.

BOYD, ELIZABETH. *The Female Page*. 1737.

BUNYAN, JOHN. *Grace Abounding*. Edited by J. Brown. 1907.
>   *The Holy War*. Edited by J. Brown. 1905.
>   *The Life and Death of Mr Badman*. Edited by J. Brown. 1905.
>   *The Pilgrim's Progress*. Edited by J. Brown. 1895.

CERVANTES SAAVEDRA, MIGUEL DE. *Complete Works*. Edited by J. Fitzmaurice Kelly. 12 vols. 1902.
>   *Don Quixote*. Translated by Thomas Shelton (Tudor Translations). 1896.

CONGREVE, WILLIAM. *Incognita ; or, Love and Duty Reconcil'd*. Edited by H. F. B. Brett-Smith. 1922.

DAVYS, MARY. *Works*. 2 vols. 1725.

HAMILTON, COUNT ANTHONY. *Memoirs of Count Grammont*. Edited by G. Goodwin. 2 vols. 1908.

HAYWOOD, ELIZA. *Secret Histories, Novels and Poems*. 1725.
>   *Bath-Intrigues*. 1725.
>   *The Fair Hebrew*. 1729.
>   *The Life of Madam de Villesache*. 1727.
>   *The Mercenary Lover*. 1728.
>   *Philidore and Placentia*. 1727.
>   *The History of Miss Betsy Thoughtless*. 1751.
>   *Jemmy and Jenny Jessamy*. 1753.

HEAD, RICHARD, and KIRKMAN, FRANCIS. *The English Rogue*. Pts. I.-IV. 1665-1671.

MANLEY, MRS DE LA RIVIÈRE. *Secret Memoirs*. 1709.
>   *Court Intrigues*. 1711.
>   *The Adventures of Rivella*. 1714.
>   *Memoirs of Mrs Manley*. 1717.
>   *The Power of Love : in Seven Novels*. 1720.
>   *A Stage-Coach Journey to Exeter*. 1725.

NEVILE, HENRY. *The Isle of Pines.* 1668.
A New and Further Discovery of the Isle of Pines in a Letter from Cornelius Van Sloetten. 1668.

OSBORNE, DOROTHY. *Letters to Sir William Temple.* Edited by E. A. Parry, 1888. Edited by G. C .Moore Smith, 1928.

PEACHAM, HENRY. *The Compleat Gentleman.* Clarendon Press, 1916.

PLANTIN, ARABELLA. *Two Novels.* 1727.

ROWE, MRS ELIZABETH. *Works.* 4 vols. 1798.

SCUDÉRY, GEORGES DE. *Zelinda.* (Modern Novels, 7.) 1692.

(*b*) STUDIES

BERNBAUM, ERNEST. *Mrs Behn's Biography a Fiction* (*Modern Language Association of America,* xxviii., 1913); " Mrs Behn's ' Oroonoko ' " (*Anniversary Papers by Colleagues and Pupils of G. L. Kittredge.* Boston, 1913).

CHARLANNE, L. *L'Influence française en Angleterre au 17ᵉ Siècle.* 1906.

DRYDEN, JOHN. *Essays.* Edited by W. P. Ker. 2 vols. 1900.

FROUDE, J. A. *John Bunyan.* (English Men of Letters.) 1880.

LE BRETON, ANDRÉ. *Le Roman au 17ᵉ Siècle.* 1898.

REYNIER, GUSTAVE. *Les Origines du Roman Réaliste.* 1912.
Le Roman Réaliste au 17ᵉ Siècle. 1914.
Le Roman Sentimental avant l'Astrée. Paris, 1908.

THOMAS, HENRY. *Spanish and Portuguese Romances.* 1920.

UPHAM, A. H. *The French Influence in English Literature from Elizabeth to the Restoration.* 1909.

URFÉ, HONORÉ D'. *La Vie et les Œuvres de Honoré d'Urfé, par le Chanoine O.-C. Reure.* Paris, 1910.

WHICHER, G. F. *Life and Romances of Mrs Eliza Haywood.* (Columbia University Studies in English and Comparative Literature. 1915.)

CHAPTERS VI.-VIII.—DEFOE AND SWIFT

(a) TEXTS

ABU BEKR IBN AL-TUFAIL, ABU JAFAR. *Philosophus Autodidactus.*
1671.
> *The History of Hai Eb'n Yockdan.* 1686.
> *The Improvement of Human Reason.* 1708.
> *The History of Hayy Ibn Magzan*: translated by Simon Ockley: revised, with introduction, by A. S. Fulton. 1929.

DEFOE, DANIEL. *Novels and Miscellaneous Works* [with Scott's prefaces]. (Bohn's Library.) 7 vols. 1854-1855.
> *Romances and Narratives.* Edited by G. A. Aitken. 16 vols. 1895.
> *The Family Instructor.* 2 vols. 1715.
> *Moll Flanders* and *Roxana.* With introduction by E. A. Baker. 1906.
> *The Earlier Life and the Chief Earlier Works of Defoe.* Edited by H. Morley. 1889.
> *Essay on Projects. True-born Englishman. Shortest Way with Dissenters. Hymn to the Pillory. The Consolidator. Apparition of Mrs Veal.*

SMEEKS, HENDRIK. *A Dutch Source for Robinson Crusoe.* The Narrative of the El Ho *Sjouke Gabbes*—an episode from the description of the mighty kingdom of Krinke Kesmes, by H. S., 1708. Translated and compared with *Robinson Crusoe*, by L. L. Hubbard. 1921.

SWIFT, JONATHAN. *Prose Works.* Edited by Temple Scott. 12 vols. 1897-1908.
> *Gulliver's Travels and other Works.* Edited by H. Morley. (Library of Early Novelists. 1906.)
> *Gulliver's Travels.* The Text of the first edition, with . . . Notes by Harold Williams. 1927.
> *A Tale of a Tub. . . . The Battle of the Books. . . .* Edited by A. C. Guthkelch and D. Nicol Smith. 1920.

(b) STUDIES

ATKINSON, GEOFFROY. *The Extraordinary Voyage in French Literature before 1700.* (Columbia University Studies in Romance, Philology, and Literature. 1920.)

BERNBAUM, ERNEST. *The Mary Carleton Narratives, 1663-1673: a missing chapter in the History of the English Novel.* 1920.

BRULÉ, ANDRÉ. *La Vie au dix-huitième Siècle: I.—Les Gens de lettres.* 1929.
I have not read this, but am informed that it develops the views outlined in this volume on authorship and the public.

CRAIK, SIR HENRY. *The Life of Jonathan Swift.* Second edition. 2 vols. 1894.

DOTTIN, PAUL. *Daniel de Foe et ses Romans.* 3 vols. 1924.
La Vie et les Aventures de Daniel de Foe. 1925.

EDDY, W. A. *Gulliver's Travels: a Critical Study.* 1923.

FIRTH, SIR C. H. "The Political Significance of 'Gulliver's Travels.'" (*Proceedings of the British Academy,* ix., 1920.)

GAUTHIER, LÉON. *Ibn Thofaïl, sa vie, ses œuvres.* 1909.

GILDON, CHARLES. *Robinson Crusoe examin'd and criticiz'd.* With an essay on Gildon's life by Paul Dottin. 1923.

HUBBARD, LUCIUS L. *Sjouke Gabbes: a Dutch Source for Robinson Crusoe.* 1921.

JERROLD, W. and C. *Five Queer Women.* 1929.
Mrs Behn, Mrs Manley, Mrs Haywood, Laetitia Pilkington, Mrs Centlivre.

MINTO, WILLIAM. *Daniel Defoe.* (English Men of Letters. 1879.)

NICHOLSON, WATSON. *The Historical Sources of Defoe's Journal of the Plague Year.* 1919.

PONS, EMILE. *Swift: I.—Les Années de Jeunesse et le "Conte du Tonneau."* (Publications de la Faculté des Lettres de l'Université de Strasbourg. 1925.)

READ, HERBERT. *English Prose Style.* 1928.
Good on the prose style and methods of narration of Bunyan, Defoe, and Swift.

SECORD, A. W. *Studies in the Narrative Method of Defoe.* (University of Illinois Studies in Language and Literature. 1924.)

STEPHEN, LESLIE. *Swift.* (English Men of Letters. 1882.)

ULLRICH, HERMANN. *Defoes Robinson Crusoe. Die Geschichte eines Weltbuches.* Leipzig, 1924.
Robinson und Robinsonaden: Bibliographie, Geschichte, Kritik. Weimar, 1898.

WOODBRIDGE, B. M. *Gatien de Courtilz.* (Johns Hopkins' Studies in Romance Literatures and Languages, vi. 1925.)

INDEX

INDEX

A

H

R

S

T

THOMSON, GEORGE, *Loimotomia*, possible source for *Journal of the Plague Year*, 200

Translations of anti-romancers, 40

Translations of Spanish picaresque novels, 44

Tufail, Ibn, *Ebn Yokdhan*, outlined, 161 ; source for *Robinson Crusoe*, 148, 160

U

UNDERDOWNE, THOMAS, his version of Heliodorus current in seventeenth century, 13

Urfé, Honoré d', *Astrée*, 15

V

VAIRASSE. *See* Allais, Denis Vairasse d'

Valentine and Orson, 13.

Vega, Garcilaso. *See* de la Vega, Garcilaso

Vincent, Thomas, *God's Terrible Voice in the City*, source for *Journal of the Plague Year*, 200

Voiture, Vincent de, *Histoire d'Alcidalis et Zélide*, used by T. D., 100

W

WACKWITZ, FRIEDRICH, 148

Walpole, Horace, *Mysterious Mother*, 114

Warren, George, source for Mrs Behn, 90

Weamys, Anne, 14, note

Wilkins, John, influence on Defoe, 134

This book may be kept

FOURTEEN DAYS

A fine will be charged for each day the book
is kept over time.

DEC 15 '75			
Bryuoy			

CAT. NO. 23 159   PRINTED IN U.S.A.